UNLOCKING THE SECRETS OF
CHINESE
FORTUNE TELLING

UNLOCKING THE SECRETS OF

CHINESE

FORTUNE TELLING

KNOW YOUR DESTINY AND PLAN YOUR LIFE

LILLIAN TOO

METRO BOOKS
NEW YORK

This 2008 edition published by Metro Books
by arrangement with Ivy Press

ISBN-13: 978-1-4351-0341-2
ISBN-10: 1-4351-0341-6

Library of Congress Cataloging-in-Publication
data available

Printed and bound in China

This book was conceived, designed, and produced
by Ixos Press, an imprint of Ivy Press
The Old Candlemakers, West Street,
Lewes, East Sussex BN7 2NZ, U.K.

Publisher David Alexander
Creative Director Peter Bridgewater
Art Director Sarah Howerd
Editorial Director Caroline Earle
Senior Project Editor Emily Gibson
Designer Ginny Zeal
Illustrator Jim Pilston
Picture Researcher Katie Greenwood

1 3 5 7 9 10 8 6 4 2

PICTURE ACKNOWLEDGMENTS

The publishers would like to thank the following agencies and organizations
for permission to use their images. Every effort has been made to trace
the copyright holder and to acknowledge the pictures, but if there are any
omissions, then please contact the publisher.

Cover: Corbis/Images.com

Art Archive/Private Collection Paris/Dagli Orti: 212

Corbis/Alexander Benz/zefa: 124; Ariel Skelley: 159; Brian A. Vikander:
40; China Photo/Reuteurs: 5, 20; Christine Schneider/zefa: 187; Images.
com: 14, 152, 188; Jim Ruymen/Reuters: 168 left; Jon Feingersh/zefa:
63; Jonathan Cavendish: 105; Jorge Uzon: 169 right; Keren Su: 132;
M. Neugebauer/zefa: 112; Marcel Hartmann: 166 right; Michael Prince:
119; Nancy Ney: 128; Nicolas Asfouri/epa: 167 left; Patrik Giardino:
11; Ragnar Schmuck/zefa: 130; Randy Faris: 5, 18; Reg Charity: 5, 97;
Ronnie Kaufman: 78; Ronnie Kaufman/zefa: 182; Royalty-Free: 211;
Rune Hellestad/Reuters: 169 left; Tim Graham: 167 right; Virgo/zefa: 54;
Wolfgang Kaehler: 154

Getty Images/Brian Stablyk/Photographer's Choice: 190; Bruno Ehrs/
Photonica: 16; Bryan Mullennix/Iconica: 136; Jade Lee/Asia Images: 8;
Juliet Coombe/Lonely Planet Images: 72; Michel Setboun/Stone: 174

Jupiter Images: 4, 26, 27, 35, 43, 67, 70, 74, 75, 77, 81, 90, 92, 106,
116, 120, 129, 131, 137, 140, 143, 144, 171

NASA: 134

Topfoto/Charles Walker: 2, 6, 9, 13

This book is dedicated with love to my wonderful team at
World of Feng Shui

Jennifer Too	Yew Sun	Jan Lim
Chris Yeo	Phillip Lim	Gopal
Nickque Tan	Han Jin	Darron Tan
Connie Leong	Kenji Chan	Anthony Teo
Cheryl Chow	Liong	Andrew Yep
Janice Yeong	Stanley Ng	Jackye Seng

CONTENTS

INTRODUCTION: DIVINING YOUR DESTINY

IN THIS BOOK YOU WILL LEARN WHAT YOUR FUTURE MIGHT HOLD. YOU WILL DISCOVER HOW TO REDUCE YOUR BAD LUCK AND HOW TO MAKE THE MOST OF YOUR GOOD LUCK. YOU WILL ALSO FIND OUT HOW TO READ THE FATE WRITTEN ON YOUR BODY AND HOW TO CONSULT ORACLES. IN SHORT, YOU WILL LEARN NEW SKILLS FOR MODERN LIVING BASED ON ANCIENT CHINESE WISDOM.

I CHING (BOOK OF CHANGES)
Consult this ancient Chinese oracle (comprising 64 hexagrams of wise advice) to solve modern-day problems.

I ntrinsic to all Chinese metaphysical systems, be it fortune telling or feng shui, is the philosophy that prevention is better than cure. The application of this philosophy to your future is not only to learn how to try to prevent or reduce the worst types of misfortune but also how to make the most of the good fortune you are destined to experience. By analyzing your birth chart, reading your body, and consulting the oracles, you will reveal your destiny and be able to plan your life.

1 ANALYZE YOUR BIRTH CHART
In Part One, we look at personal destiny charts and find out what kind of luck is coming your way. Your paht chee ("eight characters") chart will reveal what life might have in store for you. You will also learn how to interpret the ten-year luck charts, which tell you when you will experience important highs and lows in your life.

The charts are useful aids to life and living. They will help you to:
• Work out when your greatest opportunities for prosperity will occur and therefore when you should be taking risks and when you should be more cautious.
• Learn what to prioritize in your life.
• Understand imbalances in your life.

You will discover:
• How to identify your self element. This will help you to determine the influences that will shape your future.
• The timing of periods of luck during the phases of your life, especially between your coming of age and your retirement.
• The kind of luck that you can expect in the following areas of life: Wealth, Financial Success; Friends, Foes, Competitors; Power, Rank, Recognition; Intelligence, Creativity; Resources, Support, Authority.
• Your Chinese animal sign and the significance of your relationships with other animal signs.
• The appearance of special stars in your paht chee chart, such as The Star of the Nobleman that signifies help is always at hand or The Star of Peach Blossom that suggests sexual attraction.
• How to make daily, monthly, and annual readings based on your Chinese animal

sign and the magic squares formed by the lo shu numbers.

• The influence of other aspects of Chinese astrology on your fate, which includes the role played by the planet Jupiter.

Along the journey, we will examine case studies that will help you to hone your chart reading skills and learn methods for improving your good luck and lessening the impact of your bad luck.

2 READ YOUR BODY

In Part Two, we look at the aspects of your fate that are revealed by your body. We consider face reading, the significance of ear and eye shape, the meanings of moles on your face and body, and signs of success in the shapes of your hands and the lines on your palms.

3 CONSULT THE ORACLES

In Part Three, you will discover oracle techniques to determine answers to short-term dilemmas. The most well known of these oracles is the *I Ching* (the *Book of Changes*), essentially a collection of practical ancient Chinese wisdom that can be

drawn on for guidance at any time. You will also learn how to consult the Wen Shu Oracle and what the Yellow Emperor Oracle indicates for your future. Finally, you will discover the fate that awaits you in a tea cup.

SAMPLE PAHT CHEE CHART

Name: Caroline
Date of birth: April 27,1967
Hour of birth: 2.53am
Gender: Female

HOUR	DAY	MONTH	YEAR
己	辛	甲	丁
YIN EARTH	YIN METAL	YANG WOOD	YIN FIRE
丑	酉	辰	未
YIN EARTH OX	YIN METAL ROOSTER	YANG EARTH DRAGON	YIN EARTH SHEEP

PAHT CHEE CHART
A sample paht chee, or destiny chart, can be download instantly from www.wofs.com based on the birth details you key in. Your destiny chart reveals the fortune map of your entire life.

CHINESE BELIEFS AND PRACTICES

IN CHINA, DESTINY ANALYSIS IS ACCORDED THE SAME RESPECT AS FENG SHUI, WITH A BELIEF IN LUCK, ESPECIALLY LUCKY AND UNLUCKY DAYS, FORMING THE BASIS OF THE ANALYSIS. LUCK PLAYS A BIG PART IN THE CHINESE ART OF LIVING, AND ADVICE FROM ASTROLOGISTS, FORTUNE TELLERS, AND PAHT CHEE EXPERTS IS TAKEN INTO ACCOUNT WHEN MAKING IMPORTANT FAMILY DECISIONS.

BABY NAMES

Destiny reading often starts when a baby is born. Parents use paht chee charts (personal destiny charts generated from the hour, day, month, and year of birth) to choose lucky names for their children.

The Chinese subscribe to the view that it is only by knowing the benchmarks and milestones in their lives as revealed in their destiny charts and in the physical signs indicated on their bodies (particularly the face and the hands) that they can be forewarned of the hurdles and obstacles that will cause aggravation during certain times of their life. Equally, the charts forewarn of periods when good fortune will bring excellence and success to enrich their lives. The Chinese therefore respect destiny analysis and fortune telling, believing that they offer efficient ways to guard against misfortune and to magnify good fortune.

The Chinese approach to destiny analysis or personal forecasting is to identify negative periods, that is, times of their life when there is good reason to be more pessimistic than at others. These are times when it is beneficial to be particularly careful, to wear protective amulets, and to refrain from taking risks. Their personal destiny charts also reveal when they will enter into their "bright" periods, times of their life when they can take risks, be extra courageous, and be able to move ahead with confidence.

MAJOR LIFE EVENTS

The Chinese consult astrologers about births and deaths and major life events at all points in between. For example, they seek guidance:

• Before selecting a name for their newborn baby. A newborn's birth chart will indicate whether one of the five elements is "missing" from the infant's fate. Compensation may be made by including a word related to the missing element as part of the child's name. ("Missing elements" are discussed in greater detail on pages 66–67.)

• When a potential marriage partner appears on the scene for any of their offspring. Parents consult an astrologer to determine the suitability and compatibility of the proposed match.

• Throughout their life. All important decisions regarding family, work, and celebrations, such as moving house, starting a new venture, and getting married, benefit from the input of astrological and destiny analysis.

• When a member of the family dies. Particular burial rituals are observed, and the timing of the rituals is based on calendar calculations to avoid negatively affecting the living, thought to happen if the timing of the burial is wrong or the charts of those present clash in terms of day and hour selected.

FORECASTING TOOLS

For overall life forecasting the Chinese depend mostly on their personal paht chee charts, which are usually read in conjunction with predictions for the vitality of particular years, months, and days (see Chapter Five). Some days are considered more auspicious for you than others, just as some years are regarded as luck-bringing years and are better than others, depending on your Chinese animal sign.

The Chinese also "read" hands and faces and the position of moles on faces and bodies when seeking to confirm a particularly good or bad personal destiny reading, but the main tool used in personal forecasting is the paht chee chart and its related readings.

The underlying belief in Chinese destiny reading skills—which echoes that of both feng shui and traditional Chinese medicine—is the philosophy that prevention is infinitely better than cure. So the Chinese approach to life and living is always to stress the prevention of bad things happening. The Chinese believe strongly in fortune telling and destiny analysis, but they are not a fatalistic people. Indeed, the ultimate reason for consulting paht chee and feng shui experts is precisely to enable them to avoid misfortunes. By knowing when a bad time will arrive, they believe that efforts can be made to ward off, or at least to reduce, the misfortune that is written into their life charts. So prevention analysis and protection techniques are included in this book.

One of the motivations for reading this book should be not just to know if and when you will get rich, or if and when you will find your great life partner, but to learn how to take steps to lessen the effect of bad times on your life. Throughout the book I suggest remedies to neutralize or overcome the bad luck periods.

TUNG SHU
Every New Year many Chinese families consult the Tung Shu (Chinese Almanac or thousand-year calendar) for advice on how to ensure a good and safe year ahead.

BE YOUR OWN FORTUNE TELLER

ANYONE CAN LEARN TO READ THE PAHT CHEE CHARTS AND BECOME ADEPT AT DETERMINING LUCK DESTINY IN THEIR LIFE. THE ANALYTICAL PROCESS AND TERMINOLOGY IN THIS BOOK HAVE BOTH BEEN SIMPLIFIED TO MAKE THE WHOLE PROCESS MORE ACCESSIBLE AND, INDEED, A FUN WAY FOR YOU TO ANALYZE YOUR OWN LIFE AND FIND OUT WHAT IS IN STORE FOR YOU IN THE COMING YEARS.

LIFE'S UPS AND DOWNS
Parents who know how to analyze destiny charts can enhance the highs and lessen the lows in their child's life by using the correct elements for the child's well-being.

T he attractive thing about Chinese fortune telling is that it focuses more directly on mapping out the highs and lows of your life than Western astrology, which focuses more on your characteristics and attitudes. The Chinese method zeros in on the prediction of times of good and uncertain fortunes. How adept you eventually become in making accurate predictions of your luck periods will depend on how much you practice. As with most things, practice makes perfect. The more paht chee readings you do, the faster you will develop a facility with the language and interpretation of the charts.

PREDICTION METHODS

Chinese fortune telling is able to offer predictions relating to wealth, power, status, and relationships as well as many other life aspirations. Misfortune is also indicated in the paht chee charts. However, for a fuller picture the paht chee and ten-year luck period, readings should be supplemented with readings of the face and the lines of the palm. The meanings of moles on the face and body will usually confirm and expand on what is already revealed in the paht chee chart.

Astrological updates will also add to the fortune telling picture. When you are able to map out your luck from year to year, from month to month and even, if you so wish, from day to day, you will be in complete control of your life and of your luck. For this part of your investigation and your use of Chinese metaphysical techniques, you will become familiar with the lo shu square, an important symbol that also features prominently in the practice of compass formula feng shui.

It is up to you how detailed you wish your fortune telling to be when you delve into what life has in store for you according to your birth data and physical markings. Do note, however, that destiny charting can rarely pinpoint the exact timing of misfortune or good fortune events in your life; it is excellent for identifying significant milestone indications of your life. What you do to enhance the opportunities revealed by your destiny charts at particular times of your life is in your hands.

USING YOUR INSTINCTS

With practice, anyone can become adept at reading paht chee charts. It is a skill that can be learned. The degree to which people bring their own instincts to the process differs from person to person. But deep within every human individual are very powerful psychic abilities that lie embedded and asleep until they become awakened with use.

Once these abilities have surfaced, the individual's higher instincts increase in strength. I have discovered that the more I have undertaken paht chee analysis (and performed the divination oracle rituals), the sharper my instincts have become over the years. This is probably because over time I have become increasingly more aware of, and therefore sensitive to, the surrounding chi energy.

Destiny, however, is only one part of the equation of life; there is also the input of your actions and the influence of your attitudes. When we are powerful and passionate enough about wanting to transform our lives, we are usually able to transform our destiny.

Of course, fate is only one part of how our future eventually pans out. Success, health, wealth, and happiness are abstractions. How much or how little we have of each and how we interpret these concepts depends entirely on ourselves. In the same way, how much is enough for us is also our own decision. In the end, it is what we make of what is given to us that decides the direction and quality of our life.

THE PURPOSE OF PREDICTION

The aim of learning destiny analysis and how to make luck predictions is to help us to improve ourselves, to enhance our lives, and to make good decisions, and then to extend this help outward toward the people we love and care about, and even to those we don't care for.

These are living skills that help us and that enable us to help others. Just like learning to drive, to read, to add, to count, to help people ... these skills make life and living a whole lot more pleasant, so they are certainly worth learning.

My motivation in writing this book is to share the results of my continuing study of Chinese metaphysical skills. I do it with a view to enable others to access the secrets of their destiny as revealed by their birth data. In this way I hope to offer a way of helping people to iron out the problems in their lives and to expand the magnitude of their good fortune.

The challenge for me is to make the learning process both fun and interesting without losing the spirit of the skills we are dealing with. I have enjoyed writing, editing, and re-editing this book very much,

PAST AND FUTURE
Chinese fortune telling is an ancient metaphysical art that originally required the expertise of learned masters. In today's knowledge economy, with books, websites and easy chart generation, destiny analysis is a practical skill that anyone can learn.

and I hope that for those new to Chinese fortune telling I have succeeded in sparking a real interest in these wonderful skills. I also hope it gives you hours of fun and that ultimately it helps many of you move more gracefully and happily through life.

BEFORE YOU START

My advice to readers is to read through Part One completely before printing out and analyzing your own paht chee charts. This will ensure that you get a comprehensive understanding. Trying to learn the method and interpret your own chart at the same time may be counterproductive to the learning process and could be very frustrating for you.

So go slowly and become familiar with the charts before you start your own analysis. Work through the examples in this book with me as you read. This will give you the practice needed in working out what to look for in your own chart.

Eventually how adept you become in making luck predictions for yourself and others depends on how familiar you are with the charts and, most important of all, how well you understand the theory of the five elements. In Chinese fortune telling, as with most skills, improvement comes with practice. Over time you will become so familiar with the theory of the five elements that interpreting a paht chee chart will become very easy. If you go slowly, you will have no difficulty in attaining familiarity with the charts and perfecting the skills that you need to become your own fortune teller and to find out what the future has in store for you.

PART ONE

THE PAHT CHEE
CHARTS

CHAPTER ONE

PAHT CHEE AND THE FIVE ELEMENTS

The five elements are wood, fire, earth, metal, and water. Understanding their meanings and their interactions is the first step in understanding your paht chee (or personal destiny) chart.

THE BENEFITS OF PAHT CHEE ANALYSIS

GETTING A PAHT CHEE OR PERSONAL DESTINY CHART READING GIVES YOU ADVANCE NOTICE OF GOOD AND BAD TIMES TO COME AT DIFFERENT AGES OF YOUR LIFE. IT CAN PREDICT WHEN MISFORTUNES MIGHT OCCUR SO THAT YOU CAN PROCEED WITH CAUTION, OR WHEN THE GOOD YEARS WILL ARRIVE AND YOU CAN BE COURAGEOUS IN TAKING CAREER OR RELATIONSHIP RISKS.

A paht chee reading will help you at all times of your life in all areas of your life, from money to marriage, from health to harmony, and from career to color therapy. You can use it to:

Improve your love life: Use a paht chee reading to analyze your compatibility with a potential marriage partner.

Improve your quality of life: Being able to predict the good and bad periods gives you a competitive edge in life. Although the occurrence of good fortune or misfortune may be part of your destiny or karma, the quality of your life, and the size of your good fortune or misfortune, are very much within your control.

Reduce your misfortune: Having prior knowledge bad luck periods, for instance, can mean the difference between losing a

PERFECT PARTNERS
Paht chee analysis is often used to check the compatibility of potential marriage partners. Compare your personal destiny chart with that of a potential love match to discover whether you have a date with destiny.

small amount of money and losing a great deal of money, or between sustaining a small fall and being involved in a larger accident. This is the secret of destiny analysis. You might not be able to fully escape experiencing an accident during a bad period, but you can, by being careful and by using a remedy wherever it is available, substantially diminish its effect.

Improve your career luck: The paht chee reading of good and bad ten-year periods is especially useful for those running businesses or planning career moves. Changing direction is always auspicious when done at the start of a good ten-year life period. It is definitely bad when you are at the tail end of a good ten-year period.

Improve your business: You can use paht chee analysis in order to determine the compatibility of a group of people thinking of going into business together. It is a great skill for human resources managers, because the chart immediately shows whether potential employees will "fit" into the culture of the company and whether they will benefit the company and/or its boss. It is always good to employ people who have just entered a favorable ten-year luck period, because their good fortune is certain to spill over. (You would, of course, need to know their time and date of birth to generate their paht chee chart.)

Bring greater peace to your life: Analyzing the paht chee alerts you to life's afflictions, prompting you to deal with them before they occur. For many people this certainly makes for a less aggravating existence. Peace is such a rare commodity these days that anything that can bring more peace into our lives must surely be very welcome.

Add to your living skills: You can even enhance your practice of feng shui through the paht chee charts. Although fortune telling and feng shui are separate practices requiring different interpretations, they are nevertheless complementary living skills. When they are used in a timely fashion they can help to maximize your success potential and happiness.

THE PAHT CHEE CHARTS

LET'S BEGIN WITH AN EXPLANATION OF WHAT PAHT CHEE ARE AND HOW THE PERSONAL DESTINY CHARTS ARE PUT TOGETHER. BASED ON THE CHINESE THOUSAND-YEAR CALENDAR, PAHT CHEE CHART CALCULATION HAS TRADITIONALLY BEEN A CUMBERSOME PROCESS. HOWEVER, THE CHARTS CAN NOW BE GENERATED BY COMPUTER WITH THE CLICK OF A MOUSE.

The paht chee ("eight characters") method of fortune telling is generally accepted by the Chinese as the most accurate and comprehensive way of predicting your future. It is a method that uses four important pieces of birth data—the hour, day, month, and year of your birth—to generate four short columns of Chinese characters known as the "four pillars of destiny" (see sample chart overleaf). The four pillars each comprise two characters, and the resulting total of eight characters are the "paht chee" of your chart. These paht chee contain the codes of your destiny.

The upper character in each of the four pillars is known as a "heavenly stem," and the lower one as an "earthly branch"—both are derived from the Chinese lunar thousand-year calendar. (The calendar is essentially a book that contains details of the heavenly stems, earthly branches, elements, and lo shu numbers of each year, month, and day for a thousand-year period. An extract from the calendar is given in the Appendix.)

Your paht chee chart sets out the heavenly stem and the earthly branch characters of your date of birth expressed as the hour, day, month, and year. This

INDIVIDUAL DESTINY
Everyone's personal future is mapped out at birth in the paht chee chart: character, circumstances, and luck are all contained within it.

HOW CHARTS ARE MADE

As consulting the Chinese thousand-year calendar can be a complex process, some have copied all the information it contains into a computer software program, which has the formula to convert a Western date of birth into a Chinese date. This program instantly calls up the three sets of elements required from your day, month, and year of birth. Then the earthly branch element of the hour of birth is extracted from the table shown here.

TIME OF BIRTH	EARTHLY BRANCH
11 P.M.—1 A.M.	RAT/YANG WATER
1 A.M.—3 A.M.	OX/YIN EARTH
3 A.M.—5 A.M.	TIGER/YANG WOOD
5 A.M.—7 A.M.	RABBIT/YIN WOOD
7 A.M.—9 A.M.	DRAGON/YANG EARTH
9 A.M.—11 A.M.	SNAKE/YIN FIRE
11 A.M.—1 P.M.	HORSE/YANG FIRE
1 P.M.—3 P.M.	SHEEP/YIN EARTH
3 P.M.—5 P.M.	MONKEY/YANG METAL
5 P.M.—7 P.M.	ROOSTER/YIN METAL
7 P.M.—9 P.M.	DOG/YANG EARTH
9 P.M.—11 P.M.	BOAR/YIN WATER

The heavenly stem of the day pillar determines the heavenly stem of your hour of birth pillar, and the computer program will calculate this for you. This fourth pillar completes the four pillars of your paht chee chart.

is done by converting your western date of birth to its equivalent date (see panel opposite for details) as presented in the Chinese lunar calendar.

BASKET OF ELEMENTS

Heavenly stems and earthly branches are each defined as yin or yang aspects of one of the five elements—wood, fire, earth, metal, or water (see The Five Elements and Their Cycles, pages 28–33). Therefore, you might for example find "yin fire" or "yang earth" in your chart. (If the heavenly stem is yin, the earthly branch will also be yin. If the stem is yang, then the branch will also be yang.)

In addition, each earthly branch is associated with one of the 12 Chinese animal signs (Rat, Ox, Tiger, Rabbit, Dragon, Snake, Horse, Sheep, Monkey, Rooster, Dog, or Boar). We will examine the significance and meaning of the elements and animal signs later in the book.

The four heavenly stems and four earthly branches are collectively referred to as the "basket of elements." They offer clues to your character, circumstances, and potential to enjoy different kinds of good fortune as well as indications of the crosses that you may have to bear at different times of your life. The basket may be balanced or favor certain elements or even be "missing" certain elements. These factors all have an impact on the kind of luck you can expect to experience in terms of wealth, relationships, and so on.

SAMPLE PAHT CHEE CHART

PAHT CHEE CHART

Four pillars of destiny

HOUR	DAY	MONTH	YEAR
YANG WATER	YANG FIRE	YANG EARTH	YANG WOOD

Heavenly stem = *yin or yang aspect of one of the five elements*

Self element

Basket of elements

DRAGON YANG EARTH	HORSE YANG FIRE	DRAGON YANG EARTH	DRAGON YANG EARTH

Earthly branch = *yin or yang aspect of one of the five elements; also one of the twelve Chinese astrological animals (Rat, Ox, Tiger, Rabbit, Dragon, Snake, Horse, Sheep, Monkey, Rooster, Dog, or Boar)*

KEY

Four pillars of destiny = hour, day, month, and year of your birth

Each pillar has two characters: a heavenly stem (upper character) and an earthly branch (lower character)

Five elements = water, wood, fire, earth, metal

Basket of elements = the collection of elements represented in the eight characters of your four pillars

Self element = day heavenly stem character (e.g. here it is yang fire)

Dominant element = the element most represented in your "basket of elements" (e.g. here it is earth)

TEN-YEAR LUCK PILLARS

Your age

3–12	13–22	23–32	33–42	43–52

First five years of ten-year period

YIN EARTH	YANG METAL	YIN METAL	YANG WATER	YIN WATER

Second five years of ten-year period

Ten-year luck pillars = eight periods of ten-year sections of your life (the first five years of each section are represented by the upper character; the second five by the lower character)

SNAKE YIN FIRE	HORSE YANG FIRE	SHEEP YIN EARTH	MONKEY YANG METAL	ROOSTER YIN METAL

AREAS OF LIFE LUCK

METAL

Wealth, Financial Success

EARTH

Intelligence, Creativity

WOOD

Resources, Support, Authority

FIRE

Friends, Foes, Competitors

WATER

Power, Rank, Recognition

Areas of life luck: each five-year period of your life is dominated by one of these areas of luck.

53–62	63–72	73–82

YANG WOOD	YIN WOOD	YANG FIRE

DOG YANG EARTH	PIG YIN WATER	RAT YANG WATER

GENERATING YOUR OWN CHART

1 To generate your own chart, you need four pieces of information about your birth, which will generate the four pillars of your destiny:

- the hour of your birth (refers to the hour of birth in the place where you were born)
- the day of your birth (refers to the day of your birth according to the Chinese calendar)
- the month of your birth (this reveals the seasonal element of your birth day)
- the year of your birth (refers to your year of birth according to the lunar Chinese calendar).

NB: It is not necessary to convert your time of birth to Greenwich Mean Time. It is the time of birth in your locality and country that counts. Thus if you were born at night then your hour of birth must reflect this in the chart. Your Western date of birth is converted to its equivalent date as presented in the Chinese lunar calendar.

2 Go to the author's website www.wofs.com and log on. (If you are not a member, you can register within minutes.) Return to the home page.

3 On the right of the home page under FS Assistant, double-click the icon "Four Pillars Calculator."

4 Enter your date and time of birth as well as your gender and click on "Calculate."

5 Within seconds you should receive a chart showing your four pillars of destiny comprising your paht chee or eight characters, as well as a chart of your ten-year luck pillars, and a list of the elements that are related to specific kinds of luck in particular areas of your life.

HEAVENLY STEMS AND EARTHLY BRANCHES

THE FOUR HEAVENLY STEMS AND FOUR EARTHLY BRANCHES FOUND IN YOUR PAHT CHEE CHART MAP OUT YOUR DESTINY. THERE FOLLOWS AN OUTLINE OF THE RANGE OF STEMS AND BRANCHES AND AN INTRODUCTION TO WHAT THEY MIGHT MEAN IF THEY APPEAR IN YOUR CHART.

THE TEN HEAVENLY STEMS

THE HEAVENLY STEMS OF THE PAHT CHEE CHART COMPRISE THE YIN AND YANG ASPECTS OF THE FIVE ELEMENTS:

HEAVENLY STEM NUMBER	CHINESE NAME	ELEMENT	
HS 1	JIA	甲	YANG WOOD
HS 2	YI	乙	YIN WOOD
HS 3	BING	丙	YANG FIRE
HS 4	DING	丁	YIN FIRE
HS 5	WU	戊	YANG EARTH
HS 6	JI	己	YIN EARTH
HS 7	GENG	庚	YANG METAL
HS 8	XIN	辛	YIN METAL
HS 9	REN	壬	YANG WATER
HS 10	GUI	癸	YIN WATER

Heavenly stems and earthly branches are terms that are found in the Chinese thousand-year calendar. In essence, there are ten heavenly stems and twelve earthly branches and they are defined by the kind of chi or energy that is represented by the five elements (water, wood, fire, earth, and metal).

THE TEN HEAVENLY STEMS

The Chinese names of the heavenly stems and earthly branches are the "characters" of the paht chee chart. Shown here are the Chinese names of the ten heavenly stem characters, their corresponding element, and their yin or yang aspect. The stems comprise the five elements manifesting in either a yin or a yang aspect. (In Chinese philosophy, yin and yang are the two fundamental principles: yin is negative, dark, passive, cold, wet, and feminine; yang is positive, bright, active, dry, hot, and masculine.)

The elements are said to interact in three different ways—described in terms of productive, exhaustive, and destructive cycles. These cycles are explained later in

THE TWELVE EARTHLY BRANCHES

EARTHLY BRANCH NUMBER	CHINESE NAME	ANIMAL		ELEMENT
EB 1	ZI	RAT	子	YANG WATER
EB 2	CHOU	OX	丑	YIN EARTH
EB 3	YIN	TIGER	寅	YANG WOOD
EB 4	MAO	RABBIT	卯	YIN WOOD
EB 5	CHEN	DRAGON	辰	YANG EARTH
EB 6	SI	SNAKE	巳	YIN FIRE
EB 7	WU	HORSE	午	YANG FIRE
EB 8	WEI	SHEEP	未	YIN EARTH
EB 9	SHEN	MONKEY	申	YANG METAL
EB 10	YOU	ROOSTER	酉	YIN METAL
EB 11	XU	DOG	戌	YANG EARTH
EB 12	HAI	BOAR	亥	YIN WATER

The earthly branches make up the four characters in the lower half of the paht chee chart. There are twelve possible branches in all. They have Chinese names as well as an equivalent astrological animal and corresponding element (also with a yin or a yang aspect).

It is easier to think of the earthly branches as the twelve animals of Chinese astrology. Each of the animals has an intrinsic element. Four animal signs have earth as their element. Two of these are yin and two are yang aspects of the element.

As with the heavenly stems, when we read paht chee charts it is necessary to look at how the elements of the earthly branches combine. When they combine in a positive way the outcome is good and when they clash the outcome is negative.

the chapter, but suffice to say that the heavenly stem elements are placed here in the conventional order of the productive cycle, starting with wood. Wood produces fire, which produces earth, which produces metal, which in turn produces water. And then water produces wood, and the cycle starts all over again.

When we come to analyze the paht chee chart, we have to look out for how the elements of the heavenly stems in each of the four pillars—hour, day, month, and year—either combine or clash with each other. When the elements combine it suggests the outcome is good; when they clash it suggests the outcome is bad. When the combination or clash is between two yang or two yin heavenly stems, the result is magnified and in the case of clashes it is more severe.

THE TEN-YEAR LUCK PILLARS AND LIFE LUCK

THE TEN-YEAR LUCK PILLARS ARE GENERATED ALONGSIDE YOUR PAHT CHEE CHART. THEY OFFER A TIMELINE OF YOUR LIFE ON WHICH ARE INDICATED SPECIFIC PERIODS WHEN PARTICULAR TYPES OF LIFE LUCK WILL BE COMING YOUR WAY.

JUMPING FOR JOY
The paht chee chart reveals the elements that are the codes to unlocking your ten-year luck pillars—the chart that tells you when you might be jumping for joy. Some people have good fortune their whole life long, but most of us have five to ten good years when we're on a roll.

While the paht chee chart indicates the strengths, weaknesses, and the potential that you are born with, the ten-year luck pillars chart indicates the energy influences that prevail in each ten-year period that will cause the good influences or bad influences of the paht chee to manifest good or bad luck. So the two charts must be read together.

The ten-year luck chart comprises eight columns (see pages 22–23). Each column comprises two characters expressed as a pair of elements—the upper heavenly stem and the lower earthly branch or the Chinese astrological sign. Each pillar represents a ten-year period in your life, the upper character representing the first five years of the period, the lower character representing the second five years—these characters show which element rules your destiny during each five-year period. The characters therefore combine to form a lifeline showing the ages when you can expect to be on a roll or when you need to brace yourself for some tough times.

The starting years of the ten-year luck pillars and elements generated for each pillar are derived from a formula using your gender and date of birth. You will easily be able to calculate how old you will be at each of stage of your life represented by each of the luck pillars.

MAP OF LIFE'S HIGHS AND LOWS
The high and low periods of your life are thus mapped out. When expertly interpreted, these charts predict the quality and success potential in your life, that is, the periods when you are likely to:
• Become successful
• Get married
• Have children
• Become wealthy
• Become powerful.

When you have learned how to read the charts, you will be able to make accurate predictions for any given year of your life and take steps to increase your good luck or reduce your bad luck.

These charts are always read in conjunction with the ruling elements of each calendar year to determine whether the year will bring good, bad, or neutral luck (see Appendix). When you know how to

interpret the elements correctly (see pages 28–33), you will be able to predict when you will attain the high point of your life just by looking at the ten-year luck pillars.

You will also be able to determine from the paht chee chart those elements that are favorable or unfavorable to your destiny luck. When the favorable elements in the yin or yang aspect show up in your ten-year luck periods and these also correspond to favorable elements in a calendar year, you will experience a rise in your fortunes.

So if you wish to look for signs of good fortune ripening in your life you must first determine the elements that are "favorable" for you at any particular period of your life. We will learn how to do this in the next chapter.

Like the four pillars of destiny in the paht chee chart, the ten-year luck pillars are also expressed as elements. These can then strengthen or weaken the person's paht chee elements. If the elements of the luck pillars trigger off the paht chee's wealth potential, that is when you will enter into a "rich period"—the ten years of your life when you are likely to get rich.

When we say a person has a "good" set of luck pillars, we mean that the pillars during the ages of about 30 to 50 years have elements that provide the missing element(s) of the paht chee chart, that is, elements that fill in what is lacking in the chart. Alternatively, it stands for wealth luck coming. Before you can read the luck periods chart correctly, you must first determine which are the elements that are deemed good for you. You will also need to identify the elements of the chart that represent wealth and other kinds of luck.

AREAS OF LIFE LUCK

Each five-year period of your life is dominated by a particular kind of luck for you, depending on the element associated with that period. The five areas of life luck are as follows:
• Wealth, Financial Success
• Friends, Foes, Competitors
• Power, Rank, Recognition
• Intelligence, Creativity
• Resources, Support, Authority.
These areas of life luck are considered in more detail in Chapter Three.

INTELLIGENCE LUCK
A specific type of luck is prominent in each five-year period of your life. If the elements are in your favor, one period could bring you great success in academia.

THE FIVE ELEMENTS AND THEIR CYCLES

THE KEY TO UNLOCKING THE MEANINGS OF PAHT CHEE CHARTS—
AND THEREFORE YOUR DESTINY—IS KNOWLEDGE OF THE FIVE
ELEMENTS AND THEIR CYCLES OF PRODUCTION, DESTRUCTION, AND
EXHAUSTION. THESE CYCLES OF INTERACTION MAKE UP THE THEORY
OF WU XING, WHICH IS CENTRAL NOT ONLY TO CHINESE FORTUNE
TELLING AND FENG SHUI BUT ALSO TO CHINESE MEDICINE.

E ssentially, *Wu* means "five" and *xing* means "elements" in the sense of different kinds of chi (energy) dominating at different times. These different energies are named after the elements to help us understand the various properties of the different types of chi. Their essential qualities are shown in the chart below.

The Chinese attach an extraordinary level of importance to the five elements, whose interaction is considered to reflect the cycles of the universe and to link the trinity of existence—heaven, earth, and humankind. The five elements thus exert a considerable influence on everyone's personal fortunes. Their significance is related to their cyclical interactions with each other, which may be productive, destructive, or exhaustive.

Generally, when any two elements are in a productive cycle they give rise to harmony, and when any two elements are in a destructive or an exhaustive cycle they give rise to conflict.

THE PRODUCTIVE CYCLE

The productive cycle is where:
- wood burns, producing fire
- fire leaves ash, producing earth
- from earth, metal is formed and mined
- metal melts, producing liquid, which is viewed as water
- water nurtures plants, producing wood, after which the cycle starts again.

Each element produces the next in a cyclical order.

Seeing things in a larger perspective, the productive cycle also reflects nature's phenomena, and this is reflected in the seasons, with each season associated with an element (see page 30). The season of

ELEMENTS: BASIC ATTRIBUTES

WATER dominates in winter; runs downward with a risk of overflowing; liberal

WOOD dominates in spring; grows upward; enduring

FIRE dominates in summer; spreads in all directions; radiant, hot, possibly uncontrollable

METAL dominates in the fall; pierces inward; sharp, pointing; can be deadly and powerful

EARTH dominates at intersection between two seasons; attracts and nourishes; stable, caring, and protective

THE CYCLES OF THE FIVE ELEMENTS

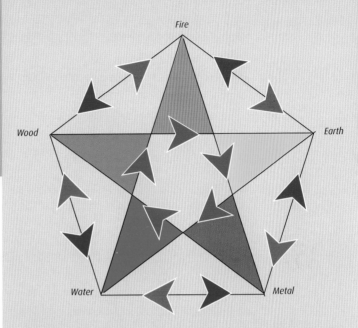

The five elements interact as three cycles: productive, exhaustive, and destructive. The outer cycle (illustrated by red arrows) indicates the **productive cycle**. Think of this as a circular flow of energy moving in a positive, clockwise direction.

When the energy starts to move in the reverse direction, that is, anticlockwise, it becomes negative: this is the **exhaustive cycle**. Here it is shown by the blue arrows.

The **destructive cycle** is indicated by the pentacle or five-pointed star placed inside the other two cycles. You can see that, when you join the elements according to this star shape, it forms the destructive cycle.

Spend a few moments learning these three cycles thoroughly—it is not difficult since they have an intrinsic logic.

growth is spring, associated with wood; then comes the heat of summer, which is fire. In the middle of the year, and in the intersections between the seasons, is earth, which is followed by the season of harvest associated with metal (because of the implements used for harvesting), and finally there is the winter season of cold, which is associated with water.

In paht chee life prediction, we have seen that the moment of a person's birth can be precisely recorded in terms of the five elements in an eight characters chart. So the year, month, day, and also the hour are expressed as one of the five elements. You can see therefore that the popular method of relying only on the animal sign of the year does not reveal a full picture of a person's destiny. However, the year animal sign does offer reliable indications of character and personality attributes and of compatibilities with other animal signs.

The fortunes of people based on animal signs follow the astrological methods of determining whether a particular year is good, bad, or indifferent. Astrological

GENERAL ATTRIBUTES OF THE FIVE ELEMENTS

ATTRIBUTE	WOOD	FIRE	EARTH	METAL	WATER
MUSICAL NOTE	E	G	C	D	A
FEELING	ANGER	JOY	CONTEMPLATION	SADNESS	FEAR
SEASON	SPRING	SUMMER	4 SEASONS	FALL	WINTER
DIRECTION	EAST	SOUTH	CENTER	WEST	NORTH
CLIMATE	WIND	HEAT	WET	DRY	COLD
TASTE	SOUR	BITTER	SWEET	PUNGENT	SALTY
COLOR	GREEN	RED	YELLOW	WHITE	BLACK/BLUE

indications address the immediate fortunes of a person, while the paht chee charts take a view of your entire life destiny.

The paht chee chart offers a tantalizing road map to making luck predictions. To interpret the elements fully, however, we need to understand their negative relationships, too. The negative cycles indicate what happens when the elements exhaust or destroy each other in your chart.

THE EXHAUSTIVE CYCLE

The exhaustive cycle of the elements is when the relationship causes energy to be depleted. Essentially, this is the productive cycle in reverse. Thus:
• wood exhausts water
• water exhausts metal
• metal exhausts earth
• earth exhausts fire
• fire exhausts wood.

This cycle features prominently in the practice of feng shui as it offers the basis for installing "cures" and "remedies" to overcome feng shui afflictions caused by the passage of time. The exhaustive cycle is the productive cycle in reverse. Thus, if wood produces fire, then we say that fire exhausts wood. Likewise, if water produces wood, then we know that wood exhausts water, and so forth.

THE DESTRUCTIVE CYCLE

The destructive cycle is when a particular combination of elements takes on a killing relationship. This is more severe than the exhaustive cycle. The destructive cycle is as follows:
• water destroys fire
• fire destroys metal
• metal destroys wood
• wood destroys earth
• earth destroys water.

Here, the logic is that wood absorbs the goodness and nutrients from the earth; the earth sullies the water, which in turn puts out the fire. Then fire reduces metal to liquid by literally melting and destroying it, and metal kills wood in the sense that it is used to chop down trees and plants.

MEANINGS OF THE CYCLES

The cycles of the five elements are best committed to memory because you need to know how particular element types might assist or obstruct one another. In interpreting the chart, for instance, you then know that a predominantly wood person would provide sustenance and resources for a fire person, or that a fire person would stimulate a lazy earth person to work and excel.

Earth types would bring stability to a rash metal person, while a metal person would make a tranquil and dreamy water-type person more action-oriented. Finally, of course, a water person would provide the sustenance for a wood person to grow.

Think through what the destructive cycle of the elements would mean for your reading of charts. A wood person is certain to drain the resources of an earth-type person; just as an earth person could well destroy a water person's life. In the same way, a water person would likely pour cold water on the fire person's enthusiasm and zest for life, and a fire person would be a formidable enemy of a metal person. A metal person would likewise be terribly harmful to a wood-type person.

There is of course a lot more to follow through. Other factors come in either to enhance or to negate the good and bad influences stated, as we will discover in the ensuing chapters.

FURTHER ATTRIBUTES OF THE FIVE ELEMENTS

We turn next to the attributes and associated attributes of the five elements. These can be abstract ideas, characteristics, or phenomena linked to and associated with each of the elements.

Since elements signify everything in the universe, they represent just about everything in existence! From body parts to compass directions to colors and shapes— opposite is a non-exhaustive tabulation of some attributes that will help you to add depth to your paht chee reading.

Use these as a key to meanings suggested with each element. Pay attention to the seasons and climatic associations because they offer clues to locations, countries, and directions, especially when the chart suggests a relocation of some kind. Also take note of the feelings associated with the elements. For instance, note that the element of fire means joy, so a person whose self element is fire will likely have a happy disposition. A person whose self element is wood tends to have a quick temper, while anyone with water as the self element will tend to be conservative, fearful of new experiences and of change. Metal self element people tend toward sadness, while earth element people tend to be philosophers. They are the thinkers of the paht chee chart.

In addition, note the colors associated with each element. These are useful when there is a need to create "balance" in your chart. Color therapy based on the five elements is especially useful when you are attempting to enhance your material luck and well-being—this means the luck of career success, marriage happiness, and health during old age. If you have determined that fire is your favorable element,

FAMILY FORTUNES

Parents can learn to balance the elements in personal destiny charts and thereby give children a head start in terms of health and happiness. When the elements are well balanced in a child's chart the early years will be enjoyable.

for instance, then wearing red or being surrounded by red will benefit you. If you discover that water is your unfavorable element, avoid wearing black or blue.

You can also use element therapy to undertake a diagnosis of your element deficiencies and excesses. Chinese healing skills depend on the five elements to aid diagnosis. In traditional Chinese medicine, the ailments of the human body are expressed in terms of either excess or lack of an identified element. For instance, the physician may find the body may have too much heat, too much cold, is too wet or too dry. Or the body could be suffering from wind. Remedies are then recommended on the basis of the elements.

In Kung Fu, martial arts moves, and in Chi Kung, breathing techniques are expressed as elements. In feng shui the

five elements hold the key to unlocking the secrets of the compass directions.

GETTING THE BALANCE RIGHT

Gaining familiarity with the elements that make up the heavenly stems and earthly branches is important because the thousand-year calendar, from which the system derives its charts, is expressed in terms of stems and branches. There are Chinese names for each of these stems and branches (see pages 24–25), but it is not vital to learn these. The most important aspect to bear in mind is that the elements of the stems and branches can be either yin or yang—opposing forces, which complement and give life to each other. Yin and yang make up the tai chi principle which stresses that having all five elements in a chart is what gives it good balance, but it is also important to see whether they are made up of all yin, all yang, or a combination of yin and yang pillars.

If there is a shortage or an excess of any element, your life is supposedly out of balance. Charts with shortages and excesses indicate lives that will have more than their fair share of obstacles and misfortunes. However, if the shortage or excess is identified it can be properly corrected and the obstacles and misfortunes reduced.

It is rare to find a chart with a perfect balance of all five elements. This is the first and most simplistic indication of a good life chart. In most people's paht chee charts there is always some element missing and therefore there will be an excess of some other element. So everyone is likely to suffer from some kind of shortage or excess of a particular element. This is usually thought to mean that some kind of affliction, aggravation, disappointment, failure, or loss will occur at some point in the person's life.

NO ONE'S LIFE IS PERFECT

When, in the old days, a child was born to a wealthy or prominent family, particularly if the child was a boy, his paht chee chart would immediately be drawn up so that the name selected could directly address any shortage or excess of elements. The remedy would be to incorporate the missing element(s) into the child's given name. (Chinese names usually incorporate the words for "water," "metal," "fire," "wood," or "gold.")

In compensating for the lack of an element in this way, the child's life would instantly become better balanced, thereby bringing good fortune. The naming of children in the old days was determined with the help of a trusted family astrologer. The practice continues to this day, especially among traditional Chinese families in Hong Kong, Taiwan, and China.

If your chart has all five elements present, this is a good indication that your life is relatively comfortable and well balanced, that you have more than enough to eat, and that you have reasonable good fortune. This good balance of element forces will also enable you to benefit from any good fortune specifically indicated in the chart. Missing elements will be dealt with in the next chapter.

GETTING A TASTE FOR THE FIVE ELEMENTS

In Chinese traditional medicine the healer may often prescribe something with a bitter taste to balance out the body of someone who has perhaps received too much sugar. The Chinese believe that when we ensure the body has a balanced supply of the five tastes symbolizing the five elements—sweet, sour, salty, spicy, and bitter—the body will enjoy peak health and will never lack energy. A great way to maintain this balance within the body is to have five types of vegetables and fruits each day, with each type representing one of the five tastes. Try, for example, this great recipe for a morning smoothie: green apples (sour); bitter gourd (bitter); star fruit (sweet); capsicum (spicy), and celery (salty).

AN INITIAL PAHT CHEE READING

THE PAHT CHEE CHART REVEALS THE WEAK AND STRONG POINTS OF YOUR LIFE DESTINY. IT INDICATES WHETHER YOUR LIFE HAS THE POTENTIAL OF WEALTH LUCK, MARRIAGE LUCK, CHILDREN LUCK, HEALTH LUCK, AND SO FORTH. IT ALSO OFFERS CLUES ON WHAT IS LACKING IN YOUR LIFE AND WHAT YOU HAVE IN EXCESS, AND THIS REVEALS YOUR FORTUNE.

Both the paht chee and the ten-year luck period charts are expressed as pairs of elements, and these refer to the five elements—water, wood, fire, earth, and metal—that feature so prominently in Chinese metaphysical practices. These elements are in turn differentiated according to whether they are heavenly stems or earthly branches. Within these stems and branches the elements are identified as being either yin or yang.

The paht chee and the ten-year luck period charts are scrutinized to obtain a general picture of your luck patterns from the time of birth until the time of death, starting with the paht chee chart.

This initial reading reveals a great deal of information about your personal life, destiny, strengths and weaknesses; it describes your luck in terms of family background, indicating the influences of the father and the mother, and even the grandparents. Your self element is represented by the **heavenly stem of the day pillar**. Other people in your life are represented by other characters in the chart, and their influence can be read in the chart (see page 36).

INFLUENCE OF SPOUSE AND CHILDREN

The charts highlight the characteristics as well as the relative importance of the potential spouse in affecting your life destiny. The spouse is represented by the **day earthly branch** character. In the lives of some people the spouse is a hugely important figure of influence while in others the spouse plays a relatively insignificant role. In addition, the life chart describes luck associated with children. When a child's influence in your life is significant this is usually also revealed in the chart. Children are represented by the **hour pillar**.

INFLUENCE OF FAMILY AND FRIENDS

Parents are represented by the **month heavenly stem** and **earthly branch** characters. The paht chee chart can show whether your parents will be supportive of or dependent on you, and whether your children will bring you honor. These aspects of your relationships will become clear when you understand the relationship of

the elements as well as the clashes and affinities of the branches. There is also a veritable gold mine of information about other relatives, friends, and sometimes even unrelated people whose influence on the self may be unusually strong.

Grandparents are represented by the **year pillar**: grandfather by the heavenly stem, grandmother by the earthly branch.

WEALTH

The charts also reveal the wealth probability of parents and sometimes they can indicate clearly whether you are born into rich or poor circumstances. The chart shows whether you are destined to become rich, and, if so, it identifies the most probable source of wealth as well as the timing of its arrival. Wealth comes in many ways—

via marriage, work, or family, for example. Endless permutations are revealed in the charts, and reading the way the elements interact within the chart will help to interpret this meaning accurately.

SUCCESS

The chart indicates whether you are destined to find recognition, becoming famous perhaps in the field of scholarship, in the performing arts, in the sciences or as a powerful captain of industry or a political leader. If you are destined to become a powerful person of influence or are destined for greatness, this too is usually revealed in the paht chee chart. Most importantly, the paht chee chart provides clues on which elements are favorable and which are unfavorable in your life.

RELATIVE ROLES

Your personal destiny chart reveals the true nature of your relationships with your relatives, including your parents, grandparents, and children. Your relationship with your spouse is the most significant, and this is revealed in the earthly branch of the day pillar.

CASE STUDY 1

HERE IS THE PAHT CHEE CHART OF SOMEONE BORN IN THE YEAR OF THE WOOD ROOSTER, DURING THE SEASON OF FALL. WE WILL EXAMINE THIS CHART STEP BY STEP TO HELP YOU UNDERSTAND HOW TO BEGIN A READING.

HOUR	DAY	MONTH	YEAR
Heavenly Stem	*Heavenly Stem*	*Heavenly Stem*	*Heavenly Stem*

YIN METAL	YANG WATER	YIN EARTH	YIN WOOD
This hour stem signifies your son	This day stem signifies your self	This month stem signifies your father	This year stem signifies your grandfather

HOUR	DAY	MONTH	YEAR
Earthly Branch	*Earthly Branch*	*Earthly Branch*	*Earthly Branch*

SNAKE YIN FIRE	MONKEY YANG METAL	OX YIN EARTH	ROOSTER YIN METAL
This hour branch signifies your daughter	This day branch signifies your spouse	This month branch signifies your mother	This year branch signifies your grandmother

HOUR HS: *Examine how this element interacts with the self element (day heavenly stem). If it supports the self element, children are a source of joy. If it clashes, offspring will cause problems.*

DAY HS: *Your self element is the most important in the chart. You must determine whether it is weak or strong and how it interacts with the surrounding elements.*

MONTH HS: *Examine how this element combines with your self element. It is good when it supports it, bad when there is a clash.*

YEAR HS: *This element has the least influence on your self element, but how it supports or clashes with other elements illuminates the chart reading.*

1. FOCUS ON THE ELEMENTS OF EACH OF THE CHARACTERS THAT MAKE UP THE CHART

Note that the heavenly stems are on the upper row, while the earthly branches (or animal signs) are on the lower row. We are looking at the basket of elements: there are 3 metal, 1 water, 2 earth, 1 wood, and 1 fire. All five elements—water, wood, fire, earth, and metal—are present, which means this is a well-balanced chart. The more balanced a chart is the better, that is, ideally it should have all five of the elements present. This is the best indication of a good life.

2. FOCUS ON THE BALANCE OF YIN AND YANG PILLARS

Again, there should ideally be a combination of both in order to create balance. When the pillars are all yin or all yang, the chart is said to be unbalanced and your life will be lacking in either yin or yang chi energy. If your life is lacking in yang chi energy, you should make up for this by systematically introducing yang elements into your surroundings, such as increasing the noise level (like keeping your radio and television turned on), increasing the amount of light in your surroundings, using yang colors such as white or red around you, and creating a lifestyle that is highly sociable whereby people visit you frequently. All this creates yang chi that will benefit you as it balances out your chart. In general, yang chi is associated with male, brightness, daytime, warmth, heat, activity, and energy, and yin chi is associated with female, silence, coldness, night, and moon. This chart has one yang pillar and three yin pillars, and this is fine because both yin and yang are present.

3. FOCUS ON THE EARTHLY BRANCHES

These are said to be beneficial when all four animal signs belong to the same affinity groups and are not hostile toward each other. This is based on the astrological grouping of friends and allies. The chart shows a triangle of affinity between the Rooster, the Snake, and the Ox. These three signs indicate this person is a deep thinker or philosopher because these three animals are the thinkers of Chinese astrology. The remaining animal sign is the Monkey, which is the secret friend of the Snake. (See Chapter Three for more information on horoscope allies among the Chinese animal signs.) The earthly branches indicate good relationships.

4. FOCUS ON THE HEAVENLY STEMS

It is best if the elements of the heavenly stems are in a productive relationship rather than a destructive one (see pages 28–33). When the stem elements harmonize, it suggests positive relationships and good family harmony. When they exhaust or destroy, it suggests underlying tensions. In this chart, metal produces water, and water produces wood, so there is some harmony here.

These initial four steps indicate things that can be picked up from the chart at a quick glance, and this is useful to do before undertaking a deeper analysis.

HOUR EB: *The child whose year of birth corresponds to the animal here will be closest to you. Examine the clashes or combination with the self element.*

DAY EB: *How this element interacts with the self and other elements will show the influence and strength of significant other parties in your life.*

MONTH EB: *How this element interacts with the self element reveals parental influence on you and the kind of luck your parents bring you.*

YEAR EB: *The influence of this element is not huge, but nonetheless it can be significant in terms of the overall fortune reading.*

CASE STUDY 2

THIS INITIAL ASSESSMENT IS DESIGNED TO LOOK AT THE OVERALL BALANCE OF THE CHART.

HOUR	DAY	MONTH	YEAR
Heavenly Stem	*Heavenly Stem*	*Heavenly Stem*	*Heavenly Stem*
YIN METAL	YIN WOOD	YIN EARTH	YIN WOOD

HOUR	DAY	MONTH	YEAR
Earthly Branch	*Earthly Branch*	*Earthly Branch*	*Earthly Branch*
SNAKE YIN FIRE	ROOSTER YIN METAL	OX YIN EARTH	ROOSTER YIN METAL

1. COUNT THE APPEARANCE OF EACH ELEMENT, NOTING ANY ABSENCES

In this chart, there are 3 metal, 2 earth, 2 wood, and 1 fire, so water is considered to be missing. Instantly we know that this person's life will be improved by incorporating the water element and thus balancing the elements, perhaps by including a water feature in the home or by living near water. Later when we delve deeper we will be able to see exactly how crucial the element of water is, and what kind of luck the element of water represents for this person. See also Missing Elements, pages 66–67.

2. NOTE WHETHER THE PILLARS ARE YIN OR YANG

A chart should ideally have a balance of yin and yang pillars. If all the pillars are yin (as is the case here), your life is sorely in need of yang energy. This can be supplied by noise, activity, being in well-lit areas or living in warm area or country rather than a cold one. If your chart has all yang characters you will benefit from peace and quiet.

3. DETERMINE YOUR SELF ELEMENT

The self element, which is the element indicated as the heavenly stem of the day pillar, plays a very important part in the reading. (In this chart, the self element is yin wood.) You will need to determine whether your self element is weak or strong, and you will find out how to do this in Chapter Two. The self element unlocks for you what the other elements in the chart represent. Since there are five elements in all, the self element will reveal five aspects of your luck, namely: Wealth, Financial Success; Friends, Foes, Competitors; Power, Rank, Recognition; Intelligence, Creativity; Resources, Support, Authority. We will examine these five types of luck in greater depth in Chapters Two and Three.

A GOOD CHART

For a chart to indicate success, wealth, happiness, or health, we need not only a well balanced and lucky set of elements in the paht chee chart, but also a set of ten-year luck pillars that support and strengthen, or balance, the elements of the paht chee chart. The ten-year luck pillars simply must indicate favorable elements that can support the person's self element for the chart to be considered good.

The elements of the ten-year luck pillars exert such a strong influence that they can cause a lucky paht chee chart to lack the strength to bring you auspicious success. Similarly, they can also bring you fantastic success even if you have an apparently weak paht chee chart. So the luck pillars offer crucial inputs into your potential for success and happiness. Often, when the elements in the luck pillars are favorable they will more than compensate for any weakness in the paht chee chart. They are then said to "remedy imbalances" in the paht chee chart.

The key to a successful reading therefore is to examine the ten-year luck pillars closely and see at what age the favorable elements required to strengthen or balance the paht chee chart make an appearance. If the required favorable elements do not make an appearance at all, then success and happiness can be elusive. However, all is not lost because then you consider the elements of calendar years (see the Appendix), for these too exert their influence on your destiny. If the elements of the calendar years are favorable the year brings good fortune. It stands to reason therefore that if both the luck pillars and the calendar years show favorable elements, then that is when you will enjoy fantastic luck! Those years do not come often and definitely do not come for everyone. This is the difference between having a good chart and being born with an unfavorable chart.

The elements of calendar years can strengthen or balance the elements in the paht chee chart, but generally if the elements in the luck pillars are unfavorable they are usually strong enough to cause misfortune or to prevent good luck from manifesting. Here is where those who know about the shortcomings in their luck pillars can do something about them. This means you can surround yourself with objects, colors, and so forth that signify the favorable element needed to improve your luck. (For a list of remedies, see pages 66–67.)

CHAPTER TWO

INTERPRETING THE ELEMENTS IN YOUR CHART

The theory of the five elements is fundamental to interpreting your paht chee chart. In this chapter you will learn what the elements might reveal about your destiny.

THE SELF ELEMENT AND ITS STRENGTH

THE PAHT CHEE CHART IS A DESTINY CHART. IT REVEALS YOUR CHARACTER, THE POTENTIAL YOU ARE BORN WITH, AND THE INFLUENCES THAT WILL DOMINATE YOUR LIFE. ALL OF THIS IS EXPRESSED AS ELEMENTS—THE ENTIRE LUCK PREDICTION EXERCISE IS BASED ON THE THEORY OF THE FIVE ELEMENTS, AND THE MOST SIGNIFICANT ELEMENT IS YOUR SELF ELEMENT.

Determining your self element is an important first step to unlocking the forces and influences that will shape your life destiny. Once you have discovered your element and determined whether it is weak or strong, and how it interacts with the other elements in your destiny, you will be able to reveal the secrets of your future, including:

• whether you will become wealthy
• what kind of success you can attain
• your most likely partner(s) and the kind of marriage you will have
• when you will meet your life partner
• the state of your health.

In the paht chee chart, your self element is the heavenly stem of the day pillar.

THE MEANING OF ELEMENT STRENGTH

Having identified your self element, the next thing to do is to determine whether it is weak or strong. The strength of the self element determines the elements that will be favorable for you as well as the elements that will hinder or block your success. In paht chee reading, no single element is intrinsically "good" or "bad"— each element interacts with others in a range of ways. You will need to be familiar with the theory of the five elements to master this aspect of paht chee reading (see The Five Elements, pages 28–33).

If the self element is weak, the element that produces it will need to be present before you can manifest whatever good luck is shown in your chart. For example, if the chart shows that you have a weak self element and also have wealth luck, this wealth can manifest only if the self element is made strong by the element that produces it being in the ten-year luck period chart or in the year chart (see the Appendix for year charts). This would mean, for example, that:

• If the self element is wood and it is weak, then it needs the water element to be present to strengthen it.
• If the self element is earth and it is weak, then it would need the fire element to strengthen it.

The water element or fire element needed may appear in the luck periods chart or in the year chart. For instance, the

PARTNER PREDICTION
Your self element (weak or strong water, wood, fire, earth, or metal) will indicate the kind of person you are most likely to spend your life with. Your ten-year luck pillar will tell you when you might meet them.

year 2006 is a fire earth year. So in 2006 if you needed the fire or earth element to strengthen a weak self element you would benefit at that time.

In 2010, which is a metal wood year, the wood element will strengthen you if your self element is weak fire. Fire destroys/dominates metal, so the metal element cannot overcome a strengthened fire. Similarly, the metal element will strengthen you if you are a weak water, and since water controls fire, a strengthened water has nothing to fear from fire. This all means that 2010 will be a beneficial year for people whose self element is either weak fire or weak water.

On the plus side, when a weak self element appears in the other pillars of the paht chee chart or in the ten-year luck pillars chart or in any year, it signifies that there are friends around to help. Having friends in this way is also interpreted as strengthening your self element.

If your self element is strong, you will find it easier to enjoy the luck indicated by the other elements. However, often when an individual's self element is strong, it indicates that there are many false friends around. There is jealousy and hidden envy. If your strong self element is wood, then when wood appears in your chart, it will always mean you will have competition. True friends are also hard to come by.

WHEN IS THE SELF ELEMENT WEAK OR STRONG?

The self element is weak when it is either exhausted or destroyed by many of the other elements around it. You need to count how many of the remaining seven elements in your paht chee chart are weakening the self element and how many are strengthening it. You may need to refer to the chart of five element cycles (on page 29) to remind yourself of the productive, destructive, and exhaustive cycles of the five elements.

The self element is strong when the surrounding elements strengthen it by either producing it or being the same element as it.

The elements of the hour and month pillars are closer to the self element than the elements of the year pillar, and they are thus said to exert greater influence on whether the self element is weak or strong. If in doubt whether your self element is strong or weak, consider the elements in the month pillar because these will exert the greatest effect on the strength or weakness of the self element.

Being able to interpret your chart accurately depends on how the elements of the chart interact with the self element and with each other, and, more particularly, how they interact with the elements that make up your ten-year luck pillars. It also depends on how they interact with the elements of each calendar year. These element interactions (or combinations) enable accurate predictions of good fortune and misfortunes for particular years.

It is important to determine correctly whether the self element is weak or strong because this has significant ramifications on subsequent readings. Case Study 3 and the case studies in the following pages will give you further practice of chart interpretation.

CASE STUDY 3

HOUR *Heavenly Stem*	**DAY** *Heavenly Stem*	**MONTH** *Heavenly Stem*	**YEAR** *Heavenly Stem*
辛	乙	己	乙
YIN METAL	YIN WOOD	YIN EARTH	YIN WOOD

HOUR *Earthly Branch*	**DAY** *Earthly Branch*	**MONTH** *Earthly Branch*	**YEAR** *Earthly Branch*
巳	酉	丑	酉
SNAKE YIN FIRE	ROOSTER YIN METAL	OX YIN EARTH	ROOSTER YIN METAL

1. DETERMINE THE SELF ELEMENT

The heavenly stem of the day pillar is yin wood, therefore the self element is yin wood.

2. EXAMINE THE ELEMENTS SURROUNDING THE SELF ELEMENT AND DETERMINE HOW THEY AFFECT IT

• The heavenly stem and earthly branch of the month pillar are yin earth. Wood destroys earth.

• The earthly branch of the day pillar is metal Rooster. Metal destroys wood.

• The hour pillar heavenly stem is metal, which destroys wood, and the earthly branch is fire, which exhausts wood.

The negative effect of these five elements closest to the self element is clear. Indeed, we can conclude from the above chart that the self element of wood is weak, as six of the seven other elements (one appearance of fire, two appearances of earth, and three of metal) are involved with wood in a destructive or exhaustive relationship.

THE ELEMENTS AND THE SEASONS

SINCE DETERMINING WHETHER THE SELF ELEMENT IS WEAK OR STRONG IS SUCH AN IMPORTANT FIRST STEP IN PAHT CHEE READING, YOU MUST ENDEAVOR TO GET IT ABSOLUTELY CORRECT. IF YOUR READING IS NOT IMMEDIATELY CLEAR, YOU CAN REFER TO THE SEASON OF BIRTH FOR FURTHER INFORMATION.

I f you are in any doubt at all about whether your self element is weak or strong, first count the elements of the chart that support and strengthen the self element before making up your mind. You can also place weighting on the season of birth based on the chart given below, which describes the strength of the elements in the seasons. So, for example, if your self element is wood, then if you were born in the spring means that instantly the season of birth makes the element strong, while being born in the fall instantly makes it very weak.

The element relating to your season of birth is shown in the earthly branch of the month pillar. Some paht chee experts maintain that the season of birth should be considered the determining factor when deciding whether a self element is weak or strong. This means that once you determine your self element you should next look at the earthly branch element of your month pillar. If this element supports the self element (either produces it or is the same element), then the self element is strong. If the season element exhausts or destroys the self element, however, then the self element is weak. According to this particular school of interpretation, it is only after you have determined the season element and if you are still uncertain that you consider the other surrounding elements.

STRENGTH OF ELEMENTS IN THE SEASONS

	METAL	WOOD	WATER	FIRE
SPRING	VERY WEAK	VERY STRONG	WEAK	STRONG
SUMMER	STRONG	WEAK	VERY WEAK	VERY STRONG
FALL	VERY STRONG	VERY WEAK	STRONG	WEAK
WINTER	WEAK	STRONG	VERY STRONG	VERY WEAK

CASE STUDY 4

THIS IS THE CHART OF PATRICK, WHO WAS BORN IN 1976, THE YEAR OF THE FIRE DRAGON.

HOUR *Heavenly Stem*	DAY *Heavenly Stem*	MONTH *Heavenly Stem*	YEAR *Heavenly Stem*
庚	丙	丁	丙
YANG METAL	YANG FIRE	YIN FIRE	YANG FIRE

HOUR *Earthly Branch*	DAY *Earthly Branch*	MONTH *Earthly Branch*	YEAR *Earthly Branch*
寅	戌	酉	辰
TIGER YANG WOOD	DOG YANG EARTH	ROOSTER YIN METAL	DRAGON YANG EARTH

1. DETERMINE THE SELF ELEMENT

Patrick's day heavenly stem reveals that his self element is yang fire.

2. DETERMINE WHETHER THIS FIRE IS WEAK OR STRONG

• The heavenly stem of the month pillar is yin fire, which strengthens the self element, but the earthly branch is metal, which is destroyed by fire.

• The earthly branch of the day pillar is earth, which exhausts fire.

• The hour heavenly stem is metal, which is destroyed by fire, and the earthly branch is wood, which produces fire.

The self element is therefore weakened by metal and earth but strengthened by wood and fire, so it is harder to determine the strength of the self element. The next step is to consider the person's month of birth more closely. Patrick was born in October, the season of fall. From the chart (left) we see that fire in the fall is weak. So Patrick's self element is weak fire.

TIMING AND ELEMENTS OF THE SEASONS

FIRST MONTH	SECOND MONTH	THIRD MONTH
SPRING		
TIGER YANG WOOD	RABBIT YIN WOOD	DRAGON YANG EARTH
February 4–March 6	*March 6–April 5*	*April 5–May 6*
SUMMER		
SNAKE YIN FIRE	HORSE YANG FIRE	SHEEP YIN EARTH
May 6–June 6	*June 6–July 7*	*July 7–August 8*
FALL		
MONKEY YANG METAL	ROOSTER YIN METAL	DOG YANG EARTH
August 8–September 8	*September 8–October 8*	*October 8–November 7*
WINTER		
BOAR YIN WATER	RAT YANG WATER	OX YIN EARTH
November 7–December 7	*December 7– January 6*	*January 6–February 4*

Another way to determine the effect of the season on the self element is to identify the element of the season, and whether it is yin or yang. Use the chart (left) to determine the season element. This method also shows how the earth element is accounted for: each season comprises three months, and the third month of each of the four seasons is said to be an earth element. Note that earth is a neutral element and its presence and influence will prevail throughout the year.

SEASONAL EFFECTS ON THE WOOD SELF ELEMENT

If your self element is wood, and you were born in the first or second months of spring, the wood element is strong and growing. The wood element brings you prosperity luck, and it strengthens your self element. This is also the best time of the year to make important decisions, start important projects, and celebrate happy occasions such as marriages, birthdays, and even have children. If you were born in the third month of spring, however, earth's influence is neutral.

If you were born in the summer, any success you experience comes only with hard work. Fire exhausts your energy.

If you were born in the fall, you will need plenty of help because this season of birth hurts you.

If you were born in the winter, during the first and second months you will be nurtured by water. Whenever you experience a difficult time in your life, you can expect some kind of reprieve or help during the winter months.

SEASONAL EFFECTS ON THE FIRE SELF ELEMENT

If your self element is fire and you were born in the first two months of the summer, the fire element is strong and there is harvesting luck; it is a time for reaping the rewards of your work. This would be a good time for you to celebrate, to get married, and to make important decisions. If you were born in the third month of summer, however, the earth element will exhaust you. The exhausting effect is less strong if your self element is yang fire. However, if earth is a favorable element for you then the effect of earth will be positive; nevertheless it will still exhaust your energies.

If you were born in the spring, the wood element of spring will nurture you. But if you were born in the fall or winter, the seasonal effect on your life is more likely to be negative. Those with weak fire as their self element need to be careful in the winter months. If they are strong fire people, however, the winter months will help by curbing their excess fire.

SEASONAL EFFECTS ON THE WATER SELF ELEMENT

If your self element is water, and you were born in the first two months of winter, then this is the season that will bring you wealth and prosperity. Everywhere there is snow and water, and these will strengthen you, more so if you are a weak water person. If you were born in the third month of winter, the effect of earth is neutral but there is the possibility it could hurt you. The earth of winter is yin earth, so any negative impact it may have on you is severe if your self element is also yin. If it is yang, the effect is greatly reduced.

Those whose self element is water will thrive in the fall and winter but will have less vitality in spring and summer. In spring they tend to feel drained by their work.

SEASONAL EFFECTS ON THE METAL SELF ELEMENT

Those whose self element is metal will do well during summer and very well in the fall, but need to work harder during the spring and winter. Those are the seasons when you will feel tired and activities will tend to leave you exhausted.

If you were born in the first two months of the fall, this is the season that will bring you lots of success and victory luck. In the fall the metal element reigns supreme, so this is the right time of year to make important decisions, start important projects, and get married. Those with metal as their self element will also find these months to be their best time (even if they were not born in the fall). If you were born in the third month, however, you will come under the influence of the earth element, which is good for weak metal people.

SEASONAL EFFECTS ON THE EARTH SELF ELEMENT

If your self element is earth, then the influence of the seasons impacts on you all through the year. Whether a season is good for you or not depends on whether your self element is weak or strong. If it is weak, the summer months will be very good for you since fire will enhance earth, while the spring will not be as great.

CASE STUDY 5

THIS IS THE PAHT CHEE CHART OF JESSICA, WHO WAS BORN IN 1979, THE YEAR OF THE EARTH SHEEP.

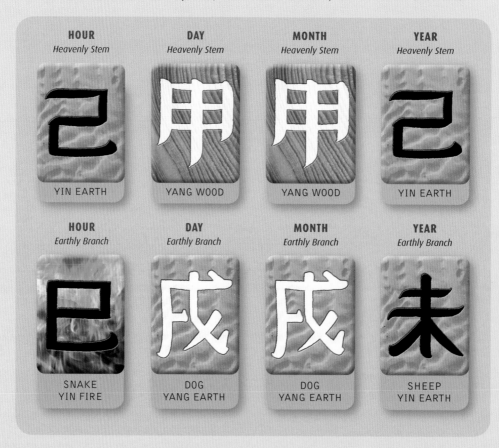

HOUR *Heavenly Stem*	DAY *Heavenly Stem*	MONTH *Heavenly Stem*	YEAR *Heavenly Stem*
己	甲	甲	己
YIN EARTH	YANG WOOD	YANG WOOD	YIN EARTH

HOUR *Earthly Branch*	DAY *Earthly Branch*	MONTH *Earthly Branch*	YEAR *Earthly Branch*
巳	戌	戌	未
SNAKE YIN FIRE	DOG YANG EARTH	DOG YANG EARTH	SHEEP YIN EARTH

1. DETERMINE THE SELF ELEMENT

Jessica's day heavenly stem reveals that her self element is yang wood.

2. DETERMINE WHETHER THIS WOOD IS WEAK OR STRONG

- The heavenly stem of the month pillar is yang wood so it complements the self element.
- The earthly branches of the day and month pillars are earth, which wood destroys (and therefore controls). The earthly branch of the month pillar also tells us that the season of birth is the third month of the fall (see chart, page 48) and Jessica's self element is influenced by yang earth (Dog). The effect is neutral. (The earth element appears at the end of each of the four seasons and it is said to have a neutral effect on the strength of the self element.)
- The hour heavenly stem is earth, which is destroyed or subdued by wood, and the hour earthly branch is fire, which exhausts wood. So these elements also weaken the self element of wood.

Jessica was born in November, the season of fall, which is when wood is very weak (see chart, page 46). So it appears that all the elements point to Jessica's self element being weak wood. She is someone who would benefit from water, but this element is missing from her chart.

3. CONSIDER THE INFLUENCE OF THE TEN-YEAR LUCK PILLAR CHART

If the ten-year luck pillars show years with water (or metal, because metal produces water), then Jessica will enjoy significant money luck during those years. This is because her wealth luck element is earth, and there are five earth elements in her chart. Because the chart has excess earth, Jessica cannot become wealthy unless her self element is strengthened. Water produces wood in the productive cycle, so she needs water.

If Jessica had plenty of water in her surroundings and had water in her ten-year luck pillars, she would benefit from the wealth indicators in her paht chee chart. Her wealth potential appears elusive, however. If she were to build a major water feature, such as a swimming pool, near her home, she would become very rich. This is indicated here by the presence of earth elements (her wealth element). Wealth luck and other kinds of luck are explored further in the next chapter.

CASE STUDY 6

THIS IS THE PAHT CHEE CHART OF KENNETH, AN UPWARDLY MOBILE INTERNET EXECUTIVE
BORN IN 1977, THE YEAR OF THE FIRE SNAKE.

HOUR *Heavenly Stem*	DAY *Heavenly Stem*	MONTH *Heavenly Stem*	YEAR *Heavenly Stem*
乙	戊	丙	丁
YIN WOOD	YANG EARTH	YANG FIRE	YIN FIRE

HOUR *Earthly Branch*	DAY *Earthly Branch*	MONTH *Earthly Branch*	YEAR *Earthly Branch*
卯	戌	午	巳
RABBIT YIN WOOD	DOG YANG EARTH	HORSE YANG FIRE	SNAKE YIN FIRE

1. DETERMINE THE SELF ELEMENT

Kenneth's day heavenly stem reveals that his self element is yang earth.

2. DETERMINE WHETHER THIS EARTH IS WEAK OR STRONG

His day earthly branch is earth and all month and year elements are fire, which produces earth. Kenneth was also born
in the summer when strong fire energy strengthens earth. This all means that the is a very strong earth person.

3. DETERMINE HIS FAVORABLE ELEMENTS

When you know the strength of your self element, you can work out which elements will be favorable and which will be unfavorable. Since Kenneth's self element is strong earth, his favorable elements will be those that destroy and exhaust the earth energy. This means that the elements that are favorable for Kenneth will be wood and metal, which destroy and exhaust earth, respectively. The reason for this is that it is only when a strong self element is kept under control that you are able to capture any good fortune that comes your way.

4. ASSESS THE BASKET OF ELEMENTS

If your paht chee chart is well balanced—with all five elements present—you are likely to have an auspicious life. It is only when the full basket of all five elements is present that the good fortune years, as indicated in your ten-year pillar luck charts, can manifest in good fortune. If elements are missing, their lack needs to be remedied. For example, Kenneth's chart has an excess of fire but is missing water and metal. To balance his chart (and therefore his life), Kenneth needs to include water and metal in his environment, otherwise there will be unexpected obstacles to his good fortune.

Kenneth's wealth luck is the water element, but water is missing from his paht chee chart. This means there is no obvious indication of wealth luck here. Kenneth has four fire elements in his chart, and fire here stands for his resources. So, Kenneth has more than enough to strengthen his earth element; this obvious strength causes his chart to be very unbalanced. Kenneth will find his friends becoming his competitors, and many will have their own secret agendas, which does not bode well for him. During fire years (see Appendix) competitive pressures will emerge that might end up "burning" Kenneth, so he needs to be extra careful during such years. The year 2006, which is an earth and fire year, will not be good for Kenneth. The year 2007, which is a water and fire year, will be a good but possibly exhausting time for him. He needs to surround himself with water and metal elements to remedy his situation. He needs to wear black, blue, and white, and it will also benefit him to go to the seaside frequently during the year. For further remedies for missing elements, see pages 66–67.

Moreover, Kenneth's strong earth energy needs wood energy in addition to water and metal. It would be a good idea for him to have plenty of growing plants in his home. With water and wood surrounding him, Kenneth will successfully bring balance into his private space and therefore overcome the bad luck caused by the elements of the year.

SUMMARY

Kenneth's charts indicate a woeful lack of the water element. There is excess of fire energy but no water. There is also no metal. Kenneth therefore needs water as well as metal and wood to ensure his chart, and therefore his life, stays balanced. In this case if his ten-year luck pillars chart shows that the crucial years of his adulthood have the required favorable elements of water and metal then—despite the highly imbalanced paht chee chart—Kenneth will enjoy good fortune.

DETERMINING FAVORABLE ELEMENTS

KNOWING YOUR SELF ELEMENT, AND KNOWING WHETHER IT IS WEAK OR STRONG, INSTANTLY TELLS YOU WHAT ELEMENTS ARE FAVORABLE FOR YOU. THIS PART OF PAHT CHEE INTERPRETATION RELIES ON THE PRINCIPLE OF THE FIVE ELEMENTS AND THEIR CYCLES OF PRODUCTION, DESTRUCTION, AND EXHAUSTION.

SELF SUPPORT

If your self element is weak fire you would benefit from surrounding yourself with living plants (and wearing green). This is because plants represent the wood element and the wood element produces the fire element—this extra fire supports the weak fire of your self element.

The guiding principle of favorable elements is that when your self element is weak, then you are said to be lacking the chi of your self element. You need, and thus will benefit from being close to and having, the element that produces your element. This element can be reflected in the things you place around you at home or in the office, and even in the way you dress and put on your make-up. It is in this sense that the paht chee chart can have important feng shui implications and far-reaching consequences.

In the case of Patrick, whose chart appears on page 47, we have noted that his self element is weak fire. In the productive cycle of elements, wood produces fire. This means that Patrick is someone who would benefit from having wood near him, so a primarily wooden house with lots of plants will benefit him. (See Missing Wood Remedies, page 66, for further wood element ideas.)

Patrick will also benefit from anyone whose self element is wood. This means that those among Patrick's close circle of friends who are wood people will be good for him. Patrick can use this information to check out his partner, his colleagues, his boss, his teachers, his professors, his parents, and his friends to see who among them will benefit him the most.

Therefore, if he is looking for a wife, he should choose a woman who has wood as her self element, or at least be born in a wood element year (see the Appendix for a list of years and their elements). Such a woman will benefit him and bring him luck. While wood element people are the most beneficial for him, the second best are people whose self element is water. This is because water produces wood, and wood produces his self element. Note that in the destructive cycle water destroys fire but in paht chee analysis, despite that being the case, this is the way to identify the second most favorable element. You look for the element that produces the most desirable element. (In any case, because water is missing from Patrick's chart water would be good for him.)

If Patrick's self element of fire had been strong instead of weak, then wood would cause him to have too much fire, which he

PAHT CHEE READING TIP

LEARNING HOW TO DECIPHER THE PAHT CHEE
CHART IS ONE THING, BUT ACCURATELY INTERPRETING THE
ELEMENTS TO MAKE LUCK PREDICTIONS TAKES TIME.
HERE'S A TIP FOR WHEN YOU GET STARTED.

Start by taking note of the general trends of your life, determining favorable and unfavorable years and so forth before looking for answers to specific questions about your love life, your marriage, your children, and your potential for work advancement and wealth enhancement. Focus initially on mastering the concept of weak and strong self elements and determining favorable and unfavorable elements. Remember that all dimensions of luck prediction that focus on aspirations of wealth and relationships are relative and hence a certain amount of subjectivity will always be involved.

does not need. Instead he would then need his self element of fire to be kept under control. In that instance, earth would be good for him, since earth exhausts fire.

DETERMINING GOOD LUCK YEARS

Knowing his favorable element will enable Patrick to identify his good years; these are years that have wood as either the heavenly stem or the earthly branch. Since his self element is weak fire, fire energy is also good for him because this would strengthen his own fire.

Thus the years 2004 and 2005 would have been good years for Patrick because the heavenly stem of these years was wood. In 2004 it was yang wood and in 2005 it was yin wood. Since Patrick is a yang fire person the year of the yang wood would have been better for him than the year of the yin wood. So 2004 was better for him than 2005.

Later we will find when we examine Patrick's ten-year luck pillars that he is experiencing a pillar which features yang metal and yang water. This means the presence of water in his luck pillar will be

helping him. The year 2006 is a fire and earth year. The presence of fire helps Patrick to strengthen his self element but on the other hand the presence of earth may exhaust him, too. Overall, 2006 is a fairly good year for him.

Patrick can use information about his favorable elements to check the calendar years, or he can use it to check his ten-year luck pillars, or he can do both. This is the way to identify the ten-year period or periods that will be his stellar years. When wood appears in both the ten-year luck pillars and also in a calendar year that falls in those ten years that will be a year when Patrick will benefit enormously. For example, that is when he could get a promotion at work, win a big contract, or simply get an offer he cannot refuse.

FAVORABLE AND UNFAVORABLE ELEMENTS

HERE ARE YOUR FIRST AND SECOND FAVORABLE ELEMENTS BASED ON YOUR WEAK OR STRONG SELF ELEMENT.

Commit your favorable elements to memory. Pay particular attention to your first favorable element and look out for years when this element occurs—either as a heavenly stem or an earthly branch—for those will usually be the years that are good for you. Note, however, that this rule is a general one and there will be charts where there are exceptions to the rule.

YOUR SELF ELEMENT	YOUR FAVORABLE ELEMENT	YOUR SECOND FAVORABLE ELEMENT	YOUR UNFAVORABLE ELEMENT	YOUR SECOND UNFAVORABLE ELEMENT
WEAK WOOD	WATER	WOOD	FIRE	METAL
STRONG WOOD	METAL	FIRE	WATER	WOOD
WEAK FIRE	WOOD	FIRE	EARTH	WATER
STRONG FIRE	WATER	EARTH	WOOD	FIRE
WEAK EARTH	FIRE	EARTH	METAL	WOOD
STRONG EARTH	WOOD	METAL	FIRE	EARTH
WEAK METAL	EARTH	METAL	WATER	FIRE
STRONG METAL	FIRE	WATER	EARTH	METAL
WEAK WATER	METAL	WATER	WOOD	EARTH
STRONG WATER	EARTH	WOOD	METAL	WATER

FINE-TUNING FAVORABLE AND UNFAVORABLE ELEMENTS

It is as important to know what your unfavorable elements are as your favorable elements, since the presence of unfavorable elements in the luck pillars or in the calendar years will alert you to the years that will be tiresome and exhausting for you. These will be the years when you should really lie low, especially if the astrological charts and your animal sign readings also indicate this.

For instance, the year 2006 is a fire earth year and thus will prove to be particularly trying for those whose self element is weak metal. The fire of the heavenly stem of 2006 will send destructive or "killing" chi to someone whose self element is weak metal. However, the earth element of the earthly branch of the year will strengthen metal.

The favorable and unfavorable elements associated with strong or weak versions of the five elements are summarized in the chart opposite. It is worth studying the chart carefully, because it contains a fundamental part of the paht chee analysis. Later on, when we go deeper into the investigation of the ten-year luck pillars, you will need to know your favorable and unfavorable elements. For example, when you analyze your paht chee chart for signs of wealth potential, fame potential, career luck, or other areas of luck, your favorable elements will play a valuable role.

Favorable and unfavorable elements are particularly important in marginal cases where you cannot quite decide whether your self element is weak or strong. In this instance, you need to study the other elements in your chart and consider the season of the month of birth. Sometimes there may be a couple of missing elements that make the chart unbalanced, and then instead of one or two favorable elements you might well need to make up for the missing elements. In such an instance the missing elements would improve the balance of elements in the paht chee. In another instance a wood person may have been born in winter when it is too cold for the wood to survive. Then, wood would need heat, and thus will benefit from fire, even though fire exhausts wood.

These are factors that require a judgmental input and, since every chart is so different, it is not possible to cover all possibilities in a book. The permutations of the paht chee chart are incredibly diverse. This is why you need to be able to reason things out logically in a comprehensive manner; only then can you have a full reading of the paht chee. However, as long as you understand the fundamentals that underpin the theory of the weak or strong self element you should have little trouble identifying your favorable and unfavorable elements. Determining this correctly is half the battle won.

WINTER WOOD

Winter-born wood element people need to boost their self element by associating with people whose self element is fire and ensuring their homes are brightly lit. Although winter represents the water element and is therefore good for a weak wood person, wood also needs fire for warmth and to balance out the season. So, even though in theory fire exhausts wood, it is nonetheless good for weak wood people in winter.

CASE STUDY 7

HOUR Heavenly Stem	DAY Heavenly Stem	MONTH Heavenly Stem	YEAR Heavenly Stem
乙	甲	辛	丙
YIN WOOD	YANG WOOD	YIN METAL	YANG FIRE

HOUR Earthly Branch	DAY Earthly Branch	MONTH Earthly Branch	YEAR Earthly Branch
亥	午	卯	申
BOAR YIN WATER	HORSE YANG FIRE	RABBIT YIN WOOD	MONKEY YANG METAL

RELATIONSHIPS IN THE CHARTS

- Hour pillar heavenly stem represents son.
- Hour pillar earthly branch represents daughter.
- Day pillar heavenly stem represents self.
- Day pillar earthly branch represents spouse.
- Month pillar heavenly stem represents father.
- Month pillar earthly branch represents mother.
- Year pillar heavenly stem represents grandfather.
- Year pillar earthly branch represents grandmother.

SELF ELEMENT AND RELATIONSHIPS

If your self element is weak, your favorable element is the element that produces it. People with the same element will be your friends. The weaker your self element, the more friends you will have. If your self element is strong, however, your favorable element is one that destroys it, and people with the same element become your competitors. Sometimes they even become your enemies. In summary, the weaker your self element, the more friends you will have in your life; the stronger your self element, the more competitors and enemies you will have in life, that is, people who will be jealous of you, or your success and your accomplishments. This does not mean that having a weak self element is better than having a strong self element. When your self element is strong it is easier for you to enjoy the different types of luck such as wealth, creativity, power and so forth. The idea is that it should simply not be "too strong." When it is only marginally strong then, although the favorable elements are those that destroy and exhaust it, such a person has the edge in that the luck indicated in the chart will manifest more easily.

The paht chee chart also reveals a great deal about the influence of particular people in our lives: parents, grandparents, spouses, and children. Your loved ones can be identified in the chart based on the element relationships as well as on the pillars themselves. The readings vary according to whether the chart belongs to a man or a woman.

FOR A MAN, THE CHART WOULD SHOW:
• Self element (heavenly stem, day pillar) is yang wood
• Wife is earth conquered by wood
• Father is also earth conquered by wood
• Mother is water, which produces wood
• Children are metal, which destroys wood
• Siblings are wood (same as the self element)
• The house of the spouse is the earthly branch of the day pillar, which in this case is Horse (yang fire).

FOR A WOMAN THE CHART WOULD READ THE SAME, EXCEPT:
• If her self element is yang wood, the husband is metal, which is the element that destroys the self element of wood.
• The offspring are fire, which is the element that exhausts the self element of wood.

Also note that the DAY pillar depicts the self and the spouse while the HOUR pillar depicts the children. The MONTH pillar depicts the parents while the YEAR pillar depicts the grandparents or ancestors. These indications are to be seen as guidelines and parents can also refer to employers or bosses. Children can be adopted or one's natural born offspring. The Master reader needs to weave all the pieces of information together to present a complete reading.

YOUR BASKET OF ELEMENTS

HOW DO YOU RESPOND TO CHALLENGES AND CHANCES? WHILE YOUR CHINESE ASTROLOGICAL ANIMAL SIGN (THE EARTHLY BRANCH OF THE YEAR PILLAR) WILL GIVE YOU A GOOD IDEA OF THE KIND OF PERSON YOU ARE, IT IS YOUR OVERALL "BASKET" OF ELEMENTS THAT WILL REVEAL HOW YOU ARE MOST LIKELY TO FACE LIFE'S ARRAY OF PROBLEMS AND OPPORTUNITIES.

The paht chee chart is what identifies the potential of your destiny, and it reveals what you are capable of when you are at your best and when you are able to rise above obstacles caused by any number of annual, astrological, or feng shui afflictions.

The paht chee chart tells you much about yourself by highlighting any shortcomings (indicated by the lack of certain elements) that block you from making the most of opportunities. It may be that you are naturally fearful of taking risks and so you will need to strengthen your courage and your vitality. Perhaps your aggressive nature rubs people up the wrong way, thereby losing you the main chance—in which case, you may have an excess of some dominant element making you come across too strong. You will need an element to suppress overexuberance. Knowing your own latent weakness, as expressed in the paht chee chart, will go a long way toward ensuring that you benefit more from the opportunities that come your way.

It is from this perspective that understanding your character and personality traits can be such a boon in helping you make better use of the resources and opportunities that come into your life. How you respond to opportunities and lucky breaks is a function of many factors. Thus, while different types of luck can act as catalysts for us to move to the next stage of our life, whether the next stage is more successful or happier depends on how we respond to the catalyst. When you weigh your basket of elements, you will discover the strength of the different elements in your basket, and this will provide you with clues to your character and your destiny, and help you consider how to respond to life's opportunities. You will also discover whether any elements are missing from your chart and what you might need to do to remedy their absence (see Missing Elements pages 66–67).

WEIGHING THE BASKET OF ELEMENTS

All five elements have a role to play in your well-being. Ideally, your chart will have a balance of the elements, bringing harmony and good fortune to your life. An excess or

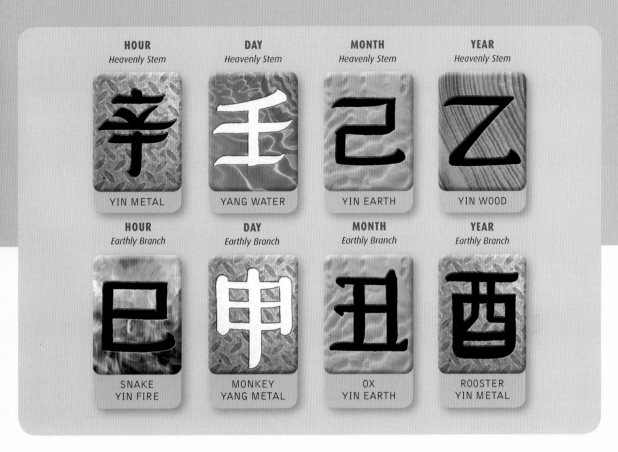

HOUR *Heavenly Stem*	**DAY** *Heavenly Stem*	**MONTH** *Heavenly Stem*	**YEAR** *Heavenly Stem*
辛	壬	己	乙
YIN METAL	YANG WATER	YIN EARTH	YIN WOOD

HOUR *Earthly Branch*	**DAY** *Earthly Branch*	**MONTH** *Earthly Branch*	**YEAR** *Earthly Branch*
巳	申	丑	酉
SNAKE YIN FIRE	MONKEY YANG METAL	OX YIN EARTH	ROOSTER YIN METAL

a complete lack of a particular element both introduce a negative note into your chart that you will need to address.

To make a character reading of your basket of elements, simply count up how many times each element makes an appearance. As a general rule, a weighting of four, that is, if an element appears four times, indicates strength as well as a positive outcome from possessing the characteristic indicated by the element. But when the weighting exceeds four, the strong point transforms into a liability. Usually the most auspicious indication is when our basket of elements has a balanced weighting of elements—this is when all five elements are present in weightings of 1s, 2s, or 3s. A more or less equal representation of all five elements indicates a well-balanced life in which all major areas—health, family, wealth, career, children—will feature positively.

When you have become more sensitive to the weighting of elements, you will be able to fine-tune the play of elements that surround you. The selection of elements is a dynamic process, changing with the season and the year. So what is "beneficial" for you is as much a function of your chart, and its basket of elements, as it is of the element that is ruling the season and the year you are going through. For instance, if your chart lacks the water element, then winter is better for you than summer, because water is the element associated with winter.

WEIGH THE BASKET

This "basket" contains 3 metal, 2 earth, 1 water, 1 wood, and 1 fire—a very balanced chart.

PERSONALITY READINGS

WHEN YOU WEIGH YOUR BASKET OF ELEMENTS, YOU ARRIVE AT A "WEIGHTING" FOR EACH OF THE ELEMENTS. THE WEIGHTINGS MIGHT INDICATE AN EXCESS OR A LACK THAT NEEDS YOUR ATTENTION. THE NUMBER OF TIMES EACH ELEMENT APPEARS IN YOUR CHART REVEALS A LOT ABOUT YOU. PERSONALITY READINGS BASED ON THE WEIGHTINGS ARE SUMMARIZED HERE.

I n reading the summary for each of the elements, it is important to bear in mind that most people demonstrate a mixture of two or three traits in different proportions. And there will usually be one or two missing elements.

It is not possible to offer a complete recipe approach to reading the paht chee, since different combinations of the elements could give rise to confusion. There will be instances when you must use your own judgment whether to put greater weight on one element rather than on another. When in doubt, you can also look to the elements prevailing in any year to give you extra leads to the reading (see Appendix).

In addition to using the following readings to interpret the dominant elements in your basket of elements, you can also apply their meanings when reading your self element (that is, the element indicated in your day heavenly stem). This element offers strong indications of your personality and character traits. It also indicates your strong and weak points and reveals the way you respond to opportunities.

WOOD

WEIGHTING: 4 +

A high wood weighting indicates a highly creative individual. You will be someone who has amazing farsightedness and vision. You are also artistic, possessing vivid powers of imagination. You strive for the stars; sometimes your ambitions may overreach your ability.

If you have a high weighting of wood it is likely that you will grab at opportunities that come your way and you will react in an imaginative and creative way that will benefit you.

If you have a wood element weighting of more than 4, then you might just be overreaching yourself. Your ambition may get the better of you. Be careful, be courageous, but never be rash. Never allow your creativity to diminish into obsessiveness, for then you will miss the wood for the trees. Your vision could get clouded when it should be crystal clear, and your creativity will be fruitless.

WEIGHTING: 2 OR 3

You demonstrate creativity and artistic leanings yet have the right amount of practical attitude to stay stable and balanced. Your reaction to opportunities will be more measured and well thought out. This is because with a rating of 2 or 3 you are also benefiting from important inputs from the other elements that appear in your paht chee chart.

WEIGHTING: 0 OR 1

If the chart is missing the wood element or has only one, it indicates a lack of creativity and imagination. You have little time for the grand vision and tend to be impatient with dreamers. You will seldom be able to take advantage of opportunities that come your way.

If this describes you, try surrounding yourself with some water element friends, or simply have water near you—live near the sea or have an aquarium or water feature in your home. Water will help you to overcome inertia in your life and make you more alert to the big breaks that come your way.

FIRE

WEIGHTING: 4 +

A high fire weighting indicates a rather extravagant as well as vivacious personality, someone who stimulates others and inspires those around them to follow suit.

You will be very charismatic, have loads of energy and vitality, and will also be highly intelligent, sharp, and incisive. You are someone to be reckoned with, but also someone whose smartness could degenerate into an overbearing attitude that puts people off.

When opportunity knocks, fire dominant people usually respond with the grand gesture. You allow your mind to expand exponentially, and when you succeed it is in a blaze of publicity. You dazzle in the limelight, and your star shines brightly.

When the fire element weighting in your paht chee chart is higher than 4, the fire element will burn itself out. This means that your time in the limelight will be shortlived.

ELEMENTAL CHARACTERS
Your paht chee chart's basket of elements reveals whether you are primarily vivacious, creative, determined, shy, or intellectual.

WEIGHTING: 2 OR 3

You are highly spirited and active. You usually respond enthusiastically but you also experience a steadying influence provided by another element, so your response is usually rather more careful than that of people with a 4 weighting in their chart. You will generally, therefore, make good use of any opportunities that come your way.

WEIGHTING: 0 OR 1

This indicates that you are a quiet, homely personality. You will usually be blind to the main chance, being rather obtuse or naïve in character. This will cause you to miss out when opportunities come—it is as if you wear blinkers.

So do note that merely having the indication of good fortune is not enough to make the most of the opportunities that come into your life. You also need to possess the sharpness of character to see, the attitude to respond, and the courage to take action—each in correct measure—to really benefit from good fortune that comes your way.

EARTH

WEIGHTING: 4+

A high earth weighting indicates that you are determined to the point of being obstinate or dogmatic. Earth is usually associated with stability and someone who is very circumspect and proper. You will seldom be the live wire of any party. Usually you will resonate with the grounding stability of earth. So when opportunity knocks the response from a dominant earth person is almost certain to be planned, calculated, and most importantly to lead to success. Sometimes, however, when the response is too measured and too well planned, the opportunity could slip through your fingers.

When the weighting in your chart is more than 4 and there is an excess of earth, success potential turns into a loss situation. Here the excess earth causes a plodding response, which translates into losing the main chance. You will experience an opportunity slipping through your fingers.

WEIGHTING: 2 OR 3

You are a particularly practical, down-to-earth person, who is also reliable and trustworthy. When helped by the presence of the fire element in equal measure, an earth person will make a great deal of the opportunity that comes into the life chart.

You will almost certainly benefit from a good luck period and will not lose out on any big break that comes your way.

WEIGHTING: 0 OR 1

You are someone who is less grounded, probably rash and perhaps unreliable. In fact, if the earth element is missing from your paht chee chart, some experts see this as indicating a tendency to dishonesty. This would be useful knowledge for a human resources manager to take note of when hiring employees!

METAL

WEIGHTING: 4+

A high weighting of the metal element is a clear indication of someone lacking in sentiments and emotions, at least publicly. You tend to be shy and cover your shyness with a brusque manner. You are comfortable in situations that do not require any show of emotion. Corporate situations will benefit you, because you will be able to safely hide behind your corporate title, business suit, and office position.

You are likely to be very competitive, businesslike, entrepreneurial, and aggressively direct in dealings with others. You are an extremely enterprising individual and can be relied upon to get the work done. You will also tend to be courageous and are the stuff of heroes.

When you enter into a period of good luck, you are literally unstoppable. You will benefit from the main chance unless your weighting is more than 4, and then surplus aggression may be a problem. In this instance, deals can fall through, and success is blocked by a dogmatism that proves negative.

WEIGHTING: 2 OR 3

You possess the same positive qualities but in smaller measure, and are thus more amenable to success. You are probably a sporting individual who is competitive but also astute—you know when to be obstinate and when to give in.

WEIGHTING: 0 OR 1

If the metal element is missing from your paht chee chart, you will demonstrate a lack of will. Your life will lack discipline and you will have a tendency to sentimentality and indecision.

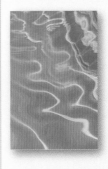

WATER

WEIGHTING: 4+

A high weighting in the water element indicates a gifted intellectual. You are someone who has amazing communicative, research, and scholarly skills. You are eloquent and adventurous, and tend to be effusive and spontaneously loud when dealing with others. You will easily grasp success opportunities.

If you have higher than a 4 rating, you could waste your good fortune through lack of focused motivation and probably also an inability to recognize your own aspirations.

WEIGHTING: 2 OR 3

You are talkative, bright, and lucid. Since intelligence is strongly associated with the water element, you will most definitely recognize opportunities that materialize and have no problem getting used to better lifestyles and enjoying your success.

WEIGHTING: 0 OR 1

You will tend to be secretive and shy. You are cautious in business and reserved socially. If you are not careful, you will lose sight of opportunities.

LIVELY LINEUP
People with a high water weighting in their basket of elements are gifted and adventurous and will easily grasp all of life's opportunities.

MISSING ELEMENTS

ONE OF THE MAIN KEYS TO INTERPRETING THE PAHT CHEE CHART IS FOUND BY COUNTING THE DIFFERENT ELEMENTS IN THE CHART. THE WEIGHING OF THE ELEMENTS NOT ONLY REVEALS THE DOMINANT ELEMENT BUT ALSO HIGHLIGHTS ANY MISSING ELEMENTS. MISSING ELEMENTS HAVE THE POTENTIAL TO CAUSE PROBLEMS IN YOUR LIFE AND NEED TO BE ADDRESSED.

The dominant element of your paht chee chart, which is not the same as the self element, is what indicates your personality traits. The strength of these traits is a direct correlation of the frequency or weight of each element in the chart. If any elements are missing from your chart, you should endeavor to compensate by using one of the remedies outlined below. The remedies include using simple color therapy in the way you dress and by applying the principles of feng shui (and thus, the five elements) in the way you create your personal space.

REMEDY PRINCIPLES

Let's take a look at what happens and what you should do when specific elements are missing from your paht chee chart. When more than one element is missing, you could either choose only the missing element that corresponds to your favorable element or incorporate both missing elements into your name. Remember to maintain a balance of elements at all times. Refrain from overdoing it. When a single element dominates, the whole chart

gets unbalanced and then obstacles can develop to bring you aggravation.

MISSING WATER REMEDIES

Incorporate a water feature in or near your home or live by a river, lake, or the sea. Wear or surround yourself with black, blue or purple.

MISSING WOOD REMEDIES

When wood is lacking it is an excellent idea to incorporate wood into the name of the person, as this will immediately bring better fortune. This could be words that suggest plants and flowers. Plants symbolize growth, while flowers symbolize harvests. Building a home where there is lavish use of wood would also be beneficial, or you could simply furnish your home with wooden furniture. Wear or surround yourself with green. Have plenty of flowers and plants around you.

MISSING FIRE REMEDIES

If the fire element is missing from your paht chee chart, keep your house well lit. Bright lights will benefit you enormously,

especially if you were also born during the winter months, because this means you need the warmth of summer. You could also incorporate fire element words into your name. These include words like "sun," "sunshine," "brightness," and so forth. You should wear or surround yourself with red, orange, and pink.

MISSING METAL REMEDIES

If the metal element is missing from your paht chee chart, introduce lots of metallic energy into your living space. Wear plenty of fine jewelry, especially made of gold. You could also incorporate the word "gold" in your name. The word "kim" is very popular with the Chinese—it means gold/metal. You should wear or surround yourself with white, silver, and gold.

MISSING EARTH REMEDIES

If earth is the missing element in your chart, let stones, crystals, and other earth materials dominate your living space. You could also incorporate earth words into your name—here it is a good idea to use words that mean precious stones, such as "diamond" or "ruby." The Chinese are also very fond of using the names of precious stones—especially "jade"—to name their children. You should wear or surround yourself with yellow and brown.

HOME REMEDY
You can compensate for the lack of wood element in your paht chee chart by surrounding yourself with wood at home in the form of décor and furniture.

CASE STUDY 8

HOUR *Heavenly Stem*	**DAY** *Heavenly Stem*	**MONTH** *Heavenly Stem*	**YEAR** *Heavenly Stem*

YIN METAL	YIN WOOD	YIN EARTH	YIN WOOD
HOUR *Earthly Branch*	**DAY** *Earthly Branch*	**MONTH** *Earthly Branch*	**YEAR** *Earthly Branch*

SNAKE YIN FIRE	ROOSTER YIN METAL	OX YIN EARTH	ROOSTER YIN METAL

RELATIONSHIPS IN THE CHARTS

- Hour pillar heavenly stem represents son.
- Hour pillar earthly branch represents daughter.
- Day pillar heavenly stem represents self.
- Day pillar earthly branch represents spouse.
- Month pillar heavenly stem represents father.
- Month pillar earthly branch represents mother.
- Year pillar heavenly stem represents grandfather.
- Year pillar earthly branch represents grandmother.

1. WEIGH THE ELEMENTS IN THE CHART

There are: 3 metal, 1 fire, 2 wood, 2 earth, and 0 water.

2. DETERMINE THE DOMINANT ELEMENT

The dominant element of this chart is metal.

3. DETERMINE ANY MISSING ELEMENTS AND ELEMENTS IN SHORT SUPPLY

The water element is missing and there is a shortage of fire.

4. DETERMINE THE COURSE OF ACTION REQUIRED, IF ANY

The chart requires water for it to be balanced. As soon as water is brought into this person's life, good fortune will arrive. For example, having a water feature in his home, such as a pool, would definitely enhance the chart and bring better all-round luck to this person. However, although water is absent from the chart, there are three metals and metal produces water. This means the person should have no difficulty in creating the presence of water to benefit his life.

HIDDEN ELEMENTS

ALTHOUGH THE PAHT CHEE CHART SHOWS EIGHT VISIBLE ELEMENTS, IT MAY ALSO CONTAIN HIDDEN ELEMENTS. FOR A MORE ACCURATE WEIGHING OF THE DOMINANT ELEMENTS OF THE CHART, AND ALSO FOR A MORE COMPLETE READING OF DESTINY AND PERSONALITY TRAITS, YOU SHOULD LOOK FOR THE HIDDEN ELEMENTS IN YOUR CHART AND ADD THEM TO YOUR BASKET.

SECRETS OF SUCCESS

If hidden elements in your personal destiny chart bring your total of wealth elements to four, you are very likely to become rich and prosperous. For this prosperity to manifest, however, you would need to make your self element strong.

Hidden elements are present when the heavenly stems and earthly branches manifest specific combinations in the chart. Your chart may include hidden heavenly stems or hidden earthly branches. First, look for these hidden elements and then see whether these elements are favorable and whether they support or clash with the other elements in your chart. Hidden elements are added to your basket of elements—they may create a better balance and hence a better life for the person or they may be harmful or cause excessive dominance of certain elements, so creating obstacles to success.

HIDDEN HEAVENLY STEM ELEMENTS

Heavenly stems produce a hidden element when a yang stem combines with a yin stem. Thus:

• When yang wood combines with yin earth the hidden element created is earth.
• When yin wood combines with yang metal the hidden element is metal.
• When yang fire combines with yin metal the hidden element created is water.

• When yin fire combines with yang water the hidden element created is wood.
• When yang earth combines with yin water the hidden element created is fire.

When hidden heavenly stems are created in your chart it is usually read as a good sign. If the element created is favorable for you and improves the overall balance of the chart it is exceptionally good. Look at the example chart shown here. Note that all the heavenly stems here are yin, so there are no hidden elements in this chart. Thus take note that hidden elements can occur only when the pillars include both yin and yang heavenly stems in the chart.

HIDDEN EARTHLY BRANCH ELEMENTS

In the case of the earthly branches, hidden elements manifest in two ways:
1 In the combination of three branches.
2 In the combination of two branches.
When hidden elements emerge as a result of three branches combining, the new hidden element created is much stronger than when it is the result of two branches combining.

DETERMINING HIDDEN ELEMENTS

HOUR *Heavenly Stem*	**DAY** *Heavenly Stem*	**MONTH** *Heavenly Stem*	**YEAR** *Heavenly Stem*

YIN METAL	YIN WOOD	YIN EARTH	YIN WOOD

HOUR *Earthly Branch*	**DAY** *Earthly Branch*	**MONTH** *Earthly Branch*	**YEAR** *Earthly Branch*

SNAKE YIN FIRE	ROOSTER YIN METAL	OX YIN EARTH	ROOSTER YIN METAL

There are four three-branch combinations. These are the combinations of the allies among the 12 animal signs:

1 When Monkey, Rat, and Dragon combine a new element of water is created.

2 When Boar, Rabbit, and Sheep combine a new element of wood is created.

3 When Snake, Rooster, and Ox combine a new element of metal is created.

4 When Tiger, Horse, and Dog combine a new element of fire is created.

There are six two-branch combinations and these are combinations of the secret friends among the 12 Chinese astrological animal signs:

1 Rat (water) combining with Ox (earth) creates hidden earth.

2 Tiger (wood) combining with Pig (water) creates hidden wood.

3 Rabbit (wood) combining with Dog (earth) creates hidden fire.

4 Dragon (earth) combining with Rooster (metal) creates hidden metal.

5 Snake (fire) combining with Monkey (metal) creates hidden water.

6 Horse (fire) combining with Sheep (earth) creates hidden fire.

The addition of hidden elements will create an entirely new basket of elements for you to analyze.

CHAPTER THREE

LUCK TYPES AND TIMING

In this chapter you will discover the five types of luck you were born with and at which stage of your life each type will be at its zenith.

YOUR FUTURE FORTUNES

YOUR PAHT CHEE CHART WILL REVEAL THE LUCK YOU ARE LIKELY TO HAVE IN THE FOLLOWING FIVE AREAS: WEALTH, FRIENDSHIP, POWER, INTELLIGENCE, AND RESOURCES. THESE LUCK CATEGORIES REPRESENT THE SUM TOTAL OF MOST PEOPLE'S ASPIRATIONS. THESE ARE THE THINGS THAT EVERYONE WANTS TO FIND OUT ABOUT WHEN THEY DECIDE TO HAVE THEIR FUTURE READ.

RICH REVELATIONS
If the wealth element is present in your paht chee chart you might be destined for great wealth. If it appears as a hidden element, it is considered to be particularly auspicious.

The paht chee chart reveals five major types of prospective luck for each individual. The potential for each type of luck is revealed via the elements, and the timing of their appearance in our lives is revealed by the ten-year luck pillar charts and also the elements of every calendar year (see Appendix).

Once you know how to identify the presence of different kinds of luck in your chart, you can proceed to undertake a detailed analysis of your luck potential, looking at both the paht chee as well as the ten-year luck pillars.

WEALTH AND FINANCIAL SUCCESS

Everyone would like to know whether it is in their destiny to become rich and, if so, at what age it would begin to happen, that is, when the money will actually start "rolling in." Many people also want to know exactly how rich they will be. How long do they have to wait and what signs can there be to indicate when they are about to strike it big?

They would also like to know how the wealth would come about—through their own efforts, intelligence, and creativity; or through making a brilliant marriage or through the help and patronage of someone, a relative, a boss, or a powerful mentor perhaps? In a paht chee reading, wealth is divided into two kinds: direct wealth and unexpected wealth.

There are so many questions we have in our heads relating to this one type of luck alone. Getting reasonably rich is something most of us aspire to, and the good thing about the paht chee chart is that, besides revealing the likelihood of wealth in our charts, it also implicitly shows us remedies and cures related to the five elements that we can put into place to "help the wealth luck along." Indeed, this is the aspect of paht chee reading that is the most exciting—the fact that we can give our wealth luck a boost.

To find out if you have wealth luck in your chart, you must first determine whether the element that represents wealth to you is present in your chart. Wealth in a paht chee chart is signified by the element that is destroyed by the self element. Therefore, if your self element is

wood, then since wood destroys earth, earth element signifies wealth in your chart and your luck pillars. It is a good idea to commit this formula to memory, because it helps you to develop an easy familiarity with the five elements.

If the wealth element is present in your paht chee chart, the next step is to find out how many times it occurs. If it occurs once, twice, or three times it indicates the potential for wealth luck, but note this indicates only the *potential* for wealth. When the wealth element can be found in the chart the potential for you being rich is said to be reflected in your chart. Sometimes when the wealth element is missing, it may show up as a hidden element. This suggests there is hidden wealth in your chart and it is therefore regarded as a very auspicious indication indeed.

It is also possible to have too much of the wealth element. For example, if wood is your wealth element and you have four or five wood in your chart, this is excessive and it becomes something negative. This may indicate an obsession with getting rich to an extent that it will harm you.

YOUR WEALTH LUCK ELEMENT

WEALTH IS SIGNIFIED BY THE ELEMENT THAT IS DESTROYED BY THE SELF ELEMENT

SELF ELEMENT	WEALTH LUCK ELEMENT
WOOD	EARTH
WATER	FIRE
METAL	WOOD
EARTH	WATER
FIRE	METAL

The remedy is to introduce the element that exhausts the wealth element in order to weaken it. The second step is to determine whether the wealth elements that appear in your chart are yin or yang. This is described as the gender of the element. If the wealth element and the self element are both yin or both yang then the wealth is unexpected wealth. If one is yin and the other is yang then the wealth is direct wealth. In your chart it is possible to have both kinds of wealth.

LUCKY WINDFALL
Your chart will show whether your wealth will be the direct result of hard work or whether it will be an unexpected windfall. If your wealth elements are both yin or both yang money comes as a windfall; if they are mixed then money is direct wealth.

FRIENDS, FOES, AND COMPETITORS

The chart can also tell you a great deal about the relationships you have with the people your life regularly touches—relatives, colleagues, and friends, who may be your allies or they may be your competitors. Indeed, the broad category of "friends" is placed under the element that is the same as the self element.

Note that friends can bring negative or positive luck into your life. How friends relate and interact with you is determined by whether your self element is weak or strong. If your self element is weak, then each time the same element occurs in your chart it means there are good, positive friends coming in to support you.

However, if your self element is strong, each time it is repeated in the chart the element will generally signify enemies and competitors, people who could well do you harm or betray you. In modern scenarios, this aptly describes politics and power play at the office.

If you look at your own circle of acquaintances, you will realize that for some people friends are always there to help, to bring comfort and assistance when they need it. For others, friends maybe stab them in the back, set themselves up as competitors, and generally cause grief and heartache.

In short, "friends" can be enemies as well. To discover what your destiny holds in store for you regarding friends, look at your paht chee chart to see whether yours is a life blessed with many good friends or whether you will always need to watch your back. Maybe friends are always seeming to compete with you, practicing one-upmanship at every possible moment.

POWER, RANK, AND RECOGNITION

Whether or not you are destined to be publicly lauded and honored, to hold high positions, and be the recipient of VIP titles is determined by the presence of the element that symbolizes such recognition in your paht chee chart. Power and rank are symbolized by the element that destroys your self element.

Thus, if your self element is wood, then if power, titles, and rank are what you

---

YOUR FRIENDSHIP LUCK ELEMENT

FRIENDS ARE SIGNIFIED BY THE ELEMENT THAT IS THE SAME AS THE SELF ELEMENT

SELF ELEMENT	FRIENDSHIP TYPE
WEAK	FRIENDS ALWAYS THERE TO HELP
STRONG	FRIENDS BECOME COMPETITORS

want in life, in your chart you must look for heavenly stems and earthly branches that are metal. Again, if the power element appears once, twice or three times, it is an excellent indication that you will attain high recognition in life.

If the power element appears four or more times in your chart, however, this would be a reason for caution to be exercised since it is now considered to be in excess. In this case you might need to introduce an element that exhausts the excessive power element.

Although you may think that you do not want or need power luck, in truth all of us do. Unless we have a certain amount of control luck, which comes with having power and influence, it is hard to get things done and it is even more difficult to live without aggravations. "Power" in this context refers not simply to political power but rather to how influential and how highly respected you are.

YOUR POWER LUCK ELEMENT

POWER IS SIGNIFIED BY THE ELEMENT THAT DESTROYS THE SELF ELEMENT

SELF ELEMENT	POWER LUCK ELEMENT
WOOD	METAL
WATER	EARTH
METAL	FIRE
EARTH	WOOD
FIRE	WATER

FRIENDLY MATCH
If your self element is weak, your friends will support you; if strong, they will compete with you.

YOUR INTELLIGENCE LUCK ELEMENT

INTELLIGENCE IS SIGNIFIED BY THE ELEMENT THAT IS
PRODUCED BY THE SELF ELEMENT

SELF ELEMENT	INTELLIGENCE LUCK ELEMENT
WOOD	FIRE
WATER	WOOD
METAL	WATER
EARTH	METAL
FIRE	EARTH

INTELLIGENCE AND CREATIVITY

Intelligence and creativity luck is considered to be the most important type of luck to have in your chart. In the paht chee chart it is signified by the element that is produced by the self element. For example, if your self element is water, then since water produces wood, it is the wood element that symbolizes your intelligence and creativity in your chart.

It is important that there is at least one such element in the paht chee chart, since its absence often indicates someone who is not particularly intelligent, unless it occurs as a hidden element either as a stem or a branch arising from the combination of any two of the stems and branches in the chart (see Hidden Elements, pages 70–71).

The presence of the intelligence element is also seen as a powerful antidote to the absence of other luck elements. For example, if the wealth element is missing from your paht chee chart, the presence of the intelligence element suggests you might be able to make good money during years when the wealth element appears in your ten-year luck pillars.

I have seen the paht chee chart of somebody whose chart showed a superficial

BRIGHT SPARK
Even a single appearance of the intelligence or creativity luck element in your chart will be enough to help you make the best of life's opportunities.

lack of wealth element among the basic eight characters but instead had three of the elements that indicate intelligence. When I examined the chart more closely, I discovered at least one hidden wealth element. With just a single wealth indicator this person used his great store of intelligence luck to carve out a great fortune for himself. What is interesting is that usually such people make their fortunes during years when the wealth element makes an appearance in the luck pillars or the calendar years.

The paht chee interpretation always acknowledges the vital influence of your own creative mind plus your intelligence and common sense. Note that the intelligence and creativity luck element, together with the element that spells resources, are the most important elements in your chart.

If there is an excess of the intelligence element, however, then the indication is mental instability. Just as the West recognizes genius as bordering on insanity, likewise when there are too many of the elements that indicate intelligence in the chart, the indications become negative, because they represent excess.

RESOURCES, SUPPORT, AND AUTHORITY

The fifth kind of luck revealed by the elements in the chart is that of resources and support. The element that shows whether you have sufficient resources and strength to manifest all the good fortune indicated in the chart is the element that produces the self element. For example, if

YOUR RESOURCES LUCK ELEMENT

RESOURCES ARE SIGNIFIED BY THE ELEMENT THAT PRODUCES THE SELF ELEMENT

SELF ELEMENT	RESOURCE LUCK ELEMENT
WOOD	WATER
WATER	METAL
METAL	EARTH
EARTH	FIRE
FIRE	WOOD

the self element is earth, then fire, which produces earth, indicates your resources.

Many paht chee experts hold the view that without sufficient resources it is simply impossible for any kind of good luck to manifest in our lives. For instance, no matter how much wealth or recognition luck may seem to be present in the paht chee chart, unless the chart also has elements that signify resources, all other kinds of good luck simply will not materialize. It is like saying, "I almost had it ..." Well, folks, a miss is as good as a mile.

The good news is that paht chee does prescribe cures that make up for vital missing elements. So, a lack of resources can always be "artificially" remedied, either by placing a reference to the element in our names, or by ensuring a good amount of it is present in our living environment. For example, if your self element is wood and your chart lacks water (your resources luck element), place a water feature such as an aquarium in your home. (See pages 66–67 for other remedies.)

FOCUS ON FINANCE LUCK

"CAN I BECOME A MILLIONAIRE?" "AT WHAT AGE CAN I MAKE MY FIRST MILLION?" "WHERE WILL MY WEALTH COME FROM?"—TO ANSWER THESE AND OTHER QUESTIONS ON WEALTH LUCK, LET'S TAKE A CLOSER LOOK AT HOW TO ESTABLISH WHETHER YOUR CHART MEANS MILLIONS ARE COMING YOUR WAY.

Signs of wealth in your paht chee chart are indicated by the presence of the element that is destroyed by your self element. So the first step to finding out whether you have the destiny to be rich is to identify the element that signifies wealth luck in your paht chee chart (see table on page 75).

Now look at your paht chee chart and count the number of times your wealth element appears among your eight characters. If your wealth element is missing, it means you do not possess any obvious wealth luck. It is probably difficult for there to be direct wealth in your destiny, but this does not necessarily mean you will be poor. Not having the wealth element does not mean having no income. It does mean, however, that you are unlikely to have your own business or possess a great deal of landed wealth or accumulate much in terms of assets. It will be difficult for you become seriously wealthy.

If your wealth element does appear in your chart, note that it best is for it to appear two or three times. More than four times is considered excessive and when it is excessive, instead of indicating wealth, it merely suggests that in your life you are likely to be near to wealth, or be near wealthy people, but you will not own or control the wealth. So it can suggest a career in banking or working for a very rich person, but it does not necessarily suggest that you will become wealthy.

Sometimes, if the wealth element appears too many times, it may even indicate loss of wealth or it may suggest that pursuing wealth can be the cause of your downfall. Whenever there is excess in paht chee, indications of good fortune transform into misfortune. In such instances you must place antidotes in position. Use the element that exhausts the wealth element in the space around you. For example, if your wealth element is wood and there is too much wood in your chart, place bright lights near you and wear lots of red to exhaust the wood energy (see pages 66–67 for more remedies).

Having said that, if your wealth element appears three or even four times in your chart, it does suggest strongly there is wealth potential in your life. You may

MILLIONAIRE MINDSET
If your wealth luck element appears in your chart three or four times, you have the potential to become very rich. For the wealth to materialize, however, you need to ensure your self element is strong.

have the destiny to become a millionaire, and probably even a multimillionaire, but for this to happen and for you to make serious money, you need to tone down the wealth element and, even more importantly, you need to be strong enough (that is, have the resources and support for your self element) for the wealth luck to materialize in your life.

This means you need to look at how the self element is doing. For instance, if your self element is weak, then to benefit from any wealth luck that appears in your chart,

your self element needs to be sustained and strengthened. This usually happens:

1 When you encounter your favorable nourishing element in a calendar year.
2 When you encounter your favorable nourishing element in your ten-year luck pillar chart.
3 When your surroundings (your home and office) are dominated by the presence of your nourishing element.
4 When a combination of all three of the above takes place.

CASE STUDY 9

SELF ELEMENT: WEAK WOOD

If your self element is weak wood, you will need water before your wealth luck of earth can manifest. What this means is that the most likely time for your wealth luck to ripen so that you get rich is during a ten-year luck pillar that includes water. It can also happen during calendar years when the water element is present. It is even better during calendar years that include both water and earth (see Appendix).

In your case, because your self element is weak wood, you cannot get rich when there is a shortage of water. During calendar years when either fire or metal is present, your wood is weakened even more, so those years do not benefit you, and in fact those years are simply not good for you. If earth is present, but is combined with fire or metal, you will not be strong enough to benefit from your wealth luck brought by the earth element. In such years surrounding yourself with water (for example, wearing blue or having water features near you) will definitely improve your wealth luck. The best remedy would be to have a swimming pool and to immerse yourself in water every day.

If weak wood is your self element, the years 2004 and 2005, being wood/metal years, were of less benefit to you and were unlikely to have been serious wealth accumulation years. These were years when you would have had problems but you would have had friends coming to your aid. This is because the wood in these years represents friends in your chart. In 2006 there is fire and earth so there is wealth luck waiting to manifest; but there is also a great deal of exhaustion caused by the fire. If you have water nearby, then you are sure to benefit from the earth element. The year 2007 has water and fire as the year elements, so there are water resources to support you but also a great deal of exhaustion caused by the fire element.

CASE STUDY 10

SELF ELEMENT: STRONG METAL

If your self element is strong metal, your wealth element is wood. Here, because your self element is strong, your wealth luck when it appears will overwhelm you and your arrogance will block the wealth from manifesting, unless your strength is lessened. So, even if wood (that is, your wealth element) appears three or four times in your paht chee chart, your wealth luck will manifest only during the ten-year luck pillar where there is the presence of fire or water or both. These elements will keep your strong metal under control, thereby enabling you to benefit from your wealth luck. The best calendar years are those years when there is the presence of fire with wood, or water with wood (see Appendix).

So if strong metal is your self element, the years 2004 and 2005 were not years when your wealth luck could have materialized, as the elements of these two years were wood and metal. There was money to be made and you could see the opportunities, but you were unable to control your strength sufficiently for the money luck to manifest. This is because your self element is too strong. There were competitors who spoiled things for you. This is because when your element makes an appearance in the chart it signifies competitors—not friends—because your element is strong. So in 2004 and 2005 the metal earthly branch brought you competitors. In 2006 the year's elements are fire and earth, so it is at best a neutral year for a person whose self element is strong metal. The year 2007 has water and fire as the year elements, so is at best a neutral year.

THE TIMING AND SOURCE OF LUCK

TO DETERMINE THE TIMING OF LUCK ARRIVAL, OR TO IDENTIFY THE GOOD AND BAD PERIODS OF YOUR LIFE, LOOK AT THE TEN-YEAR LUCK PILLARS THAT COME WITH YOUR PAHT CHEE CHART AND SEARCH FOR A PILLAR THAT INCLUDES YOUR MOST FAVORABLE ELEMENTS. TO DETERMINE THE SOURCE OF YOUR LUCK, YOU NEED ONLY ESTABLISH THE ELEMENT OF YOUR WEALTH LUCK.

PROFITABLE PROFESSION

If your wealth luck element is wood or earth, then gardening would be a wise profession to choose to actualize your potential riches.

Your favorable element depends on your self element and on whether it is weak or strong (see pages 54–57). It is during the ten-year luck period when your favorable element appears, either as the earthly branch or as the heavenly stem, that your luck during that ten-year period will be good enough to trigger the ripening of your wealth luck. If it appears as the heavenly stem, wealth luck manifests during the first five years, and if it is your earthly branch then wealth luck gets activated during the second five years of your ten-year luck pillar.

When both the stem and branch are your favorable elements, your luck is truly great because you will have a run of ten auspicious years when you may accumulate extensive wealth.

It is important to note, however, that when the wealth element is present in your paht chee chart it does not always suggest wealth. You must also look at the weighting in your basket of elements. If you have only a single wealth element, it is not sufficient to bring you much wealth. A weighting of two or three, however, is a good indication of strong wealth luck. Usually, having three of the wealth element is sufficient to indicate serious wealth, but you must also look at the ten-year luck pillars to see whether you also have the auspicious pillars necessary to cause your wealth luck element to ripen into reality.

If you have any hidden elements either as heavenly stems or earthly branches, and these signify wealth luck, then your wealth will come to you from unexpected quarters. Hidden wealth luck elements are very strong indicators of wealth potential.

You also need to look at the calendar years (see Appendix) and check their heavenly stem and earthly branch elements. The elements of any given year will either strengthen or weaken the elements of your luck pillar. They will also impact on the self element.

The self element must be strong (but not too strong) to benefit from any kind of luck and this includes wealth luck. Some paht chee experts place such heavy weighting on the influence of the calendar years that they believe wealth luck (or any kind of luck for that matter) will simply not

ELEMENTS AND SOURCES OF WEALTH

WOOD	FIRE	WATER	METAL	EARTH

Associated with wood, plants, and anything that grows, for example, plantations, printing, publishing, gardens, landscape businesses	Associated with electricity, restaurants, lights, lamps, and anything with sunshine and fire energy	Associated with water, such as fishing, shipping, cruises, aqua cultures, bars, beverages, water bottling	Associated with construction, weapons, buildings, planes, vehicles, trains, machines, computers, construction	Associated with land, property, real estate, mining, farming

Those whose wealth element is earth can also make money from the other element-related industries. This is because earth is believed to be inherent in all five elements and to lie at the core of material luck.

actualize when the elements of the year hurt the self element. This is the dynamic of paht chee reading. It suggests that you will always need to take account of the elements that are ruling during any given year. It also suggests that the ruling elements of even the month and day will also impact on the self element, thereby having a bearing on your luck in that month or on that day.

Note: This is the method that Chinese luck prediction experts use to calculate the truly brilliant days of the year for anyone. The ruling elements of the year are far too important to ignore, although, of course, out of expediency, many of us ignore the month and the day elements. However, if you wish to do so, you can use the thousand-year calendar to pull out the ruling elements of any month or day and use these elements to analyze your own good and bad days. The elements of the years for over a hundred years are in the Appendix at the end of this book.

If the year elements hurt the self element, you can use a variety of remedies (see pages 66–67) to counteract this.

THE SOURCE OF YOUR WEALTH

The element that symbolizes your wealth element will indicate the source of your wealth. If your wealth element is present in your chart in an auspicious way, then wealth is likely to come your way from the sources shown in the chart (above).

CASE STUDY 11

HOUR *Heavenly Stem*	**DAY** *Heavenly Stem*	**MONTH** *Heavenly Stem*	**YEAR** *Heavenly Stem*

YANG METAL	YANG FIRE	YIN FIRE	YANG FIRE

HOUR *Earthly Branch*	**DAY** *Earthly Branch*	**MONTH** *Earthly Branch*	**YEAR** *Earthly Branch*

TIGER YANG WOOD	DOG YANG EARTH	ROOSTER YIN METAL	DRAGON YANG EARTH

AREAS OF LIFE LUCK

EARTH	WOOD	WATER	METAL	FIRE
Intelligence, *Creativity*	*Resource,* *Support, Authority*	*Recognition,* *Power, Rank*	*Wealth,* *Financial success*	*Friends,* *Competitors, Foe,* *Colleagues*

To assist you to make a reading of your wealth potential, here is a sample reading. This is the chart of Patrick, whose chart we first saw in the previous chapter. Let us examine the paht chee chart and the ten-year luck pillars to investigate whether there is wealth potential in his chart.

1. DETERMINE HIS SELF ELEMENT
Patrick's self element is weak fire.

2. DETERMINE HIS FAVORABLE ELEMENTS
They are wood and water.

3. DETERMINE HIS BASKET OF ELEMENTS
Metal 2, wood 1, fire 3, earth 2, water 0. Note that his chart is lacking in water.

4. CONSIDER HIS WEALTH ELEMENT
His wealth element is metal. This appears twice in his chart, so there is definitely wealth potential.

5. DETERMINE THE STRENGTH OF HIS SELF ELEMENT AND RESOURCES
His fire self, although weak (due to the presence of earth and metal in his chart and also him being born in the fall), nevertheless has two other appearances of fire to keep him reasonably strong. There is also wood to produce fire. This suggests that he has enough resources to actualize his wealth potential with little difficulty.

6. DETERMINE THE SOURCE OF HIS WEALTH
The chart shows that his wealth is partly made by him (as indicated by the yang metal in the hour pillar) and partly inherited (as indicated by the Rooster yin metal in the month pillar) from his mother or another matriarchal figure, such as a grandmother or an aunt. The element itself is metal, which suggests that his wealth will be made from buildings or construction, or another metal-related industry.

7. DETERMINE THE PRESENCE OF HIDDEN ELEMENTS
Patrick's chart indicates powerful hidden wealth luck. Hidden metal is created by the combination of Rooster and Dragon, which suggests that his wealth comes from someone born with one of these animal signs in their chart. Hidden wealth elements are potent indicators of wealth.

8. CONSIDER ANY MISSING ELEMENTS
Any analysis always takes a big picture look at the paht chee chart before moving on to the ten-year luck pillars, because it is very important to look at the complete basket of elements. Patrick's chart lacks water so water in the luck pillars is good for Patrick, even though water can weaken his self element. Here, therefore, we look on water as enhancing wood, which in turn strengthens fire.

CASE STUDY 11 (continued)

9. CONSIDER THE TEN-YEAR LUCK PILLARS FOR HIS LIFELONG LUCK

Patrick's luck pillars suggest he has some excellent periods when luck is on his side. Remember his favorable element is wood and his second favorable element is water. These elements will strengthen him. He needs them in his luck pillars for him to actualize the promise of wealth luck in his chart. Based on this premise we draw the following conclusions about the timing of his luck:

• **First main pillar (Patrick aged 22–31):** His excellent years for making money start here when water and metal are present. Water is a balancing element that balances his basket of elements and strengthens him, while the presence of metal brings the promise of financial success. He still needs wood, so he will benefit during years that also feature the wood element.

• **Second main pillar (Patrick aged 32–41):** During this time Patrick also has the potential for making money and accumulating wealth. The presence of the Ox yin earth here suggests that these are years when he will demonstrate great creativity and intelligence to create wealth. This is because earth, being the element that is produced by the self element, signifies intelligence. The motivating force behind Patrick's determination to make money will be his children. This is because earth also signifies his children.

• **Third main pillar (Patrick aged 42–51) and fourth main pillar (Patrick aged 52–61):** Big money is likely to materialize during the years when both wood and water are present. These are the ten years when Patrick is between 42 and 51 and also between

PATRICK'S TEN-YEAR LUCK PILLARS

AGE (YEARS)	12–21	22–31 ★	32–41
HEAVENLY STEM	己 YIN EARTH	庚 YANG METAL	辛 YIN METAL
EARTHLY BRANCH	亥 BOAR YIN WATER	子 RAT YANG WATER	丑 OX YIN EARTH

NB: ★ = good/auspicious pillar

52 and 61 years old. These two periods coincide with his two favorable elements of wood and water. He is a yang fire person so the yang years (between the ages of 42 and 51) are favored for making money. The yin years (between the ages of 52 and 61) favor family. To pinpoint the exact year and age when Patrick will strike it big, we will need to look at the hundred-year calendar (see Appendix).

CALENDAR CONSIDERATIONS

Patrick was born in 1976, so he will be between 42 and 51 years of age during the years 2018 to 2027. The hundred-year calendar reveals that the elements will be favorable for Patrick in the years 2022 and 2023, because their elements are wood and water. This means that Patrick's most successful years from a financial viewpoint will be when he is 46 and 47 years old.

10. CONSIDER THE CHART FOR IMMINENT PROSPECTS

In 2006 the elements are fire and earth. Fire signifies friends for Patrick and it also strengthens his self element, but earth exhausts him. It is also the year of the Dog, who is the natural enemy of the Dragon. So the year 2006 is a year when Patrick needs to be extra careful and watch his back. This is not a year to take risks, indulge in dangerous sport, or start any new ventures.

42-51 ★	52-61 ★	62-71	72-81
壬	癸	甲	乙
YANG WATER	YIN WATER	YANG WOOD	YIN WOOD
寅	卯	辰	巳
TIGER YANG WOOD	RABBIT YIN WOOD	DRAGON YANG EARTH	SNAKE YIN FIRE

FOLLOW MY LEADER LUCK

IF YOUR WEALTH LUCK ELEMENT IS MISSING FROM YOUR PAHT CHEE CHART, YOU MUST ACTIVATE "FOLLOW MY LEADER" LUCK. THIS MEANS YOU MUST CAUSE YOUR SUCCESS LUCK TO BE REFLECTED TO YOU FROM SOMEONE ELSE—YOUR MENTOR, YOUR BOSS, OR SOMEONE YOU RESPECT IN AUTHORITY OVER YOU. THIS CAN CAUSE WEALTH LUCK TO MATERIALIZE FOR YOU.

MOMENTOUS MENTOR
Work with others who have wealth luck and who are your astrological allies in order to enhance your chances of money and career success.

Follow my leader luck is wealth luck that comes when there is only hidden wealth luck in your chart, that is, the wealth luck is in the hidden elements of your eight characters. The hidden elements are created from the combination of the heavenly stem or earthly branch elements (see pages 70–71).

If your paht chee chart shows no signs of wealth luck, it can mean that your wealth luck potential is not immediately obvious. It does not mean you will never become comfortably rich.

Remember that in luck prediction success does not necessarily equate with money. Nor does money necessarily go hand in hand with status, power, or fame. Each of these aspects of life is a different type of energy. So it is possible to be rich without being famous, skilled without being rich, or powerful and influential without being very clever. Wealth does not necessarily equate with happiness. Hence it is a balanced basket of elements that signifies a really good life, not one that is weighted too heavily in only one single aspect of happiness.

The best way to activate follow my leader luck in your life is to associate yourself with people whose self element is favorable to yours. This could be a little difficult as most people's self element is not immediately accessible. You need to generate their paht chee chart before you can determine their self element. This is where knowing about horoscope allies and secret friends among the Chinese animal signs can be so useful.

If you find yourself lacking wealth luck, look for mentor luck by associating with others who have it and whose animal sign can benefit you due to intrinsic astrological affinity. If their animal sign, which is based on their year earthly branch, has an affinity with your Chinese animal sign, then working for them or going into partnership with them would be extremely beneficial to you.

When you are in a "follow my leader" situation, you have to activate your allies' luck. The way to do this is to place images of horoscope allies on your desk and develop a career with people who are your horoscope allies (see the chart opposite).

HOROSCOPE ALLIES

DRAGON	MONKEY	RAT
HORSE	TIGER	DOG
BOAR	RABBIT	SHEEP
OX	SNAKE	ROOSTER

PARTNERS IN PROSPERITY

In addition to the horoscope allies are the secret friends of the horoscope—pairs of signs that are usually very auspicious. Partnerships between such pairs usually bring financial gain. When the Rat combines with the Ox, there will always be harmony. What results is earth, and if this is also your wealth luck element then the combination will bring financial benefits.

A combination of the Tiger and the Boar results in wood being the element created. If wood is your wealth element, your secret friend will bring you financial gains.

The Rabbit and the Dog combining results in the fire element and these allies also bring an unexpected windfall. This is an excellent combination, especially if your wealth element is fire.

The Dragon and the Rooster are divine friends, and their combination results in metal. If this is your wealth element, the combination brings prosperity to you.

The Snake and the Monkey create the water element, and if this is your wealth luck element the combination will bring you a great deal of speculative luck.

Finally, the Horse combines with the Sheep to produce the fire element, and this brings you the luck of a powerful patron, someone rich and influential who will benefit you both. If fire is also your wealth luck element there are financial benefits as well.

The combination of the secret friends of the Chinese horoscope is one of the most powerfully beneficial combinations of earthly branches in the eight characters system. You may also recall that having two animal signs that correspond to secret friends in the paht chee chart creates a new and hidden element (see pages 70–71).

Use the Horoscope Secret Friends chart to help you find a business or life partner who is compatible with you and with whom you will have great success luck.

Start with your animal horoscope sign based on your year of birth, and then determine whether the secret friend allied to your animal sign results in a combination that also signifies your wealth element. If it does, then seek out someone who is your secret friend. Forming a joint venture with this secret friend is sure to bring you financial benefits.

PROFITABLE PAIRS

Business partnerships based on secret horoscope friendships can result in great riches. Set up a joint venture with someone whose astrological animal combines with yours to produce your wealth luck element.

HOROSCOPE SECRET FRIENDS

EARTH
Harmony

RAT WATER + OX EARTH

WOOD
Secret Friends

TIGER WOOD + BOAR WATER

FIRE
Unexpected Windfall

RABBIT WOOD + DOG EARTH

METAL
Finding Allies

DRAGON EARTH + ROOSTER METAL

WATER
Speculative Luck

SNAKE FIRE + MONKEY METAL

FIRE
Helpful Patron

HORSE FIRE + SHEEP EARTH

CASE STUDY 12

HOUR *Heavenly Stem*	DAY *Heavenly Stem*	MONTH *Heavenly Stem*	YEAR *Heavenly Stem*
庚	丙	丁	丙
YANG METAL	YANG FIRE	YIN FIRE	YANG FIRE

HOUR *Earthly Branch*	DAY *Earthly Branch*	MONTH *Earthly Branch*	YEAR *Earthly Branch*
寅	戌	酉	辰
TIGER YANG WOOD	DOG YANG EARTH	ROOSTER YIN METAL	DRAGON YANG EARTH

Let's consider Patrick's chart once again. He is a fire Dragon. His wealth element is metal, so he needs to look for someone whose animal sign is Rooster and then go into partnership with that person. Their partnership will bear financial fruits if it is a business partnership. If the union is one of marriage, their combined luck is certain to bring wealth and also attract many new allies into their lives.

CASE STUDY 13

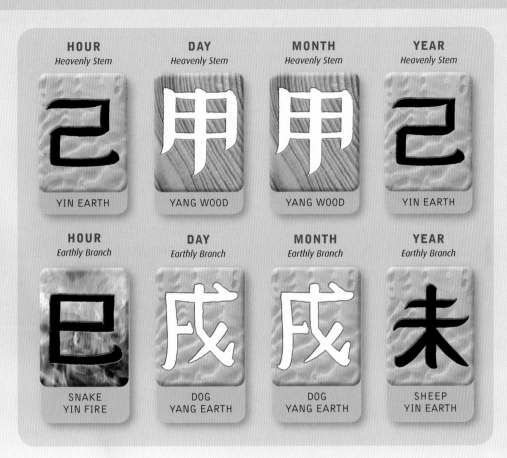

HOUR *Heavenly Stem*	DAY *Heavenly Stem*	MONTH *Heavenly Stem*	YEAR *Heavenly Stem*
己	甲	甲	己
YIN EARTH	YANG WOOD	YANG WOOD	YIN EARTH

HOUR *Earthly Branch*	DAY *Earthly Branch*	MONTH *Earthly Branch*	YEAR *Earthly Branch*
巳	戌	戌	未
SNAKE YIN FIRE	DOG YANG EARTH	DOG YANG EARTH	SHEEP YIN EARTH

Here is the paht chee chart of Jessica, who is an earth Sheep. Her wealth element is earth. Her secret friend is the Horse and, while allying with a Horse person is excellent for her, it does not result in financial gain. Instead it results in fire, which to Jessica signifies intelligence, creativity, and aspirations. This suggests that a joint venture or a marriage union with a Horse will inspire Jessica to great heights, even though it will not bring her wealth.

PHASES OF LIFE

"WHEN WILL MY GOOD YEARS BEGIN?" "WHEN WILL I GET MY BIG BREAK?" THE ANSWERS TO THESE QUESTIONS CAN BE FOUND BY LEARNING HOW TO INTERPRET THE TIMING CLUES IN YOUR PAHT CHEE CHART AND DISCOVERING WHICH TYPES OF LUCK CHI MAY BE ACTIVATED AT WHICH PHASE OF YOUR LIFE.

The Chinese contend that your life begins at the time of conception and ends at the time of burial. This is your life span, and for purposes of luck prediction your life span is divided into twelve distinct phases. The length of each phase is unequal. The early part of life comprises the first five phases from conception through to babyhood, infancy, childhood, and adolescence; together these last for approximately twenty years.

So it may be said that life really "starts" around the age of 21 years, when the life cycle reaches the "coming of age" phase, which is when you are deemed to have come to adulthood. This is the age when you will benefit most from any good luck potential that lies inherent in your chart. This is because it is at this age that you have the most amount of *sheng chi* or "growth energy."

The coming of age phase is the time when you will benefit enormously if your life chart reveals good luck forces, as indicated in the elements of your paht chee chart and ten-year luck pillars. The coming of age phase is followed by adulthood, maturity, and retirement. After that, the life cycle goes into decline and is characterized by aging and sickness, culminating naturally in death.

The Chinese focus on the 30 to 40 years of life that fall between the coming of age phase and the retirement phase. These are your active years. Good fortune sheng chi and favorable element years (as indicated in the charts) are most beneficial when they occur during these active years, so when you come to interpret your ten-year luck pillars focus in on these years. If good luck comes too early, you are too young to make the most of it, and if it comes too late you might be too old and too unhealthy to enjoy it. It is also considered to be a better life chart if the later years look better than the early years. This is because it is believed that older people are more affected by a hard life than children are.

The important years to focus on in your ten-year luck pillars are thus the "active" years of your life span. For instance, wealth or career luck is of little use if it occurs in the chart during the age of decline. When you are old you are unlikely to be able to

FIRST PHASE

According to Chinese astrology, the first phase of life comprises conception, babyhood, infancy, childhood, and adolescence. This phase lasts until your coming of age at about 21—the time when you can start to benefit from the good luck potential in your paht chee chart.

fully benefit from any kind of luck. If wealth luck shows up too early in your chart, it is also of little use, since it will not mean you are wealthy, but only indicate that your growing up years were spent in wealthy surroundings. You may have lived in a mansion, but you might have been the child of the housekeeper and not the child of the owner. In any case, wealth luck at too early an age is considered premature.

The same is true for relationships and family luck. It is best that indications of marriage and children luck should show up during the coming of age period of your life. If it comes too late in life it suggests that you will miss out on some crucial years. So for luck predictions to be meaningful, the issue of timing is important.

The answer to the question, "When will my luck begin?" is: "Your luck should begin when you come of age at around 21 years old." More to the point is: "What kind of good luck will come my way as soon as I come of age, that is, as soon as I am in a position to benefit from it?" This is the crucial question, and the answer to this lies in the analysis of the five forces of chi, which we shall examine next.

FIVE FORCES OF CHI

THERE ARE FIVE IMPORTANT KINDS OF LUCK OR CHI ENERGY WITH WHICH WE ARE ALL BORN. THESE FIVE FORCES OF CHI CAN BE ROUGHLY TRANSLATED AS FATE CHI, FAMILY CHI, MENTOR CHI, PROSPERITY CHI, AND OPPORTUNITY CHI. THEY OCCUR DURING DIFFERENT PHASES OF YOUR LIFE AND ARE IMPORTANT IN TERMS OF DECIPHERING YOUR DESTINY AND RELATIONSHIPS.

T he five kinds of chi energy found in your destiny chart are different from the five types of luck dealt with earlier in this chapter. According to Chinese luck prediction, everyone is born with these five types of chi energy in their charts. The difference between people's charts is that each of these different types of chi occurs at different times of life for different people. Some people start life with prosperity chi, others with family chi, and so forth. This is what determines the timing of your success in life.

Moreover, each person, at best, benefits from only three types of chi during the "active" period between the coming of age years and retirement years. So, in everyone's life there will always be two

kinds of chi that kick in either too early (during childhood) or too late (during the declining years). This means that we will benefit from three out of the five types of chi luck.

IDENTIFYING YOUR FIVE TYPES OF CHI LUCK

To identify the kind of chi that enters your life chart during the coming of age phase, and the other phases of your life, you need to become familiar with the five types of chi luck, and to determine which element represents your fate chi. The five types of chi are represented by the five elements. First you need to determine your fate element, because fate is the premier chi and it determines the element of the other chi luck forces. This is straightforward because your fate element is the element of the earthly branch of your year of birth (which is also the element of your Chinese astrological animal sign).

Once you know your fate element you can determine the corresponding elements of the four remaining types of chi luck by referring to the chart given here (left).

THE FIVE TYPES OF CHI LUCK

Fate chi	WOOD	FIRE	EARTH	METAL	WATER
Family chi	FIRE	EARTH	METAL	WATER	WOOD
Mentor chi	EARTH	METAL	WATER	WOOD	FIRE
Prosperity chi	METAL	WATER	WOOD	FIRE	EARTH
Opportunity chi	WATER	WOOD	FIRE	EARTH	METAL

Then you need to determine when each of the five types of chi luck will make its appearance in your life. This will indicate when each type of chi will bring helpful sheng chi to strengthen and assist you. Determining this requires two additional pieces of information from your paht chee chart, namely:

1 The element of the earthly branch of your month pillar.

2 The element of the heavenly stem of your year pillar.

FAMILY CHI

If your coming of age element represents family luck, you could begin adult life with a happy marriage and start a family at a young age.

YOUR COMING OF AGE ELEMENT

Hour Pillar	Day Pillar	Month Pillar	Year Pillar
HEAVENLY STEM	HEAVENLY STEM	HEAVENLY STEM	**HEAVENLY STEM (2)**
EARTHLY BRANCH	EARTHLY BRANCH	**EARTHLY BRANCH (1)**	EARTHLY BRANCH

These two elements will combine to reveal your coming of age element. Once you know this element, you can use it to determine the chi luck that will be at its zenith when you are at the coming of age phase of your life, that is, when you are 21 years of age. You will need your fate element as well to determine this and then refer to the table of heavenly stem and earthly branch elements to determine which new element is created from the combination (see overleaf).

ELEMENTS PRODUCED BY HEAVENLY STEM/EARTHLY BRANCH

Earthly Branch	Heavenly Stem				
	YANG WOOD	YIN WOOD	YANG FIRE	YIN FIRE	YANG EARTH
RAT YANG WATER	Water*	Wood	Wood*	Fire	Earth
OX YIN EARTH	Water	Wood	Wood*	Fire	Fire*
TIGER YANG WOOD	Water	Wood	Wood	Wood*	Fire
RABBIT YIN WOOD	Water	Wood	Wood	Wood	Fire
DRAGON YANG EARTH	Water	Wood*	Wood*	Wood	Fire
SNAKE YIN FIRE	Water	Wood	Wood	Wood	Fire
HORSE YANG FIRE	Metal*	Water	Water	Wood	Wood
SHEEP YIN EARTH	Metal	Water	Water	Wood	Wood
MONKEY YANG METAL	Metal	Water	Water	Wood	Wood
ROOSTER YIN METAL	Metal	Water	Water	Water*	Wood
DOG YANG EARTH	Metal	Metal	Water	Water	Wood
BOAR YIN WATER	Metal	Metal	Water	Water	Wood

Key

Water* means the coming of age element can be water or wood. Wood* means the coming of age element can be wood or fire. Fire* means the coming of age element can be fire or earth. Earth* means the coming of age element can be earth or metal. Metal* means the coming of age element can be metal or water.

INATIONS

YIN EARTH	YANG METAL	Heavenly Stem YIN METAL	YANG WATER	YIN WATER
Earth	Earth	Metal	Water*	Water
Earth	Earth	Fire	Metal	Water
Earth	Earth	Metal	Metal	Water
Earth	Earth	Earth*	Metal	Water
Earth	Earth	Earth*	Metal	Water
Earth	Earth	Earth*	Metal	Water
Fire	Fire*	Earth	Metal	Metal
Fire	Fire	Earth	Earth*	Metal
Fire	Fire	Earth	Earth	Water
Wood*	Fire	Earth	Earth	Earth*
Wood	Fire	Fire*	Earth	Earth
Wood	Fire	Fire	Earth	Earth

Note that when the coming of age has two elements both types of chi luck resulting from the combination will exert their influence. (See case study overleaf.)

CASE STUDY 14

HOUR Heavenly Stem	DAY Heavenly Stem	MONTH Heavenly Stem	YEAR Heavenly Stem
YANG METAL	YANG FIRE	YIN FIRE	YANG FIRE

HOUR Earthly Branch	DAY Earthly Branch	MONTH Earthly Branch	YEAR Earthly Branch
TIGER YANG WOOD	DOG YANG EARTH	ROOSTER YIN METAL	DRAGON YANG EARTH

1. DETERMINE PATRICK'S FATE ELEMENT

His fate element is earth, which is the element of the Dragon (the earthly branch of the year of birth).

2. DETERMINE PATRICK'S COMING OF AGE ELEMENT

For this we need to determine the earthly branch of the month pillar (which is Rooster yin metal), and the heavenly stem of the year pillar (which is yang fire). Then, referring to the chart on pages 100–101, we discover which element is created by combining the heavenly stem yang fire with the Rooster yin metal earthly branch of the month pillar. You can see that Patrick's coming of age element is water.

3. DETERMINE PATRICK'S COMING OF AGE CHI LUCK

Patrick's fate element is earth (that is, the earthly branch of his year of birth pillar), and his coming of age element is water. Referring to The Five Types of Chi Luck table (on page 98), we discover that Patrick's mentor luck chi force will be at its zenith during his coming of age. This is because Patrick's mentor luck is represented by water.

4. DETERMINE THE MEANING OF THIS FOR PATRICK'S LIFE

What this suggests is that Patrick benefits from the help of someone influential and important who will act as a mentor at this crucial time of his life. The mentor (or mentors, as there may be more than one) may be a relative or other significant person who will give him the means to get started in life. The mentor luck will give Patrick a good helping hand to jump-start his career. Occurring at this stage of life means the mentor luck is very beneficial to Patrick—mentor luck at this life phase usually suggests financial aid to further studies or a job opportunity that brings many new possibilities.

5. DETERMINE THE TWO OTHER TYPES OF LUCK MOST RELEVANT TO PATRICK'S LIFE

Once you have determined the chi luck that starts your life, you can then identify the elements that signify the other two types of chi luck that will be at their zenith during your adult and mature phases. Based on the order they appear in the table (that is, fate chi, family chi, mentor chi, prosperity chi, opportunity chi, fate chi again, and so on), Patrick's mentor luck chi is followed by prosperity chi luck (wood), and then by opportunity chi luck (fire). Patrick will benefit most from his mentor luck and his prosperity luck forces. The opportunity luck coming late in maturity will not be of much benefit, since by then Patrick will already be nearing retirement and will probably not have the energy to make fullest use of it.

6. DETERMINE THE STRENGTH OF THE IMPORTANT CHI LUCK FORCES

Once Patrick has identified the element that represents the important chi luck forces in his life, he can look out for these elements in his ten-year luck pillars. In this instance we are looking for water, which represents his mentor luck, and wood, which represents his wealth luck. If we find these elements also make an appearance in his luck pillars then the sheng chi representing these forces will strengthen considerably. If we do not find them, then they will be lacking in their influence because the chi energy is then said to be weak.

YOUR CHI LUCK AND YOU

CONSIDER YOUR OWN CHI LUCK BEFORE PROCEEDING FURTHER. GATHER THE INFORMATION FROM YOUR OWN PAHT CHEE CHART, AND IDENTIFY THE ELEMENTS THAT SIGNIFY THE DIFFERENT TYPES OF CHI LUCK FORCES FOR YOU. THEN CONSIDER YOUR RELATIONSHIP TO THE LUCK IN YOUR LIFE.

F irst determine which type of chi luck dominates your chart during your coming of age phase. The coming of age element reveals the kind of head start you will get at the point of time you are going out into the world. This is a very important time in everyone's life, and paht chee destiny prediction best starts at this point. For instance, if you are lucky enough to begin life with prosperity luck (probably rich parents or a rich benefactor) or with opportunity luck (such as getting an excellent job offer), then you will be getting off to a great start in life.

However, it is up to you to make the best of any initial good fortune that comes your way. Everyone starts with at least some weighting of one the five types of luck. The difference between people is how much use they make of the luck, because in fact all of the five forces of luck bring good fortune.

MAKE THE MOST OF YOUR LUCK CHI

Some people fritter away their good resources at the start of life. Others work at enhancing their good fortune. This aspect—your own actions, attitudes, and ethics—will be what determines the results of your initial good fortune. Destiny prediction may show you your potential heaven luck and offer you clues on how to improve your material earth luck, but your own decisions and the quality of your work are what create the humankind luck that will transform your good fortune into great success as you grow into maturity. On the other hand, you could simply waste it all through your attitude and lack of effort. It is up to you.

If your coming of age element happens to correspond to the element of family luck it means your family is supportive of you. It can also indicate that you start life with a happy marriage and enter into a nesting period when you will be bringing up a family. Many experts also suggest that this kind of luck is excellent when it appears at around your retirement or declining years, since it suggests good health and a happy family life in your declining years. It is during these years that this kind of luck is most auspicious.

Meanwhile, if you start out with fate luck, it usually indicates a turning point of some kind. This generally manifests as a momentous and happy occasion but it could also manifest as a major tragedy.

Fate luck chi almost always appears as some kind of traumatic moment of your life, a time when an important decision is either made by you or is forced upon you. So if it occurs at the start of life it is probably a great deal more meaningful, since it is then that we have the energy and resilience to benefit from any traumatic or life-changing event.

When the coming of age chi luck force is mentor luck this indicates a helpful person opening doors to opportunity, power, and influence for you. It is patronage at its best. It is an exceptionally good luck force to have either at the start of your adult life or during the years that correspond to your adult and mature years, as it will benefit your active years.

CAREER BOOST

If your coming of age element represents mentor luck, then a powerful patron will open doors to opportunity, power, and influence for you.

BLOOMING ROMANCE
To make love grow if your chart lacks family luck, try activating peach blossom luck by placing a representation of the appropriate astrological animal in the correct area of your bedroom.

THE CYCLE OF LUCK CHI

Once you know the luck force that corresponds with your coming of age, you can identify when other types of luck will occur. This is based on the natural cycle of elements. Thus fate luck is followed by family chi, which in turn is followed by mentor chi, then prosperity chi, and then opportunity chi (see table, page 98).

Thus, when your luck force at the coming of age is mentor chi, then in the next phase of life, which is adulthood, you will enjoy wealth chi, and in your mature years you will enjoy opportunity chi. Generally the other two types of chi are regarded as being inaccessible to your current life since they occur during the childhood phase or during your declining years. Always follow the sequence:

FATE–FAMILY–MENTOR
PROSPERITY–OPPORTUNITY–FATE
and so on.

POSITIVE EFFECTS

The mere occurrence and timing of the five types of chi luck in your paht chee chart does not guarantee that you will become rich during a prosperity chi luck phase or get married during a family chi luck phase, for example. The manifestation of the types of chi luck indicated depends also on their appearance in your ten-year luck pillars, and when they ripen the effects can be positive or negative.

The effect is positive when the element that corresponds to the chi luck indicated has a strong weighting in your chart (that is, at least two or three) but not more than four and definitely not fewer than two appearances. For example, if earth indicates prosperity luck for you, and you have three or four earth elements in your paht chee chart, and the prosperity luck force enters your chart during the adulthood phase of your life, it is very likely that you will become rich. Why is this? Because all of the elements are working in your favor!

HOW THE FIVE TYPES OF CHI MANIFEST FOR YOU

The five types of luck are fate, family, mentor, prosperity, and opportunity luck. We have seen that how these luck forces manifest in your life depends as much on the timing of their appearance as on the number of times their equivalent element appears in the paht chee chart. This is referred to as weighting in the chart.

These two pieces of information indicate the strength, magnitude, and nature of the luck. When the weighting of the element in question is zero, you can ignore it altogether. For example, if metal stands for your prosperity luck and there is no sign of any metal in your chart, you can conclude it is not in your destiny to become rich. This does not mean you will be poor; it merely means you will not have a windfall or accumulate assets. You will probably have other types of luck. Sometimes there may be other signs of wealth luck on your chart related to your self element.

Similarly, if your family luck element is wood (or any of the other elements) and this element is missing from your chart, it suggests that you are lacking in marriage and family luck. Chances are, you are unlikely to marry. You will have to look then for other indications of marriage and family luck related to your self element or you could activate peach blossom luck based on your earthly branch (animal sign) of your year pillar (see panel).

PEACH BLOSSOM LUCK

Peach blossom luck is used by those lacking family luck and those who are having difficulty finding a partner to activate or speed up their marriage luck. Astrological forces indicate that peach blossom luck is strong every nine years, and the luck is particularly strong in these years (the next year will be 2014). However, activating peach blossom luck can be done anytime, and it always brings excellent family chi luck, which implies marriage luck for those who are single.

To activate peach blossom luck, you need to place a representation of a specific Chinese astrological animal in a specific area of your bedroom, as follows:

- If you are an Ox, Snake, or Rooster, place a red Horse in the south of your bedroom.

- If you are a Rat, Dragon, or Monkey, place a golden Rooster in the west of your bedroom.

- If you are a Rabbit, Sheep, or Boar, place a blue Rat in the north of your bedroom.

- If you are a Tiger, Horse, or Dog, place a green Rabbit in the east of your bedroom.

HOW CHI LUCK MATERIALIZES

HAVING DETERMINED WHICH TYPES OF LUCK WILL MANIFEST AT DIFFERENT PHASES OF YOUR LIFE, LET'S LOOK MORE DEEPLY AT WHAT THE APPEARANCE OF EACH OF THE FIVE KINDS OF CHI MEAN FOR YOU DEPENDING ON WHICH ELEMENT THEY ARE ASSOCIATED WITH IN YOUR CHART.

FATE LUCK

Fate luck is probably the most dramatic of the five luck forces. Usually it suggests a particular moment in your life that signifies a major turning point. This can mean anything from an unexpected inheritance, a stroke of fortune, a tragedy, a death in the family, a marriage, the entrée of a special new person into your life, a new job, a change of country, a transformation of lifestyle—anything at all that suggests a major change in your life. The magnitude and nature of the change are affected by the weighting of the element that corresponds to the fate element.

WOOD FATE ELEMENT

Usually when the fate element is wood it refers to something in the creative field, such as painting, dancing, or any kind of performing arts. Some experts equate wood with areas of industry that are based on plants, such as paper, furniture, or plantation businesses. This is certainly a plausible interpretation. In addition, wood suggests a growth spurt. This means any event or incident that causes you to grow up fast. Teenage children who lose their parents, for instance, are forced to grow up overnight as they come to terms with tragedy. So, losing a parent, or parents separating, or being forced to live in another country—these and other similar dramatic events are the kind of traumatic events that are suggested by fate luck chi represented by wood.

FIRE FATE ELEMENT

If the fate element is fire, it suggests a change of direction in your career—perhaps a transfer, a new job, or being made an amazing offer. The offer could well be related to areas of industry that signify fire, such as bright lights, or a restaurant business. The fire element might refer to a hot climate, so you might be working in hot countries. Your interpretation can be as creative as you wish, but your imagination should never get out of control, which is the danger of fire. Fire chi can also suggest tragedy associated with fire.

EARTH FATE ELEMENT

If your fate element is earth, it usually means the successful, and perhaps the unexpected, acquisition of land. A turning point could occur that has its source in something to do with the land.

METAL FATE ELEMENT

If your fate element is metal it means a sudden fortune, a windfall of sorts that results in increased income levels. Usually this element is associated with the creation of wealth, and here do note that wealth is a little different from income. Wealth means assets, and is often associated with a windfall. It also suggests a commercial business or project, rather than a career. Therefore, this can mean an unexpected inheritance, winning the lottery, getting a fat profitable contract, or the sudden success of something you have invested in.

WATER FATE ELEMENT

If your fate element is water it always means a journey of some kind, a change of direction that involves travel. Water also refers to communication or enhanced income levels. Anything that suggests a flow is associated with this element, so a transformation that brings an enhanced flow of income could well be indicated by the water element. The journey can have negative or positive connotations: how the journey turns out (whether for good or bad) again depends on the way in which you react to it.

NEW GROWTH
If your fate element is wood, it suggests a growth spurt—an event in your life that will make you grow up fast.

HAPPY HOME LIFE
The appearance of family luck in your chart generally means that you will experience satisfaction and contentment at home during the time of your life indicated in the ten-year luck pillars.

FAMILY LUCK

Family luck generally indicates a nesting period. If it occurs at the start of adulthood it can be predicting a forthcoming happy love affair or marriage, which brings benefits and fulfillment. If it comes at the end of a life span, then it suggests a happy retirement where good health and happiness prevail. Family luck always indicates a sense of contentment, a feeling of satisfaction, and great happiness. Once again, the magnitude of its manifestation is directly related to the weighting of the element that corresponds to it in the chart.

If family luck occurs during childhood, it means your family looked after you well. If it occurs in your declining years it can mean that you are well looked after during

your old age. But family luck chi occurring during childhood or old age can also suggest a lack of family (that is, it implies little probability of getting married or having children). Another way to interpret this is that if the element that signifies family luck chi is missing from the paht chee chart and missing from the ten-year luck pillars, then this is a strong indication that marriage and family luck are lacking.

Signs of romance, love, and marriage in your paht chee chart are indicated by the presence of the element that represents family in your chart. Therefore, the first step to finding out whether it lies in your destiny to get married is to identify whether the element that signifies family luck is present in your chart. If it is not present in the paht chee, then it should at least make an appearance in your ten-year luck pillars chart.

If your chart indicates that you are unlikely to find romance and get married, don't despair! There are remedies you can try to replace the missing luck. (See Peach Blossom Luck, page 107.)

WOOD FAMILY ELEMENT

If your family luck element is wood, it indicates pleasurable pursuits of family life. Wood also suggests growth, and here it means growth in the family's fortunes as well as growth in the size of the family. The wood element as family luck always suggests good descendants and especially good sons who will bring honor to the family. If you are the patriarch of a family, getting family luck In your retirement years in the wood element means you will live long enough to see your children and grandchildren bringing honor to the family name. You will participate in their success as much as they participate in your good name, and your good health.

FIRE FAMILY ELEMENT

If your family luck element is fire, it means the family becomes better off due to career success. Fire always suggests the attainment of heights of recognition and fame, so that when it indicates your family it suggests a family project or business enjoying a spurt of success. It also suggests that the family gains recognition and success as an entity. People will look up to you and you will have a good name and honor.

EARTH FAMILY ELEMENT

If the family luck element in your paht chee chart is earth, it suggests meditative and spiritual pursuits. Here earth suggests a period of being grounded when thoughts turn to the fundamental things of life.

Sometimes the earth element means the rise of spirituality and spiritual pursuits in your life. It could indicate a time of retreat when you go within yourself in search of spiritual truths, possibly taking time off from pursuing material success in your everyday life.

Although family luck would seem to suggest enhanced bonding with family, sometimes it can mean a "turning inward," if the indicative element is fire.

METAL FAMILY ELEMENT

If the family luck element is metal, it indicates that the family's possessions will increase and lifestyle will take a quantum leap. This is the element that suggests wealth and asset enhancement. It can also mean finding a new project or business that benefits the entire family, bringing all the members closer together, and enhancing their collective good fortune.

WATER FAMILY ELEMENT

If the family luck element is water, it means the family will gain in prestige as a result of you being honored. This is a particularly good reading if the family luck occurs toward the ending phase of your life, because then it tends to suggest reaping the benefits of a life well lived. Water also means being well-off materially and financially.

MENTOR LUCK

WOOD AWARDS
If you have wood element mentor luck in your chart you are likely to gain recognition for your creativity, possibly in the world of the performing arts.

Mentor luck usually refers to the arrival of a powerful and influential patron in your life. It can also refer to getting assistance from a public official, or you catching the eye of a powerful man or woman. It usually manifests in the form of an elevation in status or a major promotion. If it appears during the coming of age phase of life it is a surefire indicator of a very successful start to your career. A powerful mentor helps you to gain recognition and acceptance.

If it appears during your childhood phase it suggests the possession of natural talent or skill. If it makes its appearance during the end of life, then it suggests that you will obtain public recognition for all your work and attainments. How long this luck lasts depends on the weighting of this element in your basket of elements, and how beneficial it will be depends on other indications in your charts.

Mentor luck is usually accompanied by a rise in social status. Often it means receiving an honorary and prestigious title, but it can also mean you are successful in obtaining a high political or corporate position.

WOOD MENTOR ELEMENT

If your mentor luck is wood it suggests gaining recognition for creative pursuits. The element of wood also suggests elevation in status in the performing arts, and when it comes to you as mentor luck your rise will be fast and phenomenal. You will be able to leapfrog over many others less fortunate than you, and you will gain the support of those whose opinion and judgments are important. How long this period lasts depends on the weighting of the elements.

FIRE MENTOR ELEMENT

If your mentor luck is fire it suggests that you will gain recognition for your community and charity work—no matter how small or insignificant your contribution, it will attract the goodwill of important people, thereby propelling you into a different status.

EARTH MENTOR ELEMENT

If your mentor luck is earth it indicates that you will receive an award or a special prestigious assignment. Sometimes when it is particularly strong in the charts, it can mean gaining an ambassadorship or a governorship, that is, a very high position, similar to the mandarins of the Chinese Court gaining high status. The appointment may be unexpected, but as long as you are within a good period of your life and the weighting of earth in your basket of elements is strong, you will enjoy all the perks of attaining high office.

METAL MENTOR ELEMENT

If your mentor luck is metal it indicates financial support for any worthy causes you are associated with.

WATER MENTOR ELEMENT

If your mentor luck element is water it suggests the attainment of great literary success and recognition.

PROSPERITY LUCK

As the name implies, prosperity luck refers to riches and wealth. If it makes an appearance at the coming of age phase of your life and its associated element has a high weighting, these are very strong indications that you will become rich. If the weighting of the wealth element is three out of eight, it is a strong indication of great wealth.

The prosperity luck element read as part of the five chi luck forces complements the wealth luck indicated in the five kinds of life luck using the relationship of the elements. When both indicators of wealth show the presence of wealth luck in the chart and they both occur during your active years, then there is a very high likelihood of you becoming rich. Wealth luck usually suggests material rewards.

Usually the exact year when the wealth is made or starts to be made will be during a calendar year that also has a similar corresponding wealth or resource element. So if wealth luck is of interest to you, investigate this in your chart. Be careful not to make mistakes in your reading—we don't want you celebrating and finding you were wrong. Nor do I want you feeling deflated because you mistakenly thought you had no wealth luck!

If prosperity luck appears at the phase of life that corresponds to the conception or childhood stage it means you are born into wealth. This situation may or may not last through your whole life. It depends on many different factors and not all of these factors are related to the destiny charts.

If prosperity luck appears at the time of burial, you could end your life with a great deal of wealth but it will not be you who will enjoy it. It will instead be your descendants who will benefit from the wealth. Thus, timing of the occurrence of the wealth luck force in your life is of the utmost importance.

Many experts in Chinese fortune telling interpret the presence of wealth luck during the coming of age phase of life to be the most superior of indications.

Generally the strongest indication of getting wealthy is when either earth or metal is the element of prosperity in your paht chee chart.

WOOD PROSPERITY ELEMENT

If your prosperity luck is represented by the wood element, then your wealth will come from the performing or creative arts. It can thus come from writing, singing, or dancing. This does not necessarily mean that you will be a performer. It is more than likely that you will be the producer or financier of a creative project.

FIRE PROSPERITY ELEMENT

If your prosperity luck is fire, then wealth comes from the corporate world or from your own entrepreneurial skills. Fire always suggests business and things commercial, for the energy of fire is soaring and upward. Thus it can represent wealth from electricity or electricity-related businesses. But fire can also burn itself out, so it needs continuous replenishment. If your

BUILDING BOON

*Construction could be your key
to riches if your prosperity luck
element is earth. The exact year
the wealth will be made is likely
to be a calendar year that has
the same wealth element.*

prosperity luck is represented by fire, it is a good idea to keep your surrounding space well lit, and ensure that your office and home are constantly bathed with powerful sunshine energy.

EARTH PROSPERITY ELEMENT

If your prosperity element is earth, the source of wealth is land, real estate ventures, or construction. Many successful property developers, especially those who spend their time speculating on land, make enormous fortunes if their wealth element is earth and if this is strongly weighted in their basket of elements. This is one of the strongest indications of wealth arising from asset appreciation.

METAL PROSPERITY ELEMENT

If your prosperity element is metal, then prosperity comes from trading and commerce or from the mining of minerals and metals from the ground. Metal can also indicate wealth made from the stock market through capital appreciation and speculation. The metal element is a hard element but it can be made into liquid energy. It is often therefore regarded as the "father of money," since water is often associated with money. Sometimes metal also indicates petroleum and gas—treasures from the earth.

WATER PROSPERITY ELEMENT

If your prosperity element is water, then wealth in this instance would come in the form of a flow of money generated from many different sources. Some paht chee experts associate water with the various communications businesses, such as television, newspaper companies, and also computers.

OPPORTUNITY LUCK

Opportunity luck is the kind that brings the opportunity of a lifetime. Unlike fate luck, it will force you into making a decision. It is best when it appears during the coming of age phase of your life. If it appears too early in your life, that is, during childhood, the opportunity probably comes from your family background. This can be manifested as inheriting the job of running the family business or the continuation of a political dynasty. How beneficial this will be for your luck depends on its weighting and the nature of the element that corresponds to it.

In many respects opportunity luck is a matter of timing. It suggests that you have the luck to strike at the right moment. From this viewpoint it is an extremely powerful force for beneficial outcomes.

WOOD OPPORTUNITY ELEMENT

If your opportunity luck element in your paht chee chart is wood, it indicates that when you have good ideas you must pursue them. Your ideas have the luck and energy to grow and take root, leading you to many other opportunities.

FIRE OPPORTUNITY ELEMENT

If your opportunity luck element is fire, it suggests you must not hesitate in changing career. Fire always suggests a transformation in this situation, and when it is representative of your opportunity luck, during the phase of your life when the chance comes you must not be afraid of accepting change and going for it.

EARTH OPPORTUNITY ELEMENT

If your opportunity luck element is earth, it indicates that a chance will come that requires you to change location and that deciding in favor of this change is good. This is similar to the fire element except that your chance of a lifetime might require you to relocate to another country. If this is the case, you can do so without hesitation. If the chance comes during a time of your life span when it is benefiting from opportunity luck, and your weighting of the element is strong, the chance will open the door to great success for you in the future.

METAL OPPORTUNITY ELEMENT

If your opportunity luck element is metal, it indicates that all your investments during the time when this luck appears in your paht chee chart will bring you profits. Your investments will also open up new opportunities for you, in that you could meet new people and have the good fortune to be involved with projects that have great potential for success.

WATER OPPORTUNITY ELEMENT

If your opportunity luck element is water it suggests that a chance to travel or move home will open up fantastic new prospects for you. Such opportunities may be to pursue further studies, take on a new appointment, or start up a new venture. If you are going through this luck phase you would be advised to grab any of the opportunities indicated.

CHAPTER FOUR

SPECIAL STARS

Twelve special stars may
appear in your paht chee
chart. Whether auspicious or
inauspicious, they will reveal
further details of your future.

REVELATIONS OF THE STARS

YOUR PAHT CHEE CHART CONTAINS SPECIAL STARS, WHOSE PRESENCE MAY BE LUCKY OR UNLUCKY ACCORDING TO ASPECTS OF YOUR DESTINY OR CHARACTER. FROM THE STAR OF THE NOBLEMAN, INDICATING THAT HELP IS AT HAND, TO THE STAR OF THE TRAVELING HORSE, WHICH INDICATES TRAVEL ABROAD, THESE STARS WILL UNRAVEL ASPECTS OF YOUR PERSONAL DESTINY.

The twelve special stars usually give clues to your character and personality and reveal the way you react to adversity and aggravations. They may also reveal a special attribute you have that can be the competitive edge you carry through life. These stars are therefore excellent additional indications of luck in reading the paht chee chart.

The presence in your paht chee chart of any of the stars described in this chapter suggests the potential for the indicated good/bad fortune to create additional influences in your life. However, these indications should always be read within the larger framework of the chart as well as the ten-year luck pillars.

THE STAR OF THE NOBLEMAN

When this star shows itself in your paht chee chart it suggests that you have the aura of a nobleman around you and, according to legend, this nobleman aura signifies there will always be someone or something that comes to your aid whenever you need help. This is said to be the luckiest indication to have in your chart, because it means that there will always be helpful people to help you resolve predicaments or overcome obstacles when you need it. The Chinese name for this star is *Tian Yi Gui Ren*, which means "helpful lord from heaven provides assistance."

Having this star in your chart also indicates that you are a very intelligent and creative person. You have the amazing skill of transforming adversity and bad luck into life-enhancing opportunities. In short, you act and react like a true nobleman, strong in the face of adversity and wise during good times. You will also have many followers and disciples—you will be generally liked and well respected in your community. You will find it easy to get support and encouragement. It is a very auspicious indication in the chart and if the element that indicates the presence of this star is also a favorable element for your chart, the good effects are magnified.

Not everyone has the star of the nobleman in their paht chee chart. To determine if you do, look at the heavenly stem in your day pillar (which is also your

self element) and the earthly branch in your year pillar. The combinations of the heavenly stem and earthly branch in the two pillars that indicate the presence of the Nobleman Star are shown below.

The Star of the Nobleman can appear in someone's paht chee chart as well as during specific years for everyone. For instance, if you have yang wood as the heavenly stem in the day pillar of your paht chee chart as well as an Ox or a Sheep in your year pillar, you possess the attributes of the nobleman, and during the years of the Ox and Sheep your success will be like

LUCKY STARS

Special stars in your paht chee chart may bestow on you the Nobleman's gift of support from helpful people throughout your life or the prizes of scholastic brilliance.

NOBLEMAN STARS

HEAVENLY STEM IN DAY PILLAR	EARTHLY BRANCH IN YEAR PILLAR	STARS APPEAR IN YEARS OF THE
YANG WOOD	OX or SHEEP	OX or SHEEP
YIN WOOD	RAT or MONKEY	RAT or MONKEY
YANG FIRE	BOAR or ROOSTER	BOAR or ROOSTER
YIN FIRE	BOAR or ROOSTER	BOAR or ROOSTER
YANG EARTH	OX or SHEEP	OX or SHEEP
YIN EARTH	RAT or MONKEY	RAT or MONKEY
YANG METAL	OX or SHEEP	OX or SHEEP
YIN METAL	HORSE or TIGER	HORSE or TIGER
YANG WATER	SNAKE or RABBIT	SNAKE or RABBIT
YIN WATER	SNAKE or RABBIT	SNAKE or RABBIT

coming from heaven, earth, and mankind. Each of these three gentlemen brings incredible talents and good fortune. When any one of them appears in your chart, it suggests you are a person of high intelligence, gifted, classy, learned, and generous. You will be sure to rise to great heights of attainments in your lifetime and no bad experiences will mar your life.

The presence of any one of the three noblemen is indicated by the presence of three arrangements of heavenly stems in the day, month, and year pillars as shown below. It is imperative that the heavenly stems appear in the sequences exactly as shown.

Of the three, the most powerful is the nobleman from heaven, who brings great attainment luck. He brings power and influence. The nobleman from earth, however, brings material luck, such as wealth and prosperity, fame and fortune, while the nobleman from mankind brings talents and skills. It is not possible to say which gifts and assets, because this depends on you. It is imperative that you try to make the fullest use of the good fortune in your life.

STELLAR SKILLS

If your chart is graced by the presence of one of the three extraordinary noblemen from heaven, earth, or mankind, you are likely to have a major talent that will bring you fame and fortune.

that of a nobleman during those years (see Appendix for calendar of animal years). If you have only yang wood in the day pillar and it is not the year of the Ox or the Sheep, you will still enjoy the attributes of the Nobleman Star whatever the year.

In addition to this particular indication of the Nobleman Star, the paht chee chart can also reveal the additional good fortune of being blessed by one of the three extraordinary noblemen who are described as

EXTRAORDINARY NOBLEMEN STARS

NOBLEMAN	HOUR PILLAR	DAY PILLAR	MONTH PILLAR	YEAR PILLAR
Nobleman from Heaven	Not applicable	YANG WOOD	YANG EARTH	YANG METAL
Nobleman from Earth	Not applicable	YIN WOOD	YANG FIRE	YIN FIRE
Nobleman from Mankind	Not applicable	YANG WATER	YIN WATER	YIN METAL

THE STAR OF SCHOLASTIC BRILLIANCE

The presence of the Star of Scholastic Brilliance in your paht chee chart suggests you are someone who has a thirst for, and an affinity with, the pursuit of knowledge. You will easily attain recognition in the academic fields of research and teaching, because you tend to be hardworking and very smart. (It should be noted that scholastic brilliance here pertains to exam results and does not necessarily indicate a genius intellect.)

You will also be lucky enough to gain honors and academic prizes awarded by international bodies. There is the promise of many accolades and achievements. As a result, you are bound to attain great heights of recognition by peers and colleagues.

This star also indicates a refined person who does not appreciate boorish behavior. You are gentle and gracious. However, do take note that when taken to extremes a person with too much of the influence of this star (that is, when there are more than two such stars in the chart) will unfortunately tend toward conceit and academic arrogance. This might cause problems in relationships.

Not everyone has the Star of Scholastic Brilliance in their paht chee chart. To determine whether you have it, look at the heavenly stem in your day pillar (which is also your self element) and search for the required earthly branch in any of the four pillars. If the required combination of heavenly stem and earthly branch is present, you are said to possess the Star of Scholastic Brilliance.

It is possible to have as many as four Stars of Scholastic Brilliance because there are four pillars. This would mean your earthly branches would all be the same animal. For example, if your self element is yang earth and your four earthly branches are Monkeys, then each Monkey in the earthly branch of each pillar creates a Star of Scholastic Brilliance.

To benefit from the Star of Scholastic Brilliance, you need only a single star present in the chart. If you have too many scholastic brilliance stars, it indicates an obsessive passion for scholarship that is unbalanced. This kind of passion is considered to be inauspicious and you would need to keep yourself in check.

SCHOLASTIC BRILLIANCE STARS

HEAVENLY STEM IN DAY PILLAR	EARTHLY BRANCH IN ANY PILLAR
YANG WOOD	SNAKE
YIN WOOD	HORSE
YANG FIRE	MONKEY
YIN FIRE	ROOSTER
YANG EARTH	MONKEY
YIN EARTH	ROOSTER
YANG METAL	BOAR
YIN METAL	RAT
YANG WATER	TIGER
YIN WATER	RABBIT

THE STAR OF THE AGGRESSIVE SWORD

AGGRESSIVE SWORD STARS

HEAVENLY STEM IN DAY PILLAR	EARTHLY BRANCH IN ANY PILLAR
YANG WOOD	RABBIT
YIN WOOD	TIGER
YANG FIRE	HORSE
YIN FIRE	SNAKE or SHEEP
YANG EARTH	HORSE
YIN EARTH	SNAKE
YANG METAL	ROOSTER
YIN METAL	MONKEY or DOG
YANG WATER	RAT
YIN WATER	BOAR or OX

The presence of this star suggests you will be intense and aggressive throughout your life. You will emerge as a champion of the underdog. At its most positive, this star suggests a powerful rebel leader or a highly respected member of the opposition, but it can be someone who seizes power by fair means or foul. The name of this star is *Yang Ren*—a sharp blade that inflicts damage.

Whether this double-edged sword brings benefits or harm depends on whether its element is favorable or unfavorable to your self element. This star is favorable to a chart where the self element is weak. In this instance, it brings confidence, thereby creating the cause for the attainment of great success. If this is you, you will always stand up for the weak. Even when the odds are against winning, you will remain steadfast. You will do very well as a political leader or a trade union boss. You have both the temperament and the staying power to become a charismatic leader. However, you are also heavy-handed and quick-tempered.

This star can be unfavorable in a chart where the self element is strong. In this instance, some kind of clash will occur, making you conceited and arrogant.

Not everyone has the Aggressive Sword Star in their paht chee chart. To determine whether you do, look at the heavenly stem in your day pillar (which is also your self element) and search for the required earthly branch in any of the four pillars. If you have too many Aggressive Sword Stars, they will turn you into such a fierce and quick-tempered person that no one will be able to reason with you.

Depending in which pillar the earthly branch appears, a more detailed reading can be made:

• Hour pillar: You will have problems with relationships with your children.

• Day pillar: There will be many petty squabbles with your spouse.

• Month pillar: You will be very aggressive. If the element is unfavorable to your self element it suggests that you will be eccentric and bad tempered.

• Year pillar: It signifies squabbles with the older patriarch of the family and a squandering of family wealth.

THE STAR OF PROSPECTS

If you possess the Star of Prospects, and it is favorable to your self element, you will possess the competitive edge in any field of endeavor you choose. You have the determination, the staying power, and the passion to succeed, and, indeed, you will succeed very well in your chosen profession—whatever it is.

If you discover this star in your paht chee chart and its element is favorable for a weak self element, the star brings strong determination that will lead to success. There is nothing that cannot be achieved then, and success will come to you after much hard work. But for you work is not a chore. Here we see the hand of ambition play a big role in your achievements.

Usually the presence of this star also suggests financial aid from friends and relatives during times of need, but for this to occur there must not be a clash of elements between the branches of the different pillars.

Not everyone has the Star of Prospects in their paht chee chart. To determine whether you do, look at the heavenly stem in your day pillar (which is also your self element) and search for the required earthly branch in any of the four pillars. If the required combination of heavenly stem and earthly branch is present, you are said to possess the Star of Prospects. You are likely to be a very willful and determined person who seldom allows anyone or anything to stand in your way.

It is possible to have as many as four Stars of Prospects because there are four pillars. This would mean that your earthly branches will be the same animal sign and your self element would be as indicated. For example, if your self element is yang water, then each Boar in the earthly branch of any of the pillars will create a Star of Prospects. To benefit from this star all you need is a single star to be present in your chart. If you have too many Stars of Prospects it is likely to make you an impossible person to live with.

Although, if you are an ambitious person, the Star of Prospects will help to take you to the high point of success you want to achieve, it can also mean that you are driven to the point of obsession if it appears too often in your chart.

PROSPECTS' STARS

HEAVENLY STEM IN DAY PILLAR	EARTHLY BRANCH IN ANY PILLAR
YANG WOOD	TIGER
YIN WOOD	RABBIT
YANG FIRE	SNAKE
YIN FIRE	HORSE
YANG EARTH	SNAKE
YIN EARTH	HORSE
YANG METAL	MONKEY
YIN METAL	ROOSTER
YANG WATER	BOAR
YIN WATER	RAT

THE STAR OF PEACH BLOSSOM

COSMIC COUPLE

The Peach Blossom Star indicates that you have a sweet, loving personality and that you are destined to find romance.

Some experts refer to this as the romance star, because it indicates a person whose disposition is sweet and loving, and who appears extremely attractive to the opposite sex. In a man's chart the presence of the romance star indicates someone who is sexually desirable and who can be very seductive. In a woman's chart, this star indicates someone who is sexually irresistible. A woman with this star will have little difficulty finding a suitable husband—many will solicit her hand in marriage. In both genders the presence of this star always suggests someone who is socially popular and attractive.

Not everyone is blessed with the Peach Blossom Star of love and romance in their

paht chee chart. To determine whether you have this star, look at the heavenly stem in your day pillar (which is also your self element) and search for the required earthly branch in any of the four pillars. If the required combination of heavenly stem and earthly branch is present, you are said to possess the Peach Blossom Star.

It is possible to have as many as four Peach Blossom Stars because there are four pillars. This would mean that your earthly branches would be the same animal sign and your self element would be as indicated. For example, if your self element is yang metal, then each Dog in the earthly branch of any of the pillars will create a Peach Blossom Star. To benefit from this star, all you need is a single star present in the chart. If you have too many Peach Blossom Stars it suggests that you might be a good-time person, rather cheaply seductive.

PEACH BLOSSOM STARS

HEAVENLY STEM IN DAY PILLAR	EARTHLY BRANCH IN ANY PILLAR
YANG WOOD	HORSE
YIN WOOD	HORSE
YANG FIRE	RABBIT
YIN FIRE	SHEEP
YANG EARTH	DRAGON
YIN EARTH	DRAGON
YANG METAL	DOG
YIN METAL	ROOSTER
YANG WATER	RAT
YIN WATER	MONKEY

THE STAR OF THE FLOWER OF ROMANCE

The Flower of Romance Star is sometimes confused with the Peach Blossom Star because they both aim to address the destiny of love.

When the Flower of Romance Star is present in the paht chee chart, it suggests that there is genuine love and caring between husband and wife. But the Flower of Romance also reveals the occurrence of extramarital affairs. The distinction is made between "internal" and "external" romance, with the latter implying the occurrence of infidelity; that is, a relationship outside the marriage.

If the Flower of Romance Star is indicated in a woman's chart it means the husband will be unfaithful and if it occurs in a man's chart it suggests that the wife will be the one straying beyond the boundaries of marriage.

To determine whether you have the Flower of Romance Star, first look at the earthly branch in your day or year pillar, then check whether you have the animal sign that signifies the Flower of Romance Star. If the animal sign appears in the month pillar it signifies you have internal Romance Star luck, which means you have a loving relationship with your spouse. If the animal sign appears in the hour pillar it signifies the external Romance Star. This suggests there could very well be infidelity in your marriage.

Infidelity can also be counterchecked by examining whether the earthly branch of the day pillar is clashing with any of the other earthly branches. This refers to the six kinds of clashes between the following pairs of animals:

1 RAT AND HORSE

2 SHEEP AND OX

3 MONKEY AND TIGER

4 ROOSTER AND RABBIT

5 DRAGON AND DOG

6 BOAR AND SNAKE.

The clash is most serious when it occurs between the animals of the month and hour pillars. This would suggest that the infidelity could lead to divorce, especially if the person is going through a luck period when the elements are unfavorable.

FLOWER OF ROMANCE STARS

EARTHLY BRANCH IN DAY OR YEAR PILLAR	EARTHLY BRANCH IN MONTH PILLAR (internal romance) OR HOUR PILLAR (external romance)
RAT	ROOSTER
OX	HORSE
TIGER	RABBIT
RABBIT	RAT
DRAGON	ROOSTER
SNAKE	HORSE
HORSE	RABBIT
SHEEP	RAT
MONKEY	ROOSTER
ROOSTER	HORSE
DOG	RABBIT
BOAR	RAT

THE COMMANDING STAR

This is an outstandingly auspicious star to have in the chart of an ambitious person because it indicates authority, power, and influence aplenty. In Chinese this star is named *Jiang Sin*, or "Commanding Star." If you have such a star in your chart it indicates that you definitely stand out in any crowd because you were born with a powerful disposition and a commanding presence. You have charisma and come across as someone very courageous—the stuff of heroes.

You will possess the easy authority of someone born to rule. You will have wealth and many followers; people will look up to you and they will expect you to have good leadership qualities.

Even if you do not demonstrate much promise as a child, you will emerge as a powerful leader in later years. Exactly when this trait shows itself depends on the elements of your ten-year luck pillars. Look for the periods when your favorable elements appear. In the modern context such a person could well be a powerful political leader or a chief executive officer of a multinational corporation—or even the minister of a country.

While this is generally an excellent star to have in the chart, if its signifying element in the hour pillar is unfavorable to the self element in the chart, then it changes from being an auspicious star to become a harmful star that will bring severe harm and obstacles into the life of the person. It is thus a very formidable star and one that must be closely monitored.

Not everyone is blessed with the Commanding Star of power and authority in their paht chee chart. To determine whether you are, look at the earthly branch in your day or year pillar and search for the required earthly branch in the hour pillar as indicated.

Note that here we are looking at the animal signs or earthly branches of three of the pillars in the paht chee chart. For example, if your year or day animal sign is Monkey, then you need a Rat in your hour pillar to be blessed with the Commanding Star. Then check that the element is favorable for your self element.

COMMANDING STARS

EARTHLY BRANCH IN DAY OR YEAR PILLAR	EARTHLY BRANCH IN HOUR PILLAR
RAT	RAT
OX	ROOSTER
TIGER	HORSE
RABBIT	RABBIT
DRAGON	RAT
SNAKE	ROOSTER
HORSE	HORSE
SHEEP	RABBIT
MONKEY	RAT
ROOSTER	ROOSTER
DOG	HORSE
BOAR	RABBIT

THE STAR OF THE TRAVELING HORSE

This star is associated with traveling luck. If you have such a star in your chart it means you will have the luck to travel far and wide beyond your shores. It also means that you could work overseas far from home for long periods of time. It is generally regarded as an auspicious star to possess. However, if it clashes with any of the other stars mentioned in this chapter it has the power to destroy the good fortune indicated by the other star, and to create misfortune in its stead. Similarly, when it meets up with a troublesome and aggravating star it will make matters even worse. In this sense, it can be a dangerous star to have.

A clash takes place when there are other good stars in your chart. The closer the star is to the Traveling Horse Star, the greater the damage to the star. Like the Horse it is named after, when it takes off, it could be galloping so fast you cannot stop and then the outcome could be disaster. It can also cause havoc when its element clashes with another element close by.

So it is perhaps not a bad thing that not everyone is blessed with the Traveling Horse Star in their paht chee chart. Indeed, if you have too many of this star in your chart it can suggest an unsettled life marked by frequent travels.

To determine whether you have this star, look at the earthly branch in your day or year pillar and search for the required earthly branch in the hour pillar as shown. If the required combination of earthly branches is present in the combinations

TRAVELING HORSE STARS

EARTHLY BRANCH IN DAY OR YEAR PILLAR	EARTHLY BRANCH IN HOUR PILLAR
RAT	TIGER
OX	BOAR
TIGER	MONKEY
RABBIT	SNAKE
DRAGON	TIGER
SNAKE	BOAR
HORSE	MONKEY
SHEEP	SNAKE
MONKEY	TIGER
ROOSTER	BOAR
DOG	MONKEY
BOAR	SNAKE

shown in the table on this page you are said to possess the Traveling Horse Star.

Note that here we are looking at the animal signs or earthly branches of three of the pillars in the paht chee chart. Here we look at the day and year pillars first and check what the animal signs of these pillars are, and then from there we proceed to check the hour pillar for the "correct" animal sign that will indicate the presence of the Traveling Horse Star in your chart. For example, if your year or day animal sign is Rat, then you would need a Tiger in your hour pillar to indicate you have the Traveling Horse Star.

THE STAR OF SPIRITUALITY

HERMIT HABIT

The Star of Spirituality means that you have a philosophical or religious nature. People with this star in their charts are often nuns, monks, or even hermits, but it may simply mean that you are a deeply thoughtful person.

The presence of the Star of Spirituality in your chart suggests that you are a philosopher, someone who enjoys thinking and developing their mind. You are definitely not much of a social person—you prefer your own company and the silence of quiet meditation.

Paht chee experts also point to this star to indicate a leaning toward the spiritual life and even suggest that it could lead to you becoming a monk or a nun. If you have this star in your chart, you have the destiny to lead a deeply religious life or even a hermit's existence.

To determine whether you have this star, look at the earthly branch in your day or year pillar and search for the required earthly branch in the hour pillar as indicated in the table shown on this page. If the required combination of earthly branches is present, you are said to possess the Star of Spirituality and will therefore be destined to be a deeply philosophical or spiritual person.

Note that here we are looking at the animal signs or earthly branches of three of the pillars in the paht chee chart. Here we look at the day and year pillars first to check what the animal signs of these pillars are, and then from there we proceed to check the hour pillar for the "correct" animal sign that will indicate the presence of the Star of Spirituality in your chart. For example, if your year or day animal sign is Horse, then if you have a Dog in your hour pillar it would indicate that you have the Star of Spirituality.

SPIRITUALITY STARS

EARTHLY BRANCH IN DAY OR YEAR PILLAR	EARTHLY BRANCH IN HOUR PILLAR
RAT	DRAGON
OX	OX
TIGER	DOG
RABBIT	SHEEP
DRAGON	DRAGON
SNAKE	OX
HORSE	DOG
SHEEP	SHEEP
MONKEY	DRAGON
ROOSTER	OX
DOG	DOG
BOAR	SHEEP

THE WAR STAR

This is akin to the general fighting a war and winning through good strategy and foresight. The presence of the War Star suggests a person of high intellect with great ability in planning and strategic defense. This is one smart person, someone crafty and elusive, who is able to play many roles like a chameleon.

In its most positive and favorable manifestation the presence of this star implies someone who can rise high up in the hierarchy of a country's defense. It is a star that suggests a person who commands an army. But it is a star that can also become unfavorable—for instance, when it is overshadowed by the Traveling Horse Star. When it becomes inauspicious, this star is considered to bring the kind of bad luck associated with robbery.

To determine whether you have this star, look at the earthly branch in your day or year pillar and search for the required earthly branch in the hour pillar.

Note that here we are looking at the animal signs or earthly branches of three of the pillars in the paht chee chart. We look at the day and year pillars first and check what the animal signs of these pillars are, and then from there we proceed to check the hour pillar for the "correct" animal sign that will indicate the presence of the War Star in your chart. For example, if your year or day animal sign is Rooster, then if you have a Tiger in your hour pillar it indicates you have the War Star—you are someone exceedingly skilled in the art of war and the use of strategy.

AIM OF THE GAME

The War Star indicates that you are an intellectual who wins life's battles through the use of effective game-playing and smart strategy.

WAR STARS

EARTHLY BRANCH IN DAY OR YEAR PILLAR	EARTHLY BRANCH IN HOUR PILLAR
RAT	SNAKE
OX	TIGER
TIGER	BOAR
RABBIT	MONKEY
DRAGON	SNAKE
SNAKE	TIGER
HORSE	BOAR
SHEEP	MONKEY
MONKEY	SNAKE
ROOSTER	TIGER
DOG	BOAR
BOAR	MONKEY

THE WARRIOR STAR

WARRIOR STARS

EARTHLY BRANCH IN DAY OR YEAR PILLAR	EARTHLY BRANCH IN HOUR PILLAR
RAT	BOAR
OX	MONKEY
TIGER	SNAKE
RABBIT	TIGER
DRAGON	BOAR
SNAKE	MONKEY
HORSE	SNAKE
SHEEP	TIGER
MONKEY	BOAR
ROOSTER	MONKEY
DOG	SNAKE
BOAR	TIGER

FIGHT FOR RIGHT

If the Warrior Star appears in your chart, it means that you are a courageous person who will do everything in your power to right wrongs and counter injustices.

This star is also referred to as the Death Star, although its presence in the chart is nowhere near as foreboding as this would suggest. The Warrior Star indicates a courageous person, someone who is ever eager to fight against injustice in the world, to fight for a cause. If it is overshadowed in any way by the presence of the Traveling Horse Star, this Warrior Star will attract court cases, litigations, and great misfortune to your spouse. This star is thus to be viewed rather suspiciously. To overcome the effects of this star it is necessary to use element remedies to suppress the hour earthly branch element (see pages 66–67 for Missing Element remedies).

To determine whether you have the Warrior Star, look at the earthly branch in your day or year pillar and search for the required earthly branch in the hour pillar as indicated in the chart given on this page. If the required combination of earthly branches is present, you are said to possess the Warrior Star.

Here we are looking once more at the animal signs or earthly branches of three of the pillars in the paht chee chart. We look at the day and year pillars first and check what the animal signs of these pillars are, and then from there we proceed to check the hour pillar for the "correct" animal sign that will indicate the presence of the Warrior Star in your chart. For example, if your year or day animal sign is Snake, then if you have a Monkey in your hour pillar it indicates you have the Warrior Star—you are exceedingly brave.

THE STAR OF POWERFUL MENTORS

In Chinese destiny analysis much is made of "mentor" luck, which in the old days was often the main success factor in the career of young scholars hoping to enjoy patronage in the Court of the Emperor. In modern times it is just as beneficial to enjoy the luck of being supported, helped, and guided by powerful benefactors. Indeed, success often comes from "who you know rather than what you know."

In the paht chee chart, the presence of powerful benefactors or patrons in your life is indicated by the presence of the Star of Powerful Mentors, which is sometimes also referred to as the Heavenly Virtue Star. When this star is present in your paht chee chart it indicates that you will always have someone powerful to help you succeed, and during times of danger there will always be someone there to help you.

To detect the presence of the Powerful Mentors' Star, check the table shown on this page. First note the earthly branch in your day or year pillar, then check the rest of the chart to see if the indicated earthly branch or heavenly stem appears in the year, month, day, or hour pillars (that is, in the rest of the chart).

POWERFUL MENTORS' STARS

EARTHLY BRANCH IN DAY OR YEAR PILLAR	EARTHLY BRANCH (EB) OR HEAVENLY STEM (HS) IN YEAR, MONTH, DAY, OR HOUR PILLAR
RAT	EB SNAKE
OX	HS YANG METAL
TIGER	HS YIN FIRE
RABBIT	EB MONKEY
DRAGON	HS YANG WATER
SNAKE	HS YIN METAL
HORSE	EB BOAR
SHEEP	HS YANG WOOD
MONKEY	HS YIN WATER
ROOSTER	EB TIGER
DOG	HS YANG FIRE
BOAR	HS YIN WOOD

BENEFACTOR BENEFITS
You will enjoy significant career success thanks to an important patron if the Star of Powerful Mentors appears in your chart.

CHAPTER FIVE

ADDITIONAL ASTROLOGY

Your paht chee chart reading is usefully supplemented by readings of the Chinese Astrology Wheel, lo shu charts, and auspicious times linked to your Chinese animal sign.

UPDATING DESTINY ANALYSIS

PAHT CHEE CHART READINGS SHOULD BE SUPPLEMENTED WITH CHINESE ASTROLOGICAL READINGS EACH YEAR IN ORDER TO UPDATE YOUR DESTINY ANALYSIS. ASTROLOGICAL FORCES HAVE A MAJOR IMPACT ON YOUR GOOD AND BAD LUCK DAYS, MONTHS, AND YEARS, AND INTERPRETING THIS IMPACT ON A DAILY, MONTHLY, OR YEARLY BASIS WILL HELP YOU TO PLAN FOR THE FUTURE.

GRAND DUKE

Jupiter, the largest and fastest planet in the solar system, is revered as the Grand Duke in Chinese astrology because of its vital influence in Chinese fortune telling.

T he passage of time can bring afflictions and dangers, which unless avoided or remedied can manifest misfortunes such as illness, accidents, setbacks, and other problems in your life. Time dimension changes in your fortunes fall broadly under the umbrella of Chinese astrology, whose origins lie in the cosmic turtle and the 12 animal signs that signify years of birth based on the lunar calendar.

In the paht chee chart your animal sign is the earthly branch character of the year pillar. In Chinese astrology the animal signs have additional connotations and attributes that offer extra information. These complement the readings of the paht chee chart and its accompanying ten-year luck pillars. You can use your animal sign based on your year of birth to determine additional dimensions that can reveal current indications of impending good fortune or misfortune.

Chinese astrology will also reveal dangerous afflictions such as illness, accidents, loss, and other manifestations of bad luck that might befall you in a particular year, and this is where the preventive dimension of Chinese fortune telling is so wonderful. As they say, forewarned is forearmed. If you know that a certain year threatens to bring you misfortune, it is possible to take precautionary measures based on element cures and remedies.

One of the astrological forces you should note in terms of yearly luck is the location of Jupiter (*Tai Sui* in Chinese) as shown on the astrology wheel. Tai Sui is one of

THE ASTROLOGY WHEEL AND TAI SUI

In Chinese astrology the 12 animal signs are associated with the 24 compass directions. Each animal sign occupies alternate 15 degrees of the compass and this corresponds to the flight path of Tai Sui (also known as the Grand Duke Jupiter).

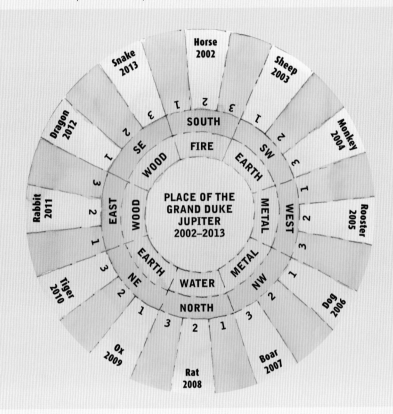

According to astronomical evidence, Tai Sui has 12 satellites and it takes 12 years to complete one full orbit around the sun. The number 12 is thus very significant, as it coincides with the Chinese system of having 12 animal signs signify the 12 "earthly branches" of their calendar. The 12 Chinese astrological signs placed around the compass indicate the location of the Tai Sui in each of the twelve years of its orbit around the sun.

Tai Sui takes the equivalent of one Chinese year to move 15 degrees of the compass. In any given year, therefore, it resides in the direction that corresponds to the animal sign of the year (see above). For example, the year 2005 was a Rooster year so Tai Sui was residing in the west, the direction of the Rooster. In 2006, the Tai Sui is in northwest 1, the location of the Dog. It is important to note that each compass direction is associated with an element. (See Cultivating the Tai Sui and Offending the Tai Sui, overleaf.)

CULTIVATING THE TAI SUI

Cultivating the Tai Sui means undertaking constructive and productive activities in the direction where the Tai Sui is located in a given year. This includes undertaking construction work, repairing as well as renovating. You will see from the Astrology Wheel on the previous page that each direction is associated with a particular element. You can earn the Tai Sui's favor through acting in accordance with the element in the appropriate section of your house or garden when Tai Sui appears in a particular year. For example, you could:

• plant a tree if the Tai Sui direction happens to fall in the wood directions of east and southeast (2011, 2012, 2013)

• install a new light when it moves to the south (2014)

• create a small mound of earth when it occupies the southwest or northeast (2009)

• install a small water feature in the north (2008).

the nine planets of our solar system. Its size is beyond imagination, and its mass is far greater than the sum of the other planets combined. Jupiter's volume is 1,400 times that of the earth. Not only is it the largest planet, it is also the fastest planet and its radiation is greater than that of the sun! It is thus a powerful influence. Ancient Romans regarded Jupiter as the leader of their entire pantheon of gods, the "God of the Universe." Its influence has thus been acknowledged in both the West and the East.

You can further interpret your yearly, as well as monthly and even daily, readings through the use of the lo shu squares and, of course, through your Chinese animal sign horoscope, all of which are explained in this chapter.

CULTIVATING AND OFFENDING THE TAI SUI

The Chinese regard the Tai Sui as the "God of the Year." Some describe him as the Commander-in-Chief of the Gods, and from ancient times Tai Sui has indeed been regarded as the most powerful of the "Earth Deities."

In reality Tai Sui refers to the planet Jupiter. In the old days, the Chinese called it the "Sui Star" or "Year Star." They believed that as they moved along their orbital paths the planets and the stars had a great influence on phenomena on earth, as well as on people's fortunes. They believed for instance that the moon not only affects the tides of the oceans and seas, but also that it subliminally influences human behavior.

Classical experts of the Chinese astrological sciences say that "the Tai Sui can sit but he cannot be confronted." In other words, nothing brings better fortune than cultivating the Tai Sui and nothing brings greater misfortune than offending and confronting the Tai Sui.

So, notwithstanding what your birth charts may be predicting, on a short-term basis it is vital note of the astrological forces of every given year and act according to the taboos associated with the astrological afflictions. One of these is the Tai Sui. Check which direction Tai Sui is in in a given year and perform an elemental action (see panel) or install an elemental remedy in that area of your property (see pages 66–67). For example, when the Tai Sui is in the west or northwest it is a good idea to place windchimes or other auspicious images (especially the Pi Yao—a kind of chimera with a dragon's head) made of metal there. If you respect the Tai Sui, it rewards you with success and good fortune. This becomes especially important for those born in the animal sign of the year.

For example in 2005, the Tai Sui occupied the west, the place of the Rooster, so those born in Rooster years should undertake productive activities in the west to enjoy the powerful good luck brought by Tai Sui. In 2006 the Tai Sui moves to the location of the Dog, which occupies northwest 1. Thus, by simply observing the Tai Sui's location, it is possible to benefit from knowledge of Chinese astrology. In 2007 Tai Sui moves to the location of the Boar, which occupies northwest 3, and in 2008 it moves to the location of the Rat in north 2.

OFFENDING THE TAI SUI

Facing or offending the Tai Sui means engaging in destructive activities in the Tai Sui's location. This includes demolishing work, digging a pond, or digging a hole. This means that if you undertake renovations in the Tai Sui locations you will experience adverse effects. This is because almost all renovation work involves some demolishing work. Some say that even chopping down a tree (especially when the Tai Sui is in the east or southeast) in the Tai Sui's direction is like offending the Tai Sui, and this can also lead to misfortune.

"When Tai Sui sits above your head, there is no happiness and only calamity will occur. When Tai Sui appears to confront your animal sign, even if you are healthy, you may encounter financial loss." ANON

MAGIC NUMBERS: THE LO SHU SQUARES

OF GREAT SIGNIFICANCE TO YOUR FORTUNES IS THE STUDY OF THE IMPACT OF THE YEAR'S FORCES ON YOUR DESTINY AND LUCK FOR THAT PARTICULAR YEAR BASED ON YOUR ASTROLOGICAL ANIMAL SIGN. ONE OF THE MOST POTENT WAYS OF UNLOCKING THE SECRETS OF THE LUCK OF THE YEAR IS AFFORDED BY THE NUMBERS OF THE LO SHU MAGIC SQUARE.

By their positioning in each different year, the nine numbers of the lo shu square unlock a great deal of vital information that can be interpreted to your advantage. All the afflictions can be noted and systematically neutralized, while auspicious aspects and indications can be taken advantage of.

ANNUAL LO SHU CHARTS

In each year a different lo shu chart "rules" the fortunes of the different directions as well as the different animal signs. The lo shu chart in every year is derived from the designated lo shu number of the year and this is extracted from the Chinese thousand-year calendar. According to this calendar the lo shu number of the year 2007 is 2 and that of 2008 is 1. The lo shu charts for 2007 and 2008 are thus derived with the numbers 2 and 1 in the center. The other numbers between 1 and 9 are then entered into the lo shu three grid by three grid square following a particular sequence. The "flight of the stars" (that is, of the numbers) is from the center to the northwest, from the northwest to the west, then to the northeast, to the

CHART MEANINGS
Generally, Three Killings, Grand Duke Jupiter (Tai Sui), and Five Yellow are inauspicious— they can mean obstacles, misfortune, difficulties, illness, and disharmony.

ANNUAL LO SHU CHART FOR 2007

SE	S	SW
1 GOOD	**6** GOOD	**8** GOOD
9 GOOD	**2** ILLNESS FIRE BOAR	**4** LOVE/ THREE KILLINGS
5 FIVE YELLOW	**7** VIOLENCE	**3** HOSTILE GRAND DUKE JUPITER
NE	N	NW

(E on left side, W on right side)

ANNUAL LO SHU CHART FOR 2008

SE	S	SW
9 GOOD	**5** THREE KILLINGS/FIVE YELLOW	**7** BAD
8 GOOD	**1** GOOD	**3** BAD
4 GOOD	**6** GOOD GRAND DUKE JUPITER	**2** BAD
NE	N	NW

(E on left side, W on right side)

south, to the north, to the southwest, to the east, and finally to the southeast.

These annual charts reveal a great deal of information about the year as well as about the outlook for individuals based on their animal sign. The key is to be able to read how each of the directional locations is affected by the characteristics and attributes of each of the nine different numbers that "fly" into the direction during the year. For example, in 2007 the lucky number eight will fly to the southwest and this means that the southwest enjoys exceptional good luck in 2007. Since this is also the location of Monkey and the Sheep born people (see the Astrology Wheel, page 135), the year 2007 is said to bring exceptional good fortune for them. In 2008 it is said to bring wealth luck for the Rabbit.

It is important to know how to draw up the annual lo shu chart to undertake annual readings for different people born under different Chinese animal signs. To do this all you need to know is the lo shu number for the year (see chart) and follow the "flight path" sequence from the center to the southeast given above.

YEARLY LO SHU NUMBERS

YEAR	REIGNING NUMBER	YEAR	REIGNING NUMBER
2005	4	2018	9
2006	3	2019	8
2007	2	2020	7
2008	1	2021	6
2009	9	2022	5
2010	8	2023	4
2011	7	2024	3
2012	6	2025	2
2013	5	2026	1
2014	4	2027	9
2015	3	2028	8
2016	2	2029	7
2017	1	2030	6

MOON MEANINGS

To interpret paht chee charts we use the Chinese lunar calendar, which is based on the cycles of the moon. Each month has an associated lo shu number that may be auspicious or inauspicious for you.

MONTHLY LO SHU CHARTS

In addition to the annual charts it is also possible to draw up the lo shu charts for each of the calendar months of the year. The annual and monthly charts are based on the Hsia or solar calendar of the Chinese system of measuring time. The Chinese have two calendars, a lunar calendar and a solar calendar. To interpret Chinese astrology we use the solar calendar. However for paht chee readings and to determine your animal sign we use the lunar calendar.

For each month as defined by the Hsia calendar there will be a ruling number and this number becomes the center number of the ruling lo shu chart for that month. To draw the monthly chart therefore, and place the numbers correctly around the nine grid chart, all you need to be familiar with is the "flight of the stars" (that is, the movement of the numbers around the grid). This enables us to place the rest of the numbers 1 to 9 around the lo shu square. The sequence is the same as the "flight of the stars" for the annual charts, i.e., from the center to the southeast.

To read the meanings of the numbers in the monthly and annual charts we need to know the meanings of the individual numbers as well as when the numbers combine. Each number has a different meaning and each number also has an element associated with it. Using the meanings of the numbers, in addition to the effect of the elements combining with the elements of your animal sign, you will be able to unlock the kind of luck you can enjoy in each month of the year.

Use the table given here to determine the lo shu numbers of the different months; then discover the meanings of the numbers in the following pages.

SAMPLE CHART
This monthly chart for June 2007 (Year of the Boar) shows the number six is in the southeast, which is auspicious for the animal signs associated with this direction (the Dragon and the Snake).

MONTHLY LO SHU NUMBERS

CHINESE MONTH	START OF MONTH	REIGNING NUMBER IN YEAR OF RAT, RABBIT, HORSE & ROOSTER	REIGNING NUMBER IN YEAR OF DOG, DRAGON, OX & SHEEP	REIGNING NUMBER IN YEAR OF TIGER, BOAR, SNAKE & MONKEY
1	FEBRUARY 4	8	5	2
2	MARCH 6	7	4	1
3	APRIL 5	6	3	9
4	MAY 6	5	2	8
5	JUNE 6	4	1	7
6	JULY 7	3	9	6
7	AUGUST 8	2	8	5
8	SEPTEMBER 8	1	7	4
9	OCTOBER 8	9	6	3
10	NOVEMBER 7	8	5	2
11	DECEMBER 7	7	4	1
12	JANUARY 6	6	3	9

Note: The above is a summary of the 10,000 year calendar. See Appendix for list of animal years.

MEANINGS OF THE LO SHU NUMBERS

For the purposes of determining your luck prospects you need first to determine the compass location of your animal sign (see the Astrology Wheel, page 135). Thus, if you were born in the year of the Rooster, your fortunes will be affected by the numbers that fly to your direction—west. As such, it is important to know what the individual numbers mean.

As a general rule, the numbers **one**, **six**, and **eight** (being the white numbers, according to the "flying star" system used to create lo shu squares) are deemed to be extremely auspicious—with the **eight** being the most auspicious—and we are now in the period of eight.

The number **eight** is an earth number, so its effect on different directions will be different. Generally speaking, the number **eight** will exhaust the south sector (fire)

and will bring good fortune to the north-west and west sectors (metal).

The number **one** indicates career success and it belongs to the water element. It thus brings excellent luck to the east and southeast sector animal signs (wood).

The number **six** belongs to the metal element and it brings excellent good fortune to the Rat born person (water).

The number **four** brings the luck of romance and literary endeavors, while the number **nine** is a magnifying number that seriously expands your good luck whenever it is accompanied and strengthened by a powerful good fortune star such as **one**, **six**, or **eight**.

The danger numbers are **two** and **five**. These will bring illness and loss respectively. The number **three** brings quarrelsome vibes, court cases, and aggravations, and finally, the number **seven** brings burglary and violence.

Chinese astrology always starts from an analysis of the lo shu numbers that affect your luck during the months of any year. It is very useful knowing what the numbers affecting us are indicating, since they offer valuable signposts and signals to what lies in store in any given year. When you are aware of the afflictions of the year you can install cures and when you are on a roll you will likewise know how beneficial it might be to be courageous in that year. Indeed, knowing with a certain amount of confidence what lies in store in any given year allows you to make decisions with greater self-assurance. Chinese astrology then becomes a valuable tool for living and working.

CHINESE TIME: PERIODS OF EIGHT

Periods of time in Chinese astrology are based on numbers one to nine. Each of the nine periods lasts 20 years, giving a complete cycle of 180 years. Each period is named after its ruling number, and we are now in a Period Eight, which began on February 4, 2004, and ends on February 4, 2024.

THE LO SHU NUMBER OF THE DAY

As with the month and the year, each day is also associated with a lo shu number that can be extracted from the 10,000-year calendar. The lo shu numbers of the day follow the ascending order of: White 1, Black 2, Blue 3, Green 4, Yellow 5, White 6, Red 7, White 8, and Purple 9.

The lo shu numbers indicate whether a particular type of activity should be carried out or avoided altogether.

WHITE 1

When the lo shu number is one you should be extra careful with young children. They should not be allowed to run about outside the house because misfortune can befall them. However, this number is excellent for bathing purification and for making ritual offerings.

BLACK 2

On this day it is a good idea not to stay out too late at night. Traveling at night is definitely advised against. This is also not a day to weep or cry, go swimming, or take physical risks. This is a good day to perform rituals that cleanse the home, so this is an excellent day to do spring cleaning and space clearing.

BLUE 3

This is a bad day to cut trees down—you should not disturb the wood element. Avoid work with plants and working in the garden. It is also not a good idea to drive nails into wood today. Keep your home well lit on this day.

GREEN 4

Keep young children indoors. It is a good day to seek medicinal cures.

YELLOW 5

Do not disturb the soil by digging, plowing, or sowing seeds. You should also not participate in festivals or invite a dog home. This is a good day for making petitions to the authorities and for undertaking virtuous and charitable acts.

WHITE 6

Keep complaints to a minimum. Make a special effort to avoid people wanting to find fault with you. This is an excellent day for making petitions to the gods and for praying in the temples.

RED 7

This is not a day to cook red meat, eat meat, or take animals to slaughter. It can potentially be a violent day. Avoid using fire on this day.

WHITE 8

This is a bad day to burn food or garbage or handle soiled objects. You should not mourn or weep because this will deplete your vitality. It is a good day to get married, perform smoke purification, and attend prayer sessions.

PURPLE 9

This is not a day to trust anyone with a special mission or to send emissaries. You can lose a great deal of money from doing so. This is a good day to recover money owing to you.

SPIRITUAL SIX
When the lo shu number of the day is White 6, you will find that it is an excellent day for making spiritual devotions such as praying in the temple.

ANALYZING DAYS OF THE WEEK

EACH OF THE TWELVE CHINESE ASTROLOGICAL ANIMAL SIGNS IS SAID TO HAVE AN "EXCELLENT" DAY, A "VITALITY" DAY, AND AN "OBSTACLE" DAY EVERY WEEK. KNOWING WHICH DAYS ARE FAVORABLE OR UNFAVORABLE TO YOUR SIGN WILL HELP WITH DAY-TO-DAY PLANNING. IF YOU WERE BORN ON ONE OF THESE DAYS, IT WILL HAVE PARTICULAR SIGNIFICANCE FOR YOU.

MONDAY MISHAPS
Avoid starting out on journeys or exercising heavily on a Monday—deemed to be the day of the moon—if this day is your obstacle day.

The good and bad days—excellent, vitality, and obstacle days—are derived from the influence of the planets and are listed by the twelve animal signs in the table shown opposite. Note the three days that are relevant to your animal sign. Excellent and vitality days are ideal for any project but avoid important projects on obstacle days.

If you were born on your obstacle day, you are recommended to wear "cures" that overcome the unfavorable aspect of the planetary influence of that day. Every year there are annual amulets that overcome misfortunes due to afflictions of bad days in that year—log on to www.wofs.com for these annual amulets. If you were not born on your obstacle day, that's great, but take note of that day and try to avoid doing anything important then.

OBSTACLE DAYS
Monday
... is deemed to be the day of the moon, also referred to as the planet of the soul of women. If this is your obstacle day, you should not take leave of loved ones, start a long journey, go to a funeral, undertake any fire rituals, or perform heavy exercise.

Tuesday
... is the day of Mars, also known as the planet of the soul of men. You should definitely not get married on this day if it is your obstacle day. Nor should you hire any new employees, make contracts, sign new agreements, or embark on a journey.

Wednesday
... is the day of Mercury, the planet of the soul of the prince. It is generally a positive day but if it is your obstacle day avoid selling anything on this day. You should also not make any offerings or gifts and you should avoid going to the doctor.

Thursday
... is the day of Jupiter, the planet of the Bodhisattva spirit. This is usually regarded as a spiritual day. If it is your obstacle day, it is advisable to take a peaceful stance. Do not quarrel or start a fight with anyone. It is also not a good time to undertake construction work, build a roof, or start

ANIMAL SIGNS: GOOD/BAD DAYS

ANIMAL SIGN:	Rat
EXCELLENT DAY:	Wednesday
VITALITY DAY:	Tuesday
OBSTACLE DAY:	Saturday

ANIMAL SIGN:	Horse
EXCELLENT DAY:	Tuesday
VITALITY DAY:	Friday
OBSTACLE DAY:	Wednesday

ANIMAL SIGN:	Ox
EXCELLENT DAY:	Saturday
VITALITY DAY:	Wednesday
OBSTACLE DAY:	Thursday

ANIMAL SIGN:	Sheep
EXCELLENT DAY:	Friday
VITALITY DAY:	Wednesday
OBSTACLE DAY:	Thursday

ANIMAL SIGN:	Tiger
EXCELLENT DAY:	Thursday
VITALITY DAY:	Saturday
OBSTACLE DAY:	Friday

ANIMAL SIGN:	Monkey
EXCELLENT DAY:	Friday
VITALITY DAY:	Thursday
OBSTACLE DAY:	Tuesday

ANIMAL SIGN:	Rabbit
EXCELLENT DAY:	Thursday
VITALITY DAY:	Saturday
OBSTACLE DAY:	Friday

ANIMAL SIGN:	Rooster
EXCELLENT DAY:	Friday
VITALITY DAY:	Thursday
OBSTACLE DAY:	Tuesday

ANIMAL SIGN:	Dragon
EXCELLENT DAY:	Sunday
VITALITY DAY:	Wednesday
OBSTACLE DAY:	Thursday

ANIMAL SIGN:	Dog
EXCELLENT DAY:	Monday
VITALITY DAY:	Wednesday
OBSTACLE DAY:	Thursday

ANIMAL SIGN:	Snake
EXCELLENT DAY:	Tuesday
VITALITY DAY:	Friday
OBSTACLE DAY:	Wednesday

ANIMAL SIGN:	Boar
EXCELLENT DAY:	Wednesday
VITALITY DAY:	Tuesday
OBSTACLE DAY:	Saturday

anything negative. It is a day when you must not do anything unkind to animals.

Friday

... is the day of Venus, also a day of magic power, a day of the soul of medicines. If it is your obstacle day, you should not spend it disputing with people or negotiating settlements with others.

Saturday

... is the day of Saturn and is also referred to as the neutral day. If it is your obstacle day, it is unfavorable for many activities, so refrain from buying or selling anything, getting into arguments, and from building, starting a project, opening a shop, or launching a new product. Do not go on a journey today, and try not to visit friends or attend festivities.

Sunday

... is the day of the sun, often referred to as the planet of the gods. This is the planet of the royal soul and is usually an important day for members of royalty. If it is your obstacle day, however, it is unfavorable, so you should not move house, change office, undertake surgical operations, go on a journey, attend a funeral, or undertake any kind of gardening activity. You should also refrain from celebrating your birthday, marriage, or christening on a Sunday.

EXCELLENT DAYS AND VITALITY DAYS

If you were born on either your excellent day or your vitality day, you are sure to be intelligent and extremely resourceful. Your life will be filled with lucky signs and good omens. You will succeed easily in everything you undertake, and you are likely to live a long and stable life. Your vitality day will also be a good day for you to undertake a large variety of activities—things will move smoothly for you on this day. So check the chart and commit your vitality day to memory. Plan important occasions to take place on this day.

The excellent day is a time when your spiritual energy will be at its highest, so this is a good day to meditate and chant special prayers.

Your vitality day is the day when your intrinsic vitality is at its highest point during the week. This is thus an excellent day to undertake any projects that require a high level of energy and concentration.

Monday

... is the day of the moon. If this is your vitality day, it is favorable for you to start new projects, for sowing seeds, adopting children, buying and selling, celebrating festivals, and for improving the feng shui of your home. Any space cleansing and purification activities will meet with great success.

Tuesday

... is the day of Mars. If this is your vitality day, it will be favorable for any activity requiring military strategy, organization, and precision. It is a particularly good day for borrowing money, for moving house, gambling, taking risks, and investing in the stock market.

Wednesday

... is the day of Mercury. If this is your vitality day, it is an excellent day to undertake interviews, make publicity, go on a journey, get married, and participate in any kind of celebration. It is also a perfect day for completing unfinished work.

Thursday

... is a day of the powerfully spiritual planet Jupiter. If this is your vitality day, it is a day favorable for undertaking activities with religious and spiritual aspirations. It is a good day to make offerings at temples, get married, start a study program, plant plants, sow seeds, prepare medicines, study divination techniques, and go horse riding. It is the kind of day that will attract new friends into your life and give your spirits a major lift.

Friday

... is a magical day that belongs to the planet Venus. If this is your vitality day, it favors you, the teacher. It is great to indulge in generosity on this day, do charity work, go for surgery, start a journey, prepare medicine, plant trees, and enter into an intimate relationship with someone.

Saturday

... is the day of the planet Saturn so it is a rather bad day. However, if this is your vitality day, it is an excellent day to commence work on building a new house, move home, transfer to another job, acquire a new pet, say prayers for a long life, and clean your house.

Sunday

... is the day of the sun and means that you have an affinity with those born into the royal houses of the world. If this is your vitality day, it is favorable for all activities connected with celebrations— marriage, birthdays, anniversaries, and any other occasions of celebration are blessed on this day for you. It is not a day to work but more a day to enjoy the pleasures of your world.

AUSPICIOUS DAYS AND ANIMAL SIGNS

SOME DAYS OF THE CHINESE MONTH ARE MORE AUSPICIOUS THAN OTHERS DEPENDING ON YOUR ANIMAL SIGN. FOR EACH ANIMAL SIGN THERE ARE THREE FAVORABLE AND THREE UNFAVORABLE DAYS EACH MONTH. SOME ACTIVITIES ARE RECOMMENDED ON YOUR FAVORABLE DAYS BUT YOU ARE ADVISED TO PROCEED WITH CAUTION ON YOUR UNFAVORABLE DAYS.

The three favorable days based on your animal sign are excellent days for you to pursue activities related to your career, your work (business), and your marriage or partnership. These are the days when your potential for success, power, and upward mobility can take root or ripen. The three unfavorable days are days when you could well succumb to obstacles, aggravations, and people with bad intentions toward you. These are the days when you are weak, so they represent a time when you should lie low and not engage in verbal or physical contact with your enemies.

The table opposite shows your auspicious and inauspicious days of the month, based on your animal sign. The numbered days indicated in the table refer to the Chinese days of the lunar month. To obtain the Chinese lunar months, refer to the new moon in the annual Almanac calendar (log onto www.wofs.com). The new moon day is always given as Day 1 of the lunar month. All other days follow from this first day.

Always try to select one of your three favorable days to embark on projects whose success is important to you and avoid new projects on obstacle and aggravation days. The luck you experience can be related to your work or to your heart. The vibrations of certain days are luckier than others for people, depending on their animal signs. For most people the time of the waxing or expanding moon seems more favorable, that is, their success days fall within the first 15 days of the month. The exception to this seems to be the 27th day for gaining power for those born under animal signs Tiger, Rabbit, and Dog. In addition, the Rooster's success day is the 25th, which falls within the period of the waning moon.

The characteristics of each of the 30 or so days of the lunar month indicate the success or obstacles you will encounter on particular days. New jobs, new projects, and renovation works on your home should ideally be started during success days to ensure the attainment of your goals. On enemy days you should avoid everything to do with discussions, meetings, court cases, and so forth; otherwise the battles you fight could well be lost.

ANIMAL SIGNS: AUSPICIOUS AND INAUSPICIOUS DAYS

	RAT	OX	TIGER	RABBIT	DRAGON	SNAKE
LUCK	20th day	17th day	5th day	11th day	3rd day	13th day
POWER	6th day	14th day	27th day	27th day	12th day	12th day
SUCCESS	3rd day	12th day	9th day	12th day	17th day	6th day
OBSTACLE	26th day	12th day	14th day	26th day	8th day	8th day
AGGRAVATION	10th day	18th day	12th day	25th day	9th day	9th day
ENEMY	23rd day	5th day	3rd day	18th day	11th day	6th day

	HORSE	SHEEP	MONKEY	ROOSTER	DOG	BOAR
LUCK	17th day	8th day	8th day	14th day	9th day	2nd day
POWER	12th day	1st day	1st day	7th day	27th day	8th day
SUCCESS	6th day	2nd day	2nd day	25th day	5th day	11th day
OBSTACLE	20th day	20th day	9th day	3rd day	11th day	26th day
AGGRAVATION	5th day	5th day	10th day	11th day	3rd day	3rd day
ENEMY	27th day	27th day	17th day	24th day	12th day	12th day

For activities related to increasing your power choose your power days. This includes times when you are standing for election, applying for a job, going for an interview, or pitching for a promotion or a contract. If election day falls on your power day you will surely be assured of success.

Note that when the weekly and this monthly cycle of good and bad days contradict each other for the same day given to any individual, then the weekly cycle is regarded as exerting the stronger influence. This is because the weekly cycles are ruled by the powerful planets. When the two influences confirm each other, both must be taken into account when making a judgment about days.

RULING ANIMAL SIGNS OF THE DAY

In the annual Almanac calendar, the ruling element and ruling animal sign of the day for the 365 days of the year are shown in the monthly calendars (go to www.wofs. com). These days have specific characteristics associated with them since the element and the animal offer clues to the energies of the day. Here is a brief description of the attributes of days ruled by the twelve animal signs:

DAY OF THE RAT

This day is favorable for engagements, marriages, the birth of a son, for trade, and important projects. It is a good day to be a vegetarian and contact with flesh should be avoided Divinations carried out today will be accurate. It is also a good day to start a journey. The conflict animal is the Horse because it is the sign that is directly opposite your own animal sign.

DAY OF THE OX

This is a good day for embarking on heavy or difficult tasks, such as road works, building a house, and resolving problems. It is not so favorable for spiritual practices.

DAY OF THE TIGER

This is favorable for prosperity rituals such as making a wealth vase (a feng shui ritual whereby you place precious things in a vase and put it in a secret place in your home), building a water feature, starting a 49-day wish list (a ritual whereby you write a wish on a piece of paper and sign it 49 times before burning it), or making fire rituals to symbolically cleanse all the negativity from your life. It is not a good day for marriages generally, celebrations, or giving birth.

DAY OF THE RABBIT

This is a good day for funerals, for royal occasions, and for buying a pet.

DAY OF THE DRAGON

This is favorable for religious practices, consecrations, and for making pujas (home worship) to get rid of negative forces . It is an excellent day to ask for favors, especially from people in higher authority. This is a great day to be courageous.

DAY OF THE SNAKE

This is a great day for making offerings and for giving gifts to friends and relatives. It is also a good day to lend or borrow money.

PERSONALIZED INTERPRETATIONS

You can make personalized readings of the element and animal sign of the day by looking at how the day's element and animal sign interact with the element and animal sign of your year of birth.

To determine if a certain day is favorable for you, examine the element relationship between your element at birth with that of the day. If the day's element produces your element, then the day is good for you. If the element is the same as your year of birth element, it means the day brings friends. If the element destroys your element, it means the day is bad for you, and if the element exhausts your year element, then it will be a very exhausting day.

If your year animal sign is friends with or allies with the animal sign of the day (see Horoscope Allies, page 91), then the day is favorable. If the animal sign of the day is in conflict with your animal sign, then the day will be very trying. The day is not good for you and you should not undertake important activities or make important decisions. If the animals are the same, then any judgment you make becomes a matter of being very careful so you would be well advised to be prudent. Remember that when the animal sign is the same it can indicate either a friend or an enemy, depending on whether your self element is weak or strong.

If you make a journey south on this particular day you will receive good news.

DAY OF THE HORSE

This day is auspicious for festivals, celebrations, and improving your relationships. It's a good time to keep in touch with overseas friends. This is a day when it is most unfavorable to cut your hair or get married. Avoid contact with blood at all costs.

DAY OF THE SHEEP

This day is suitable for ceremonies and for upgrading the household. Also, any work connected with the earth, such as planting, building, and digging, is favorable. But this is not a good day to have surgery or for going into hospital.

DAY OF THE MONKEY

This day is favorable for all manner of pleasurable activities, sports, music, and games of chance. It is also excellent for marriage feasts and other celebrations. It is not a good day to be honored or to accept bigger responsibilities.

DAY OF THE ROOSTER

This is an excellent day to prepare and take medicines, go to hospital, give aid to those in need, and to do charity and important communication work. Large festivals and celebrations are best avoided.

DAY OF THE DOG

This is a favorable day for undertaking prosperity rituals and other prayers. But it is a very bad day to cut or wash hair.

DAY OF THE BOAR

This is favorable for the handing over of your power and for welcoming ceremonies. It is a good day to open a new building or launch a new product. However, all contact with the earth should be avoided—so no planting, digging, or building.

PART TWO

FACE, HAND, AND BODY READING

CHAPTER SIX

FACE AND HEAD READING

The shape and spacing of your facial features and the characteristics of your ears and eyes are all thought to reveal aspects of your future. What do yours say about you?

INDICATIONS OF WEALTH ON YOUR FACE

MOST PAHT CHEE AND ASTROLOGY EXPERTS SUPPLEMENT READINGS OF THE CHARTS WITH A DETAILED READING OF THE FACE. THE CHINESE STRONGLY BELIEVE IN LUCKY AND UNLUCKY FACES, AND MUCH IS MADE OF THE SYMBOLIC "MOUNTAINS" AND "RIVERS" OF THE FACE (RAISED AND INDENTED FEATURES), SEEN AS INDICATORS OF WEALTH AND GOOD FORTUNE.

In general the central axis of the face is deemed to be the crucial beginning point of a person's destiny. When this appears to balance both sides of the face, the powerful trinity of luck is regarded as being properly aligned for prosperity. So the first requirement of a "wealthy face" is symmetry of both sides of the face. If this is obviously not the case, the Chinese believe that an unbalanced, and therefore a difficult life lies ahead of the person.

1: THE FOREHEAD

A reliable indicator of wealth is said to be a person's forehead—the first wealth spot on the face. This is the part of the face that represents the luck from heaven. It is the foremost mountain of the face and ideally it should be gently curved, round, high, and slightly protruding. This kind of forehead indicates power, wealth, and great authority. A perfect forehead is rare, but as long as it protrudes and looks prominent and wide, then genuine good fortune is indicated. A high forehead is also an indicator of high intelligence and

intellectual capability. The Chinese believe that a good forehead supports all the other luck features of the face because it also signifies the place of the heavenly celestial Dragon.

This is a yang spot on the face (most of the auspicious spots on the face are yang spots) and means a great deal in terms of your luck potential.

Everyone should take care of their forehead and keep it clear of blemishes and unsightly spots. Use artificial aids to ensure a smooth forehead if necessary.

Moles on the forehead are acceptable unless they are placed dead in the center, in which case they should be removed. Black moles here are deemed by the Chinese to be most inauspicious.

2: THE MIDDLE SPACE ABOVE THE NOSE

The second wealth spot on the face is the space above the nose. Good fortune is always expressed as being a perfect blend of the trinity of luck. This is expressed in terms of *Tien*, *Ti*, and *Ren*—heaven, earth, and mankind luck—with man in the

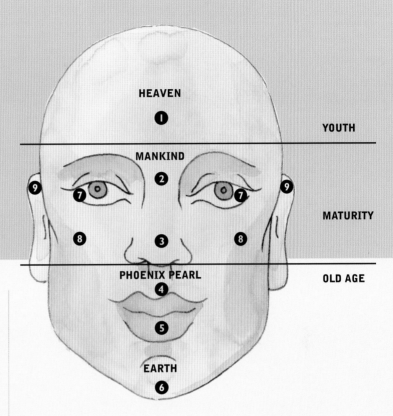

HEAVEN ❶

YOUTH

MANKIND ❷

❾ ❼ ❼ ❾

MATURITY

❽ ❸ ❽

PHOENIX PEARL ❹

OLD AGE

❺

EARTH ❻

center, located at the middle space above the nose and between the eyes. This is the man spot or *Ren* in Chinese, also referred to as the "life palace." Here the space should be clear, bright, and luminous if it is to represent a life of good fortune. There should be no hair, no unsightly coloring, no spots or blemishes, or moles in this area, because these are all signs that depict obstacles in life. Collectively or by themselves they signify hindrances in your life and blockages to your luck. If this space is clear and luminous it suggests a life of great affluence and easy influence.

3: THE NOSE

The nose is the third wealth spot on the face. The Chinese have a great preoccupation with the nose, generally regarding it as the most reliable indicator of wealth accumulation on a person's face. This is deemed to be a yin spot, and it signifies one of the important rivers of the face. In the Chinese classical texts on face reading, the nose signifies the River Jie, which brings great wealth. The rounder and

fleshier the nose looks, the greater is the wealth luck indicated. Nostrils should never be too small nor too large. The key to good fortune is always a balance and symmetry that suggests a good union of the yin with the yang.

Therefore, the nose must look balanced and smooth. Spots—white or black—are seen as obstacles, and moles at the tip of the nose are regarded as a major sign of misfortune in your life.

The Chinese always regard a big nose with some indulgence, no matter how out of proportion it may look on the face. This is because the nose is seen as the repository of money fortune and it indicates wealth from many different sources. This indicator of wealth is said to be more reliable on a woman's face than on a man's face.

FACIAL FORTUNE
Your face is divided into three to represent the three main phases of life: youth, maturity, and old age. There are nine "wealth spots" on your face (mostly in the maturity section), indicating the likelihood of you becoming rich at different times of your life.

4: THE PEARL ON YOUR MOUTH

Directly below the nose is the tip of the lips, and if you are deemed to possess the gift of the gab—tremendous prosperity luck that comes from speaking—you will see here what is termed the "phoenix pearl." It looks round and is slightly protruding, and usually those who have it will probably have had it from childhood, in fact from the time they were born. This sign is always very prominent in a newly born baby.

Like a cleft chin or a dimple, the pearl is deemed also to be a beauty spot. It brings good fortune in both men and women. The pearl is considered the fourth wealth feature on the face and is highly valued on the face of a woman, particularly a prospective daughter-in-law, as she is said to bring good luck to her husband.

5: THE MOUTH

Directly below the pearl is the mouth, which is considered the second river on the face. It is known as the River Huai. The mouth is considered lucky and auspicious when it is soft and succulent. Irrespective of its size, the mouth must never appear dry, since this indicates loss of luck. As long as the mouth is always moist, it indicates money luck. This is why it is such a good idea for men and women alike to use lip balm. This keeps lips perpetually moist. Women have the added advantage of using lip gloss, and this is said to attract great good fortune in your life.

The mouth is the fifth wealth spot on the face. Moles around the mouth, as long as they are not black, are deemed to enhance the good luck of the mouth. Often small red moles around the mouth indicate that the person will never lack food.

6: THE CHIN

The chin is the second mountain on the face and this is also regarded as the sixth wealth spot. The chin is the place of earth in the trinity of *tien ti ren* and is sometimes viewed as the jawline. To be auspicious, the chin should be slightly protruding and prominent. A receding jawline is a sign of misfortune in old age, or it can even be a sign of premature death. A prominent chin indicates a strong base mountain, and this is also suggestive of a long, stable, and fruitful life.

7: THE EYES

The seventh wealth spot on the face is the eyes. The eyes are said to indicate great good fortune when they shine and are slightly moist—what may be described as being bright-eyed. It does not matter what shape, size, or color the eyes are. What is most significant is the inner vitality that shines through. When the eyes are bright and are well protected by arched eyebrows, the life of the owner is said to be healthy and prosperous.

Eyebrows should never be overly plucked or shaved. Indeed, when a face lacks eyebrows the person simply cannot climb up the ladder of success. The person without eyebrows will also become vulnerable to "attacks" by others. If you have to pluck your eyebrows you should never remove hairs above the brows. This action will instantly curtail your good fortune.

When one eye is smaller than the other, it is a good idea to use eyeliners to correct the imbalance. Once again it is symmetry that suggests good fortune. It does not matter if your eyes lack the double eyelid of Caucasian faces. What is important is the shine and luminosity of the eyes.

8: THE CHEEKBONES

The eighth wealth spot on the face is the cheekbones. In terms of age luck (see page 161), you enter into the center section of the face, which indicates the maturing years, after the age of 21.

If the cheekbones stand out prominently and appear bright and shiny, it is one of the surest signs that serious wealth luck is about to manifest in your life.

Cheekbones should always have flesh. They should never look bony, since this is an indication of excessive and harmful yang energy in your life. The color of the cheekbones is also important. Cheekbones that look pink and luminous are indicators of good fortune. Cheekbones that appear sallow and dry suggest that you are experiencing a loss of vitality and chi energy.

9: THE EARS

The ninth and final wealth indicator is the ears. If your ears are well formed and in proportion, they indicate great good fortune and wisdom. They are said to represent the flow of the Yellow River. The Chinese have a great preference for long ears because these kinds of ears remind them of Buddha's. Long, well-defined ears that are not overly fleshy or large are a sign of class and the high born.

SUMMARY

Of the nine wealth features only one is placed in the youth section of the face and two in the old age section (see page 157). This suggests that our destiny manifests mostly during the time of life between youth and old age—this is named the age of maturity. Thus while face reading gives us a good idea of luck potential, it is essential to note that the bridge between heaven and earth is mankind. It is mankind luck that has the most impact on our destiny as it unfolds. The face over time can undergo change—just as mountains can flatten and rivers can run dry. It is vital to stay ever watchful, as much over our physical bodies as over the luck that we are constantly creating for ourselves.

BRIGHT EYES

If your inner vitality is clearly evident in your eyes, you are likely to be healthy and prosperous.

LIFE STAGES ON THE FACE

FACE READING CATEGORIZES INDIVIDUAL FACIAL FEATURES ACCORDING TO COLOR, SHAPE, DISFIGUREMENTS, AND BIRTHMARKS, AND THE MEANINGS OF THESE INDICATIONS VARY DEPENDING ON THE SPECIFIC AREAS OF THE FACE WHERE THEY APPEAR.

The Chinese art of face reading has always been considered an indispensable tool to understanding the human psyche and the fate that lies ahead of us. Chinese philosophers (such as Gui-Gu Tzu) who specialize in face reading have had much of their knowledge preserved in books and there are ancient texts on face reading, such as *Xiang Bian Wei Mang*, that are still in print today.

One of the more popular methods used in face reading is to determine the luck at different times of your life. This is considered accurate in pinpointing the times when you will face difficulties, and when you will sail through. This face reading method involves the demarcation of the plane of the face into different age periods (see the illustration opposite).

DIFFERENT LIFE STAGES

In general, your ears and the top part of your face represent the early years of your life when you are in your preteens, teens, and early twenties. As you grow older your destiny gets recorded progressively down your face toward your eyebrows, nose,

cheeks, lips, and, finally, your chin. The illustration shows in more detail the part of the face that identifies the fate of your current age:

• If your current age is on the right-hand side of your face, then leisure dominates your time.

• If it is on the left side of your face, work and career matters take up your attention and your time.

• If it is on the center part of your face, you are said to be at a crossroads, and some important decisions confront you.

SIGNS OF MISFORTUNES

Marks, discolorations, spots, creases, and indentations indicate problems. Where they are found on your face gives you an idea at what age you will be facing such problems. Problems can manifest as illness, bad relationships, accidents, money troubles, and so on. The bigger and darker the mark on your face, the more serious the problem you will face. The Chinese usually take the sudden appearance of dark marks as a portent and sponsor prayers to "avert" some bad karma ripening.

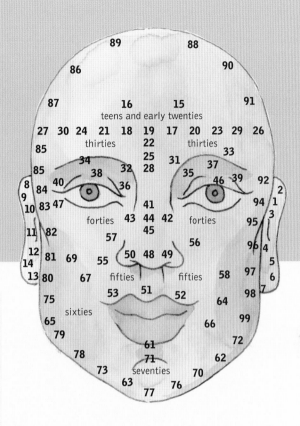

If you have a birthmark on one of your ears, for example, this indicates a difficult time during your childhood years. Marks on the bridge of your nose indicate a tough time in your twenties marked by uncertainties and obstacles. Discolorations at the end of your nose point to troubles during your forties, perhaps to do with your family or with your financial stability. Issues will arise that are likely to cause you worry and aggravations.

Generally, when your forehead is flawed, it means you will have a difficult relationship with your parents. (Or it could indicate you were a bit of a rebel when you were a troublesome teen!) If your forehead is small or bony, it indicates that your parents were not well heeled and could not afford expensive school fees. A skinny looking forehead is almost always an indication of something lacking in your life during your childhood and adolescence. If you have a broad, round, and smooth forehead, it indicates a very easy and pampered period during your growing-up years.

Markings, spots, scars, and indentations in your face can change over time, which denotes that your life fate is not fixed, but can change through the years. This usually reflects the result of the trinity of luck working simultaneously, whereby good mankind and earth luck influences your heaven luck.

If you find you are at a difficult period in your life, one way to deal with it is to grit your teeth and be even more determined to improve the other two-thirds of your luck to compensate for the unlucky events and outcomes.

You can get a bottle of moisturizing cream or book a facial at your nearest beauty salon to iron out the trouble spots on your facial features. Strange as it may sound, when you take good care of the physical face, the psyche also benefits—it is like attracting good chi with a smooth and unblemished complexion.

FACE FATE

Specific areas of your face represent different periods or years of your life, according to face-reading experts. They believe that marks and creases on a particular spot indicate problems at that time in your life.

THE MEANINGS OF FACIAL MOLES

WE TURN TO THE CHINESE ALMANAC, ALSO KNOWN AS THE TUNG SHU AND COMMONLY REFERRED TO AS A "BOOK OF AUSPICIOUS AND INAUSPICIOUS DATES," FOR THE MEANINGS OF FACIAL MOLES. THE MOLES FOUND ON THE FACE MAY SIGNIFY CHARACTERISTICS SUCH AS CREATIVITY AND INTELLIGENCE AND TYPES OF LUCK SUCH AS WEALTH AND HEALTH LUCK.

N ot many people realize that there is so much more to the *Tung Shu* than simply identifying good and bad dates. The Almanac is a vast mine of information relating to astrology, codes, and symbols, derived from the wise sages and philosophers of ancient China. Here, we delve into the secret meanings of moles when they appear on your face. Moles have different and subtle meanings depending on which part of your face they appear.

Check your face for moles, and then look at the illustration opposite to identify the numbers that are the closest match to the position of the moles on your face. Usually, the moles hold meaning for you only if they are prominent and not widespread. If your face if full of spots, acne, or "little" moles, they do not count for interpretation purposes. When you've ascertained which position corresponds to your facial mole, refer to the meanings below.

MOLES 1 to 3

As a child, you were somewhat rebellious and a free spirit. You have an innate creativity and work best when you are

given a free hand. Generally, your superiors like your avant garde approach to life. If you have a mole here, you are far better off in business and being your own boss rather than working for somebody else. What is promising is that you have the luck to be your own boss.

MOLE 4

You are an impulsive person, often acting with a flamboyance that gives you charisma and a sparkling personality, but you can be difficult when there are too many opinions. You tend to be argumentative, but never hold grudges. This mole tends to give you an explosive temper. Should you decide to have it removed, you will find yourself becoming calmer and more at peace with the world.

MOLE 5

A mole above the eyebrow indicates that there is wealth luck in your life, but you will need to earn it and work harder than most people to attain it. All the income you make must be carefully kept because there are people who are jealous of you who might attempt to sweet talk you into parting with your wealth. Be wary of those who try to interest you in any get-rich-quick schemes. If you have a mole here, it is advisable not to be too trusting of others. Follow your instincts and be cautious. Never allow other people to control your finances.

MOLE 6

A mole here indicates intelligence, creativity, and skill as an artist. Your artistic talent can bring you wealth, fame, and success. It also indicates wealth luck, but this can be fully realized only if you follow your heart rather than stick to conventional means of making a living. Success will come if you are brave.

MOLE 7

Moles under the eyebrows indicate arguments within the extended family that cause you grief and unhappiness. These arguments will affect your work and livelihood. It is advisable to settle any differences you have with your relatives if you want peace of mind to move ahead.

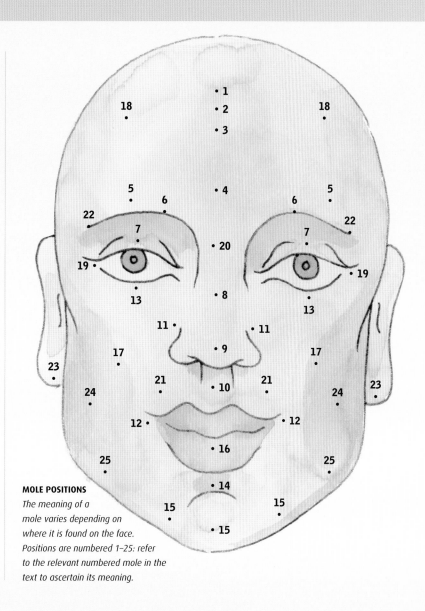

MOLE POSITIONS
The meaning of a mole varies depending on where it is found on the face. Positions are numbered 1–25: refer to the relevant numbered mole in the text to ascertain its meaning.

MOLE 8

This is not a very good position for a mole. Your financial position will constantly be under strain because of a tendency to overspend. You also have a penchant for gambling. You need to learn when to stop. Someone with a mole here also has a tendency to flirt with members of the opposite sex as well as with members of the same sex. Better be a little discerning where you exert your charms, or you might get into trouble.

MOLE 9

This mole position suggests sexual and other problems. It is an unfortunate mole and you are well advised to get rid of it, if possible. It brings a litany of woes and a parade of problems.

MOLE 10

A mole here just under the nose indicates excellent descendants' luck. You are surrounded by family at all times and will have many children and grandchildren. You have the support of those close to you and will be both materially and emotionally fulfilled.

MOLE 11

A mole here suggests a tendency to succumb to illness. It is a good idea to have this mole removed, especially if it is a large, dark-colored mole. Otherwise use lots of foundation to cover it, if appropriate.

MOLE 12

A mole here foretells a successful and also a very balanced life. You are likely to be not just rich, but famous as well. Although you have every opportunity to live the high life, however, you will have a satisfying home and family life as well. Women with moles in this position are particularly lucky and tend to be beautiful and glamorous as well.

MOLE 13

Your children will be a big worry in your life. Your relationship with them will not be good. There is nothing much you can do about this except to learn tolerance.

MOLE 14

A mole here suggests a vulnerability to food that can be a big problem in your life. You may have allergies to certain foods or you may simply eat too much.

MOLE 15

You are always on the move and are constantly renovating and redesigning your house. You like to be introduced to new things and see new places. You are not happy if you remain in one place for long. You enjoy travel and adventure, and have a very observant eye.

MOLE 16

You need to be careful when it comes to eating, and also when it comes to your sex life. These are your two biggest problems. You tend to have weight issues, which can make you depressed. You enjoy romance, sometimes with more than one person, but because you are a person with some morality, you will feel guilty about it, and this will cause you much stress.

ROULETTE RISK
If you have a mole on the bridge of your nose (Mole 8), beware of a penchant for gambling.

MOLE 17

You will be someone of great social prominence. You are active on the social scene and you are an excellent conversationalist. There is a tendency to become bigheaded about your success, which could lose you your good name. This loss of reputation will affect you deeply because you draw your confidence and self-worth from what others think of you.

MOLE 18

You are always on the move. There is a great deal of overseas travel in your life, but you should take extra care each time you cross the great waters, as your mole prefers you to stay at home.

MOLE 19

You have money luck and many good friends, so this is a very auspicious mole to have. Your weakness is that you tend to succumb to the charms of the opposite sex far too much. In your life, it is this that could get you into hot water, so do attempt to cool your ardor!

MOLE 20

A mole here can be very lucky or very unlucky. You are destined for either extreme fame or infamy. You have great creative flair and are also highly intelligent, but your talents can be used for both good and bad. You are not a person to be trifled with, for you are no pushover and you do not forgive and forget easily. This mole is a mark of someone who will go down in history—and it could be either as a great person or as a tyrant!

MOLE 21

This is a very auspicious mole to have on your face because it suggests plenty to eat and drink throughout your life. This mole is also likely to signal the arrival of fame and recognition in your life.

MOLE 22

Your life is always happy and things go smoothly for you. You could well become a sports superstar if you have the passion for this field of endeavor. Moles at the end of eyebrows also suggest a person of authority and power. This means that if you are the chief executive officer of a company, you will do very well.

MOLE 23

You have a high IQ, and you are both brain-smart and street-smart. You have a highly developed survival instinct and this characteristic means that you are going to lead a meaningful and long life. You will be active until a very old age and will have plenty of friends and family around you till the very end.

MOLE 24

You will achieve fame and fortune in your early life and you are advised to use this period to safeguard your old age, as people with moles here tend to have a harder life as they get older.

MOLE 25

You will enjoy good prosperity and recognition luck, but do be careful of excesses. Stay traditional in your attitudes and you will have a long and fruitful life.

YOUR EARS AND THE INNER YOU

IF YOU HAVE LONG EARLOBES LIKE THOSE ON A BUDDHA, YOU ARE PREDICTED TO ENJOY A LONG AND MEANINGFUL LIFE. THOSE WITH FLESHY EARS ARE SAID TO BE EXTREMELY SEXY, WHILE THOSE WITH HARD, THICK EARS ARE PREDICTED TO BE RICH. WHAT KIND OF EARS DO YOU HAVE AND WHAT DO THEY SAY ABOUT YOU? HERE'S WHAT THE CHINESE ALMANAC AND CULTURAL ENCYCLOPEDIA HAVE TO SAY.

LARGE, FLESHY EARS

Large, fleshy ears are best for those born in the years of the Ox, Horse, Rooster, and Monkey. Large ears like these, however, are not so suitable for those born in Rabbit and Tiger years. Despite all their riches, they will lead busy but lonely lives. Takeshi Kaneshiro has ears that are thick, large, fleshy, and quite reddish in color. It is said that such ears will bring great prosperity. Takeshi will live to an old age and is likely to reach a high position in life. Starting off his career as a model, he launched a successful singing career in both Mandarin and Cantonese. His versatility has seen him portray his characters with much depth in both Chinese and Japanese movies.

HIGH-POSITIONED EARS

Ears positioned high above the eyebrows with light-colored lobes and large ear holes stand for wealth, prosperity, and longevity luck. Steven Spielberg has ears like these. This world-renowned director is reported to have a personal fortune worth over US$2 billion! From *E.T.* to *Saving Private Ryan*, Spielberg has produced one hit after another. For those with similar ear types, if your eyes are brown in color, you will be an upper-class socialite. If your nose and mouth are in good shape, you will get support from relatives. As a safe measure, avoid shaping your brow sloping downward, as this could indicate suffering even though you are wealthy.

SMALL, HARD EARS

Petite, pert, and sexy, Kylie Minogue has small, hard ears. Matched with a small figure and thin body shape, these ears bring accomplishment. Kylie's life, although peppered with both successes and disappointments, can only be described as one of achievement. She has made it big on the world stage as an A-list singer and entertainer. Ranked one of the sexiest women in the world, she is enjoying her stardom. These ears don't sit well on a plump, tall person, where they suggest a short life. Someone with this kind of ear—small with a small earhole—is wily and clever. They may appear innocent, but often know more than they let on.

KINGLY EARS

These well-proportioned ears indicate someone who has been born into an aristocratic family. They are described as a king's ears. It is therefore apt that Prince William has ears like these. Being second in line to the throne, it augurs well for the British royal family that Prince William's ears are long, hard, and thick, with the whole ear very well positioned. This adds auspicious balance to the prince's face and indicates a person with sound common sense and morality.

Prince William's ears also suggest someone of great compassion with the potential for great wisdom to arise during their older years.

BIG EARS WITH LARGE EARHOLES

A large ear with a large earhole is not a very good sign. With this ear type, wealth luck does not last for very long. Jessica Simpson has ears of this type. Fortunately, with her slim figure, this bad luck is not very pronounced. Being a popular and sexy star, Jessica will want to look her slimmest best at all times.

Jessica's claim to fame has been from *Newlyweds: Nick and Jessica*, a successful reality TV show featuring her wedded life with 98° singer, Nick Lachey.

The series, which proved to be popular worldwide, involved the couple allowing cameras to document their everyday life. Although Jessica has worked very hard for her success (and continues to do so), according to the advice of the Chinese Almanac for people with her ear type, she would be well advised not to become complacent in the future.

Those with this ear type should guard against taking success for granted. These ears bring potential for wealth, but only for those prepared to work hard. There is a danger of losing that wealth if you become complacent. There is also potential conflict with relatives and with your partner.

WIDE, THIN EARS

People whose ears are wide and thin have plenty of good luck when they are young. Being the daughter of actor Jon Voight, actress Angelina Jolie certainly had a better start to life than most people do.

This ear type has a small lobe and the upper part is larger than the lower part. These ears are pale in color with a large earhole. If the person has a sharp forehead, it indicates that they could face difficulties in their late teens and it also suggests that they might well leave home in search of independence. This ear type brings fame and fortune to those people who are born in Rat, Rabbit, and Horse years.

Angelina, a wood Rabbit, got her first break in the critically acclaimed HBO movie, *Gia*. Her kick-ass attitude in *Tomb Raider* sealed her fame and her movie *Alexander* was also a success. Angelina has overtaken her father as a household name, and in recent years she has even become infamous for being the third party in the Brad Pitt/Jennifer Aniston divorce. It is possible that she could suffer much heartache in later life, especially with respect to problems associated with her children, as is often the case for people who have wide, thin ears.

BIG-LOBED EARS

Ears with big lobes like those belonging to American actress Sarah Michelle Gellar are a sign of great and strategic intelligence. Better known as Buffy the Vampire Slayer from the hit television series, Sarah brilliantly scored a Grade Point Average (GPA) of 4.0 and graduated high school two years early from the Professional Children's School in New York.

Ears such as these are set level with or higher than the eyebrows and they tend to be thick. The ear color is a shade paler than the face color.

Big-lobed ears bring exceptional good luck to people born in the years of the following Chinese horoscope animals:

• Dragon
• Ox
• Dog
• Sheep.

Even though she is a Lady Snake, Sarah has been enjoying a great deal of luck with her successful acting career. Her movie *The Grudge* raked in the profits.

This ear type is not so suitable for those born in the years of the Rabbit and Tiger, bringing them loss and bad luck. For them, it is an indication of poverty.

ELF-LIKE EARS

Paris Hilton, hotel heiress and star of TV reality show *The Simple Life*, possesses elfin ears. Like an elf, she dances her way through life.

These ears indicate someone with a very complex, mixed-up personality who suffers from moods and ambivalence. At times, she acts like a spoilt brat; other times, she flashes her huge smile and comes across both sweet and innocent. Her ears are long, with the upper part quite sharp. This indicates a busy life filled with unpredictability. This certainly seems to describe Ms Hilton's jet-setting lifestyle.

These ears are best suited to those born in the years of the Horse, Rabbit, or Tiger. Paris—being a metal Rooster—may not have the ideal pair of ears for her animal sign, but nevertheless she is enjoying her own notoriety, which, as a Rooster, she carries off magnificently. Paris also has the kind of confidence that arises from having been born into great wealth. This ear type indicates a volatile life, where, in spite of great riches, there is also great loneliness. Paris may have the Hilton empire waiting for her, but her ears suggest that it will take more than money to make her happy.

YOUR EYES AND YOUR FUTURE

THE CHINESE BELIEVE THAT YOUR EYES OFFER CLUES TO YOUR PERSONALITY AS WELL AS TO WHAT YOUR FUTURE HAS IN STORE. THEY BELIEVE THEY REVEAL THE HIDDEN ATTRIBUTES AND SUCCESS POTENTIAL OF A PERSON—THAT WHICH IS NOT IMMEDIATELY OBVIOUS. WHAT DO YOUR EYES SAY ABOUT YOU AND WHAT DO THEY REVEAL ABOUT YOUR DESTINY?

Your eyes are a window into your covert agendas and your hidden passions. Even as you mature (and possibly change the way you make up your eyes), you will find yourself changing along with them. Use the five categorizations of eyes presented here to check out things you did not know about yourself and about your loved ones, and let them provide a clue to what kind of life and lifestyle you will have. Here, we refer to five kinds of eyes most commonly found in successful people to help in our analysis.

PHOENIX EYES

Phoenix eyes tend to be triangular in shape. They sometimes resemble almonds with well-defined irises. People with eyes like this are usually described as having beautiful, large expressive eyes that strike you as being very alert, healthy, serious-looking. At their most extreme, these eyes can suddenly turn fiery, and then they become a shade deeper and darker in color. When the corners of these eyes curve upward, their owners will enjoy immense good fortune.

People with these eyes will grow in self-confidence as they grow older. If they also have prominent eyebrows, these people will probably be intensely ambitious. Phoenix-eyed people can be very demanding and hot-tempered, quick to take offence, but are also incredibly charming. They are courageous, ambitious, and optimistic in their outlook, and these are the attributes that take them to the very pinnacle of their professions.

If you are a woman and have eyes like a phoenix, it is likely that men will find you irresistible. However, you are the emotional type and would not succumb to superficial wooing. Indeed, women with phoenix eyes can turn incredibly nasty when they are crossed.

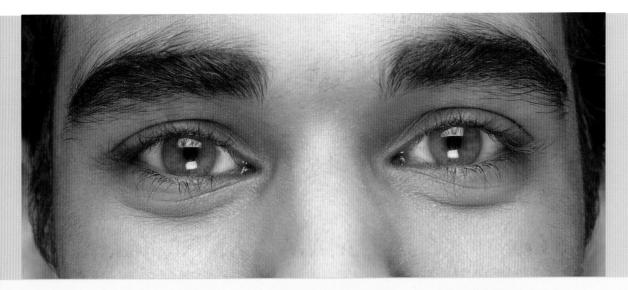

If you are a man with phoenix eyes, it is likely that your work will override any emotional entanglement you might have. There is plenty of power in your future and also a great deal of influence.

When the corners of phoenix eyes droop downward, the person tends to be impatient and selfish. The character of phoenix-eyed people is that they more often than not wear their hearts quite arrogantly on their sleeves.

They are straightforward, and they make much of their self-declared sincerity so they tend to be socially very successful. They also make loyal friends. These people will have a good life if they ensure their eyes stay bright and their ends are made up to flip upward rather than droop (if they use make-up, of course). Otherwise, they can end up lonely and sad.

When phoenix-eyed people have extra-large irises, they are very aggressive and are usually not close to their siblings. Such people also tend to be very independent. It is as if in some way they are born to succeed since success sits particularly well on their shoulders.

DRAGON EYES

Dragon eyes are big and appear to be full of energy, usually dominating the face. Eyes like this tend to be long and full and generally curving upward. The dragon stare is full of power and great vitality, almost piercing in its intensity.

People who have dragon eyes show a high degree of determination, courage, and perseverance. They will appear mesmerizing to those they focus on and their appearance will grow on anyone who sets eyes on them. When dragon-eyed people are riled, their eyes take on even deeper intensity. They reach the height of their power toward their late thirties, and by middle age they are usually already very successful.

People with dragon eyes are sure to enjoy success and prosperity. The size of

EYE INDICATIONS
Your eyes reveal clues to your character, including your level of self-confidence, courage, warmth, friendliness, and passion. Determine which kind of animal eyes you have and what that means about your personality.

their success depends on their other physical indicators, for example, on their face and hands as well as what is revealed in their paht chee charts.

Note, however, that if the lower eyelids curve upward, the indications are even more auspicious, as they suggest a well-balanced personality, which sits well with a powerful and courageous intellect. People with dragon eyes are kind and compassionate and get along with most people. They have power and authority, but they are also humble in their general demeanor. They come across as attractive and magnetic. The female of the species is particularly hard to resist.

TIGER EYES

These are oval-shaped eyes that appear large and penetrating in their gaze. Tiger-eyed people are not as wide-eyed as dragon-eyed people and their eyes tend to appear longer and less broad. Tiger eyes sit well on incredibly cool people, who may come across as being devoid of emotion. In women, tiger eyes can seem extremely intimidating and, indeed, they can be dangerous to those they associate with. Be careful of them and give them a long leash. Tiger eyes on Tiger-born people can be tough to handle. They tend to bring

trouble and bad luck, especially to those involved in a love relationship with them.

Men with tiger eyes tend to lead very complicated lives. They are successful in business, but generally devoid of warmth. Their success is based on cold calculation and strategic moves. They avoid direct confrontation, but when forced to respond, they are hostile and can be deadly. Never confront a person with tiger eyes, as you are sure to face a challenge. They rarely play by the rules, so you must be very careful. On the positive side, tiger-eyed people are usually determined. If you have them on your side, they make a formidable ally.

Tiger-eyed people can have eyes that tend to narrow, looking either downward or upward. If their irises appear nearer to the lower eyelid, they seem to be looking downward and you should be careful of them. Those tiger-eyed people whose irises are nearer their upper eyelid tend to be overconfident and also rather offensive, so they usually encounter obstacles in their interpersonal relationships.

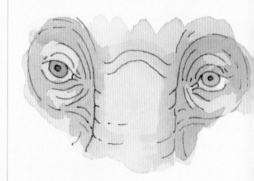

ELEPHANT EYES

Eyes like these are usually set quite far apart an tend to be rounded and sloping. They are ey that appear perpetually at peace with the worl

Their wide-eyed look is incredibly appealing and those whose ends taper gently will attain great fame as well.

The elephant eye gaze is very penetrating, but there is also an indifference in the look of the elephant-eyed people. They are not generally unpleasant, but it is hard to get close to them.

Elephant-eyed people come across as friendly, approachable, and eager to please, but do not be fooled, because in truth they become uncomfortable whenever anyone becomes too friendly. They are adept at dealing with the many superficial friendships that touch their lives but it is all general good comradeship, not friendship based on heartwarming closeness. People with elephant eyes rarely get involved in an intimate sort of friendship with the people they meet.

If elephant-eyed people appear to have well-delineated eyelids, their eyes look harmonious. Such people tend to be outwardly amicable and highly intelligent. They will have a creative side and feel the need for self expression. They also have a knack for appearing to be prosperous. People who belong to this group often possess leadership qualities and can climb the political ladder with success.

Women with elephant eyes tend to be spoilt and rather aloof. Men with elephant eyes tend to stay silent most of the time. If the paht chee chart indicates that an individual will attain great fame in their life, it is certain to happen. However, do not expect it to be profitable in any major way for those men and women who have elephant eyes.

TORTOISE EYES

People with eyes that resemble those of a tortoise usually have smaller irises. These often reveal a repressed or otherwise laid-back attitude, yet tortoise-eyed people possess vitality and astuteness. People with tortoise eyes often have hidden agendas, although they appear to be fluid and easygoing.

Hidden within their depths are feelings, opinions, and loyalties that you will know nothing about unless you get to know them very well. Tortoise-eyed people play their cards close to their chest.

At their worst, tortoise-eyed people can be rather unforgiving and even vindictive. But this is when there is more white in their eyes. When the black and white of the eyes is evenly balanced, tortoise-eyed people are incredibly perceptive and sharp. Tortoise-eyed people make good partners and business associates.

People who possess tortoise eyes are usually lacking when it comes to their sex drives. They prefer working and immersing themselves in their jobs rather than indulging in sex-oriented pursuits. They make excellent parents and are usually faithful to their spouses, but they tend to lack passion.

CHAPTER SEVEN

HAND, PALM, AND BODY READING

The shape of your hands, the lines on your palms, and the moles on your body can all reveal aspects of your destiny.

SUCCESS IN YOUR HAND SHAPE

THE CHINESE BELIEVE THAT FORTUNE TELLING USING THE PAHT CHEE CHARTS AND FACE READING TO DETERMINE GOOD FORTUNE IS WELL SUPPLEMENTED BY STUDYING THE EXTREMITIES OF THE HUMAN BODY—MORE SPECIFICALLY BY LOOKING FOR SIGNS AND SYMBOLS IN THE SHAPE AND APPEARANCE OF YOUR PALMS, WHICH ARE ALSO LINKED TO THE ELEMENTS.

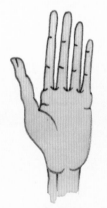

SLENDER PALM

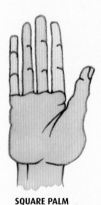

SQUARE PALM

L ines and indentations on your hands are believed to reveal a great deal about how successful you will be in all your life areas, including how successful you can expect to be during specific times of your life. Hands will also show when you might have a career change and when you can expect to ride high at work.

The Chinese believe that there is a direct communication between your hands and your mind, body, and spirit at all times, so that their appearance, shape, and lines, as well as telltale signs and symbols on the palm, offer remarkably accurate clues to your fortunes and misfortunes.

Over time, the Chinese have developed guidelines and principles for analyzing the lines of the palm and the appearance of the hands in order to assess what they reveal about your destiny.

The shape and appearance of your palms may be slender, square, heavy, elongated, or fleshy—whatever shape they are will offer insights into your life and destiny. First, consider the shape of your palms using the images to guide you. Then discover what the shape means.

CATEGORIZING YOUR HAND ELEMENT

As with face reading, feng shui, and other astrological practices and Chinese tradition, the principles that underpin hand analysis are related to the categorization of hands according to the five elements. Thus, all hands are classified according to the elements of wood, fire, earth, metal, and water. Knowing your hand element gives you insights into your personality and also into the type of profession that would suit you best, and in which you are most likely to succeed.

SLENDER PALMS: WOOD ELEMENT

If you have slender palms, you will thrive in professions that require you to work with or near the element of water. Such industries will enhance your chances of success and will therefore suit you best. Water industries include banking and financial services, consumer goods, import/export, trading, insurance, fishing, and everything related to shipping, transport, forwarding, and commerce.

SQUARE PALMS: METAL ELEMENT

If you have square palms, professions and work that require you to be in contact with earth element energy will suit you best, thereby enhancing your chances of success. Earth-related professions include architecture, engineering, and anything to do with real estate and property development. Road and infrastructure construction as well as all building-related businesses, such as factories that manufacture cement, floor tiles, wall tiles, and roof tiles, all fall within the earth category of businesses that would bring out the best from a person with metal-type hands.

HEAVY PALMS: EARTH ELEMENT

If you have heavy palms, being involved in work related to the fire element would be most suitable. Professionally such work would bring you into contact with fire energy. Acting, show business—all entertainment work, in fact—advertising, the mass media, the food industry (including restaurant work), and electronics would

all fall into the category of work that would harmonize with this hand type.

ELONGATED PALMS: FIRE ELEMENT

People with elongated palms will do well at work that brings them into close proximity with wood energy. Professions would include all agricultural ventures, such as garden nurseries and plantations, furniture businesses, publishing, textiles, writing, and so forth. Being near to wood will enhance the fire energy of your hands, thereby adding to your success potential.

FLESHY PALMS: WATER ELEMENT

If you have fleshy palms, you will thrive in metal-type professions and industries. Metal industries include computer, electronic components, engineering, and other hi-tech businesses. You can also find potential for advancement in information technology, the legal profession, mining, and the motor and automobile industries. Working in a factory environment is also an excellent option.

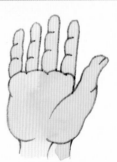

HEAVY PALM

ELONGATED PALM

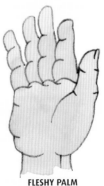

FLESHY PALM

PALM READING

THE THREE PRINCIPAL LINES ON YOUR PALM—THE HEART, HEAD, AND LIFE LINES—ARE REGARDED AS HEAVEN, MANKIND, AND EARTH LINES IN CHINESE PALM READING. IF THESE MAIN LINES ARE DEEP, CLEAR, AND HAVE NO INTERRUPTIONS, IT IS A SURE SIGN OF A SMOOTH AND SUCCESSFUL LIFE. BUT WHAT DO THE LINES AND SHAPES APPEARING ON YOUR PALM MEAN FOR YOUR FUTURE?

HANDY HINTS

Symbols of success and lucky lines appearing on your palm will offer clues to your future.

KEY

Ψ Trident
◊ Island
φ Fish
△ Triangle
Grid lines
／ Small line
⌂ Temple
≶ Feathery lines
🕱 Joining lines

All secondary lines branching off the main lines of heaven, mankind, and earth are good when they run upward and bad when they cross the main lines. Joining lines (also known as root lines) mean you have helpful people joining your camp to assist you. There are also distinct symbols of success to be found on palms. Lucky indications are tridents, fish, and temples. Roots and islands on the other hand are unlucky signs. Here is a brief guide to interpreting your own palms.

TRIDENTS

These are symbols of power and of unanticipated good luck. When a trident falls along the fate line, it usually indicates a promotion or unexpected windfall. The presence of a trident on your hand is a sure indication that you will always be in a position of power, and that you are a very influential person. Usually the trident indicates three types of luck—wealth, power, and influence. When it appears as shown in the illustration it indicates the fulfillment of your ambitions.

ISLANDS

An island on your career line usually means a dismissal or a severe illness that could cut short your career. Or you could be the victim of vicious politics. The island is always regarded as a very inauspicious symbol. Wherever it appears on the hand always suggests some kind of obstacle during that period of your life.

THE FISH

This is a sign of great prosperity and wealth. When this is found along your career line, it

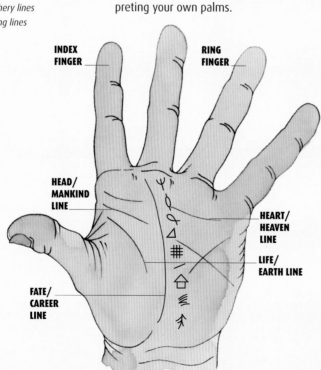

INDEX FINGER

RING FINGER

HEAD/ MANKIND LINE

HEART/ HEAVEN LINE

LIFE/ EARTH LINE

FATE/ CAREER LINE

FINGERS OF FATE

Not only do your hand shapes and the lines on your palms reveal a lot about you, but the length of your index and ring fingers can also give you a clue to your destiny.

INDEX FINGER

If your index finger is longer than your ring finger, this indicates natural leadership ability. You swiftly identify what has to be done and are capable of directing and motivating others in helping you achieve your goals. You will do well in a job that allows your natural leadership to unfold. Your weakness is that you may be hot-tempered and overly quick to react when you feel your position threatened.

RING FINGER

If your ring finger is longer than your index finger, this indicates you have plenty of creative and original ideas. You are good at marketing yourself and you thrive on other people's appreciation of your talents. You will enjoy a job where you can demonstrate your talents and skills. Your weakness under stress is that you become defensive when you fear that people will reject your work.

indicates that massive wealth will come from your work or career. The fish sign can also be seen in other parts of the hand— wherever it appears it is an indicator of expanding wealth. The fish stands for abundance, and in the old days experts in palmistry would advise keeping fish to activate the signs of abundance shown in the palm. If you keep lively goldfish you will activate the fish signs on your palms.

TRIANGLES

These are signs of achievement and success. On your fate line, triangles also signify a turning point in your career, something that changes your work direction for the better. Triangles always signify recognition of some kind. If you are fortunate enough to have a triangle sign, you should feel very blessed.

GRID LINES

These are signs of being stuck or stifled. When found on the career line, they may symbolize a jealous colleague politicking against you, a middle manager stifling your creativity, or an unfulfilling job.

SMALL LINES

When these cross the main lines, they signify obstacles and difficulties.

THE TEMPLE

This is a rare symbol of great influence that relates to your own spirituality. It suggests a state of blissful realizations.

FEATHERY LINES

These indicate worry and warn of some- thing causing you torment at work.

JOINING LINES

Also known as "root lines," they symbolize helpful people entering your life.

HIDDEN MEANINGS OF BODY MOLES

THE CHINESE BELIEVE THAT MOLES CAN BE LUCKY OR UNLUCKY
DEPENDING ON THE PART OF THE BODY THEY APPEAR, THE INTENSITY
OF THEIR COLOR, AND THEIR SIZE IN PROPORTION TO THE BODY.
ACCORDING TO THE INFORMATION HERE, BASED ON INFORMATION
FROM THE CHINESE CHARACTER OF "TUNG SHU" AND OTHER TAOIST
SOURCES, WHAT DO YOUR MOLES REVEAL ABOUT YOUR DESTINY?

A mole can be a tiny black speck on the feet signifying opportunities for travel, or it can be a dark red dot on the hand, often interpreted as indicating a particular skill or luck associated with your hands. Moles on the back generally denote some kind of burden or heartache to be carried through life; moles on the front of the body are said to attract success luck.

Some say that the moles on our bodies are in reality secret imprints carried over from our previous lives, stamps of some past karmic deed—good as well as bad—meant to ripen in this life. Others contend that moles are messages of good fortune and misfortune that reflect important turning points of our life. Each noticeable mole on our body carries a hidden meaning, or depicts some secret obstacle or unexpected help from someone.

In certain traditions, the messages of moles were so significant they could even be read as bringing bad luck to the family, or so highly regarded that the member of the family with the mole would be revered. In many parts of China it is believed that the larger and more prominent the mole,

the greater is its power. Another widely held belief is that lighter-colored moles spell better fortune.

MOLES ON THE FRONT OF THE BODY

MOLE 1

Life will be quite a challenge for you and there will be times when things will not be easy. The good news is that if the mole is red and appears more toward the front than the back, you will rise easily to whatever challenges may face you.

MOLE 2

You are easily stressed. Take a deep breath each time you feel unbearably pressured by your loved ones.

MOLE 3

You are popular and efficient and your life is one busy challenge after another. You do not lack for work and are much in demand at social events. This is probably because you are likely to hold a high position with responsibilities to match.

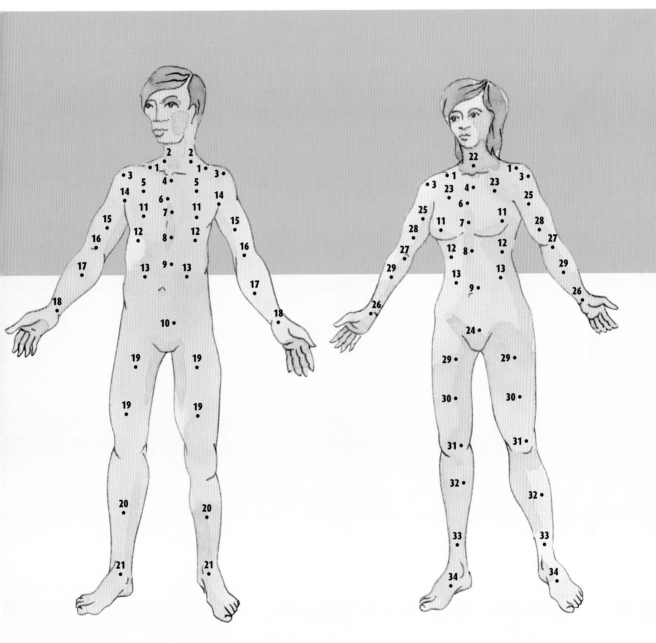

MOLE 4

Be careful about your eating habits, especially if the mole is black and prominent. If the mole is light-colored, it means your spouse loves you very much.

MOLE 5

A mole on the upper breast suggests a happy life with few worries. But you need to take care of your health in your fifties.

MOLE 6

This is the sign of a very ambitious person with big dreams. If there are other indications of success on your palm or paht chee chart, you could rise to great prominence.

MOLE 7

A mole here suggests someone who is generous and kind at heart. You are honorable when conducting business.

MOLE POSITIONS

The meaning of a mole varies depending on where it is found on the front of the body and whether it is on a man or a woman. Positions are numbered 1–34: refer to the relevant numbered mole in the text to ascertain its meaning.

FATHERHOOD FORTUNE
A man with a mole in the genital area (Mole 10) will be blessed with many children.

MOLE 8

A mole on the stomach signifies you have everything going for you; your life will be smooth and safe.

MOLE 9

A mole here on your stomach signifies you will enjoy great wealth luck. The smaller the mole, the better, but it should be dark and clearly visible. If it touches your navel, you will rise to become seriously wealthy.

MOLE 10

The man who finds a mole here will be blessed with many children.

MOLE 11

A mole here suggests you will be blessed with obedient children who will bring you much happiness.

MOLE 12

A mole here will bring plenty of good fortune. Everything will move smoothly in your life and there will also be unexpected windfalls. When moles here appear as a pair, they indicate extreme good fortune.

MOLE 13

A mole near either side of your lower abdominal area means you will have a handsome husband or a beautiful wife. You will also be blessed with good looks.

MOLE 14

A mole near the armpits is a sign of good fortune luck for males. If the mole is hidden deep inside the armpit, it means you will attain a high rank in life.

MOLE 15

A mole on this part of the arm suggests that you need to work hard for everything you get. You could also be involved in a very physical kind of work.

MOLE 16

A mole on the inside of your elbow suggests that it is hard for you to get the recognition that you deserve for the hard work you do. Getting the results you want could be elusive.

MOLE 17

A mole on the inside lower arm area suggests that you will deal with money all your life, although the money will not necessarily be yours. You should be careful in all your financial dealings, as this is a warning mole.

MOLE 18

A mole on your inside wrist means you love spending money and will have a hard time hanging onto your wealth. Practice giving to charity, and this will ensure you have plenty of money to spend and to give away. When the mole is on the left hand, it means money flows out faster than you can make it. On the right hand, some say this mole attracts a flow of money.

MOLE 19

A mole found on a man's inner thigh is an indication of inheritance luck, so there is a possibility of a relative leaving you a small fortune. For women, however, this mole suggests that wealth will come from your own efforts.

MOLE 20

Moles on the lower leg are not such a good indication, as these suggest you will have to endure hardship and suffering in the course of your life.

MOLE 21

A mole near the upper part of a man's feet denotes a life filled with travel both for pleasure and work. If the mole is small and is a dot, it suggests happiness in travel. If the mole is very large, it suggests that travel brings problems.

MOLE 22

A mole found on the base of your neck can sometimes indicate a short life, with the possibility of being highly stressed-out. Learn to relax.

MOLE 23

This mole suggests you will be entrusted with the responsibility of taking care of your family. It is also an indication that you will do an excellent job and will be well rewarded in later life.

MOLE 24

This mole indicates that you are very passionate and have a high sex drive.

MOLE 25

This mole suggests you love children and have a great affinity with them.

MOLE 26

This mole indicates that you have unstable characteristics and also that you have a tendency to overspend.

MOLE 27

This mole means that you cannot keep a secret. You do not mean any harm but you love to talk.

MOLE 28

A mole here suggests you should take care of your money, or you could find yourself losing some of your hard-earned cash.

MOLE 29

This mole is a very reliable indicator of prosperity and wealth.

MOLE 30

This mole suggests a sunny disposition and that you treat everyone with respect and are in turn well respected.

MOLE 31

A mole on your knee means you will need to work extremely hard to succeed in life.

MOLE 32

A mole here indicates you are not a very ambitious person. Knowing this, perhaps it's time to start setting goals in life.

MOLE 33

This mole signifies that you can be rather heartless at times.

MOLE 34

A mole on the top of your foot indicates that your love life does not run smoothly. However, if the mole is red, it means you will be successful in love but the problem will be that you are too flirtatious to have a monogamous relationship.

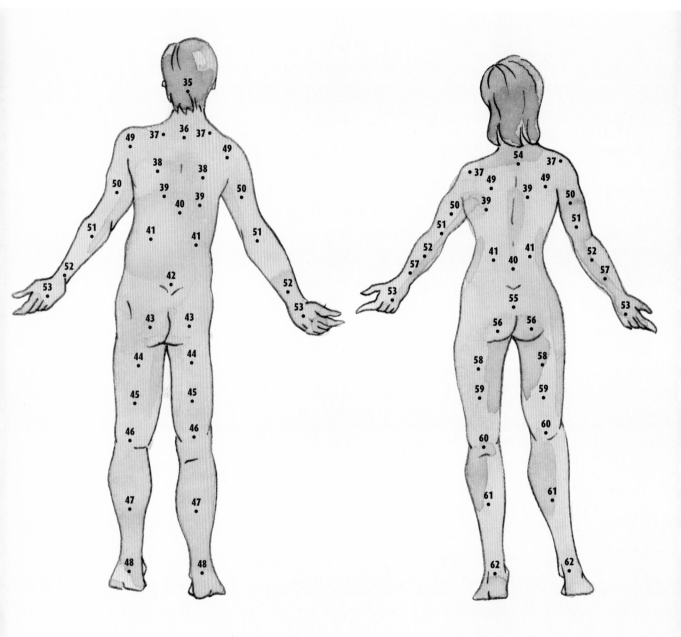

MOLE POSITIONS

The meaning of a mole varies depending on where it is found on the back of the body and whether it is on a man or a woman. Positions are numbered 35–62: refer to the relevant numbered mole in the text to ascertain its meaning.

MOLES ON THE BACK OF THE BODY

MOLE 35

A mole at the nape of your neck is a good mole that indicates you will have every-thing you need to equip yourself with all the basic necessities of life. There is a like-lihood that you will be rich or at least that you will not lack for money.

MOLE 36

A mole positioned at the top of the spine in the center of the back has unfortunate implications for both men and women. For men, it's health problems; for women, marriage problems.

Men who have a mole at the center of their back will constantly be plagued by backache. Their life is likely to be about dealing with one problem after another.

In the old days, a mole such as this would have been cauterized and removed.

MOLE 37

A mole on the back of the shoulder suggests that you will have to bear the burden of many heavy responsibilities, including having to swallow many indignities during the course of your life. Again, this is a mole that is best removed, if this is appropriate and possible for you.

MOLE 38

Moles found here will generally invite backstabbing, betrayal, and politicking. You will have a hard time escaping the slings and arrows that are aimed at you unless you remove this mole.

MOLE 39

A mole located in this position suggests a lack of prosperity luck. It is likely you will find it difficult to hold onto your job, either because you do not like it, or the job does not like you.

MOLE 40

A mole located in this position is thought to be inauspicious—it generally brings gastric and stomach problems.

MOLE 41

A mole here indicates a lack of ambition, indecisiveness, and a general tendency to prevaricate. You will find that you lack the motivation to carry on and will constantly need pushing to get on with your life. But this mole also suggests you have spouse luck, a good indication.

MOLE 42

This mole suggests the potential for success and wealth. There is plenty of good fortune in running your own business. If you have such a mole, you should be an entrepreneur rather than working for someone else.

MOLE 43

A mole on your buttocks is an excellent indicator of intelligence, wisdom, and creativity. You will rise to prominence and be highly respected.

MOLE 44

Moles on the back of the thighs indicate that you will enjoy plenty of good fortune during the course of your life. You will also be charismatic and popular.

MOLE 45

Located slightly lower at the back of the thighs, this mole suggests you are very knowledgeable and intelligent. You can also be depended upon.

MOLE 46

Sadly, if your mole is located on the back of your knee, it is said that you will have to endure a life that is lacking in the good things. You may want to consider having this mole removed.

MOLE 47

Located at the back of the calf, this is a mole that suggests you are very busy, but it is a "good" type of busy, because it also brings recognition. You will enjoy good relationships with most people.

MOLE 48

A man who possesses a mole on the back of his ankle will be one who tends to stay away from home and could even move far away. This is a mole that suggests someone always on the move.

MOLE 49

This mole indicates that you are perceived as having no class or finesse. This mole should ideally not be revealed. It is better to cover it.

MOLE 50

You will experience love and marriage dilemmas; if the mole is dark, the portents are even more negative.

MOLE 51

If you have a mole in this inauspicious location, you have a tendency to be messy and slovenly.

MOLE 52

A mole on the outside of the wrist indicates that you will possibly experience a broken marriage or at least a very unstable love life during your forties. If you cover the mole with long sleeves, though, the instability could calm down.

MOLE 53

If you have a mole on the back of your hand, keep it, for it means you will be earning lots of money!

GOOD COMPANY
Women with a mole on the middle of their calves (Mole 61) will never want for supportive friends during their lives.

MOLE 54

A mole here implies a marriage that could involve unfortunate circumstances.

MOLE 55

A mole here suggests someone who is reliable, trustworthy, and pays attention to their work.

MOLE 56

Finding a mole on your behind means that you will experience a sheltered life blessed with good fortune.

MOLE 57

You will have to endure lots of gossiping and backstabbing in your life if you have this mole.

MOLE 58

This mole indicates that you have plenty of patience, but when pushed to the limit you can snap.

MOLE 59

You will make an efficient accountant, as this mole indicates someone who is good with numbers and managing money.

MOLE 60

A mole on the back of your knee reveals that you will have excellent interpersonal skills and enjoy good relationships with most people.

MOLE 61

This mole indicates that you have plenty of friends who will always be there for you. This is a very auspicious mole indeed.

MOLE 62

You need to work hard but you have good relationships with people.

PART THREE

RITUAL ORACLE DIVINATION

CHAPTER EIGHT

CONSULTING THE ORACLES

For the everyday problems and questions posed by life in the modern world, try asking an ancient source of wisdom for advice and guidance. You may find answers in the *I Ching* (*Book of Changes*) or by consulting the Yellow Emperor, Wen Shu, or even your tea cup.

HOW TO CONSULT THE *I CHING*

THE *I CHING* (*BOOK OF CHANGES*) IS A COLLECTION OF PRACTICAL WISDOM PERTAINING TO THE HUMAN CONDITION. AT LEAST 5,000 YEARS OLD, IT IS A METHOD OF DIVINATION THAT GUIDES US TO THE SOLUTION OF OUR EVERYDAY PROBLEMS. UNLIKE PERSONAL FORECASTING METHODS BASED ON CHARTS OR READING FACES, IT OFFERS AN IMMEDIATE RESPONSE TO A SPECIFIC QUESTION.

The key to *I Ching* oracle consultation is in the creation of the predictive hexagram (six lines that may be broken or unbroken). The hexagram offers answers to specific questions. There are 64 hexagrams altogether and these offer a great deal of information that is related to the texts of the *I Ching*. There are two sets of three lines in each hexagram. A set of three lines is called a trigram, and there are eight possible trigrams, each with its own Chinese name (see chart, page 195).

There are several accepted ways of creating the lines that make up the trigrams and predictive hexagrams: we focus on the use of three coins, as this is simple.

Serious practitioners of the coin method use ancient Chinese coins. According to them, antique coins—especially those taken from temples—are deemed to offer more reliable answers. Chinese coins from the nine prosperous dynasties are regarded as very auspicious. These are round with a square hole in the center. The round shape symbolizes heaven (signified by the trigram Chien), while the square hole stands for earth (signified by the trigram Kun). The yang or positive side usually has four characters written in Chinese, which carry the meaning "your luck has arrived."

The yin or negative side has two characters, and these characters added to the four characters of the yang side make a sum of six characters, which symbolically reflects the six lines of the hexagrams.

Using three coins also symbolizes the trinity of heaven, earth, and mankind, as well as the lines of the trigrams. If old coins are not available it is perfectly acceptable to use normal everyday modern coins. Heads stand for yang positive, while tails stand for yin negative.

THE COINS RITUAL

Before tossing the three coins, you should calm your mind and focus inward. If you have an altar at home, you could precede consultations with prayer. Look on the *I Ching* as a communication channel to a higher being. Think through the various aspects of the dilemma for which advice and guidance are being sought.

Take out your coins and lay them on a red velvet or silk cloth. When you are ready, put them in a metal container and shake them vigorously, while concentrating on the question and asking for a clear, easy-to-understand answer. Then toss the coins onto the cloth. (It is acceptable to shake the coins in your hand but this is not considered to be as efficient.)

You will have to toss the three coins six times in order to construct the six lines of the hexagram. After each throw, analyze how the coins fall—each throw represents one line of the hexagram.

CONSTRUCTING THE HEXAGRAM

In the coin method the hexagram is constructed from the bottom up. The first line is the bottom line, and each line is determined by the way the coins fall after each throw, up to the top line, which is the sixth (see Sample Hexagrams, overleaf).

Each time the coins are thrown there are four possible combinations, which each result in a broken or unbroken line. The lines may be unbroken (yang) or broken (yin) and changing or unchanging. A changing line is one that changes from yin to yang or vice versa. As you will see, when a line changes it results in another hexagram. This new hexagram should be studied in conjunction with the first hexagram for a full consultation.

TIPS ON USING THE I CHING

Be relaxed. Be focused, serious, and calm. If you are agitated the mood is sure to spill over into the reading. So compose yourself before directing your concentration to the question you ask.

- Be specific. Ask a clear, unambiguous question. Be clear in your mind what you really want to know. Never consult the oracle frivolously. Instead, formulate your inquiry carefully. Meditate on the matter for a while before proceeding with any consultation. This allows your mind to reflect on the question seriously, in the process igniting deeper wisdoms from inside you to surface.

- Write your question down. If you put your question in a notebook this gives the mind a visual imprint of the question. Putting pen to paper also forces you to gather your thoughts in an organized way.

THE FOUR POSSIBLE COMBINATIONS OF THROWING COINS ARE AS FOLLOWS:

1 Young Yang: one yang and two yin (or one head and two tails)

· Represents an unchanging solid yang line (unbroken)

2 Young Yin: one yin and two yang (or one tail and two heads)

· Represents an unchanging broken yin line (broken)

3 Old Yang: three yang (or three heads)

· Represents a changing solid yang line (unbroken)

4 Old Yin: three yin (or three tails)

· Represents a changing yin line (broken).

Construct your hexagram according to the lines described above. Remember to start at the bottom. Here is what a typical hexagram resulting from tossing the coins might look like:

SAMPLE HEXAGRAMS

		FIRST HEXAGRAM	NEW HEXAGRAM
Unchanging line	6		
Unchanging line	5		
Changing line X →	4		
Changing line X →	3		
Unchanging line	2		
Unchanging line	1		

The first hexagram focuses more on the current dilemma in the situation; the second hexagram usually describes the predicted outcome of the situation. The changing lines themselves can sometimes offer clues to the likely outcomes of the situation about which you are consulting the *I Ching*. For instance, if the third line is a changing line, read the prediction represented by the third line. If there is more than one changing line, read all the predictions indicated by the changing lines and try to formulate a pattern to the answer being given. Mark all changing lines with a cross or an asterisk as you go for your own reference.

When you have successfully generated the hexagram(s) in answer to your question, use the chart shown opposite to find the number of your hexagram. Then look up the hexagram in the following pages and find the answers to your question. Remember, the bottom three lines of your hexagram are the lower trigram and the top three are the upper trigram.

INTERPRETING ANSWERS

The *I Ching* can be used as a life-planning tool. It can tell you when it is not a good time to start new ventures, get married, or make fresh commitments. It is a good idea to check with the *I Ching* before taking significant action that has long-term consequences. You can also ask the *I Ching* whether your reading of your paht chee chart is accurate or not. This is a straightforward question that usually prompts an accurate answer.

I Ching interpretation is straightforward. Most of the time it advises on timing, but it can also point the way to other possibilities, and the things to consider when making choices—you can use a series of questions to get your answer, and start a conversation with the *I Ching*.

TABLE OF HEXAGRAMS

LOWER TRIGRAM \ UPPER TRIGRAM	CHIEN	CHEN	KAN	KEN	KUN	SUN	LI	TUI
CHIEN	1	34	5	26	11	9	14	43
CHEN	25	51	3	27	24	42	21	17
KAN	6	40	29	4	7	59	64	47
KEN	33	62	39	52	15	53	56	31
KUN	12	16	8	23	2	20	35	45
SUN	44	32	48	18	46	57	50	28
LI	13	55	63	22	36	37	30	49
TUI	10	54	60	41	19	61	38	58

Hexagrams are made up of two trigrams (a group of three lines), divided into the top three lines (upper trigram) and bottom three lines (lower trigram). To find the number of your hexagram, first match the upper trigram on the table with that of your hexagram and then combine with the lower trigram. The resulting number on the table is the number of the hexagram you should consult.

THE 64 HEXAGRAM PREDICTIONS

1 CHIEN: CREATIVE
THE POWER OF HEAVEN IS AWESOME AND ACCURATE

6 Good fortune is definitely coming your way.

5 Every disagreement can be harmoniously resolved.

4 You will find a remedy to your problem.

3 Operations at work produce good results and proceed smoothly.

2 There is happiness and success ahead.

1 You are right to be optimistic in your expectations.

2 KUN: RECEPTIVE
HUNGER GETS APPEASED AND THE BELLY IS FULL

6 A happy time when mothers give a helping hand.

5 You receive the promotion you want.

4 Bad news turns out to be frivolous—no cause for alarm.

3 Troubles and problems get solved with little difficulty.

2 You get an appointment with an important person.

1 Favors women—there is good news coming.

3 CHUN: INITIAL HARDSHIP
THE IMAGE OF AN ILL WIND THAT BLOWS NO GOOD

6 There is chaos from the start—be wary!

5 Entanglements cause you to have a frustrating time.

4 Sickness does not find immediate relief.

3 Disputes get worse before they get better—jealousy.

2 There is a danger of gossip getting out of hand.

1 Fair-weather friends disappoint you. No need to react.

4 MENG: IMMATURITY
THE IMAGE OF YOUTHFUL FOOLISHNESS

6 It seems you are wasting your time and effort.

5 Your social life is riddled with idle gossip.

4 You have to confront serious setbacks.

3 There is a need for great caution.

2 Be prepared for a shortage of money.

1 You have to endure a loss of wealth.

5 HSU: WAITING
THE IMAGE OF A DRAGON WITH ITS PEARL BRINGS SUCCESS

6 A brilliant realization makes you happy—good news.

5 The merger you seek will take place. Be happy.

4 Your new business venture brings good profits.

3 Relationship happiness is coming your way.

2 The project you are working on will succeed.

1 If you persevere and work hard there are sure to be benefits.

6 SUNG: CONFLICT
THE IMAGE SUGGESTS CONFLICT AND HOSTILE VIBRATIONS

6 Indications suggest a waste of your time and money.

5 Your spouse causes you distress.

4 Business partners create misfortunes.

3 New commitments do not bring satisfaction.

2 You experience a cash flow problem.

1 Obstacles block everything you do.

7 SHIH: COMPETITION
DRIED LEAVES WITHER IN THE PERIOD OF DROUGHT

6 Help comes after a bad time; everything gets easier.

5 A period of frustration ends. Good news is coming to you.

4 Worries and problems get transformed into happiness.

3 There is a good harvest for all your efforts.

2 Plans find a favorable response.

1 At work things begin to look up for you.

8 PI: UNION
THE DRAGON BOAT IS LOADED WITH GOLD INGOTS

6 An auspicious wind blows good fortune into your home.

5 There is plenty of goodwill and rejoicing.

4 Legal problems get resolved.

3 Money owed to you is recovered.

2 Marriage plans proceed smoothly.

1 A double happiness (hei see) occasion takes place: birthdays, a new baby, a marriage.

9 HSIAO CHU: TAMING THE SMALL
TAMING THE SMALL SUGGESTS A NEED FOR PATIENCE

6 Better to watch, wait, and consolidate.

5 Going to see the great man brings no benefits.

4 Crossing the great waters does you no good.

3 Relationships are in a state of suspension.

2 Business travels do not yield good results.

1 This is a bad time to expand.

10 LU: INACTIVITY
BIRDS DROOP THEIR HEADS IN THE SHADE

6 There will be a period of inactivity.

5 This is a time to prolong negotiation if you want benefits.

4 Travel is advisable; there will be new avenues to investigate.

3 A good time to focus on your studies.

2 If you are well prepared the sky is the limit.

1 When you have mastered the skills, money will be plentiful.

11 TAI: PEACE
GREAT GOOD NEWS COMES THREE TIMES TO YOU

6 There is continuous good fortune.

5 Peace and harmony prevail in your environment.

4 Business and travel luck favors you.

3 Troubles and disputes find a quick solution.

2 Associates are agreeable to your plans.

1 There are good indications of a forthcoming marriage.

12 PI: STAGNATION
THE DRAGON IS CAPTURED — PROGRESS COMES TO AN INSTANT HALT

6 Ideas and actions are useless in the face of bad luck.

5 Success is hard to come by; it is better to wait.

4 Your love life is stagnating—best to go with the flow.

3 When things come to a standstill, look within for solutions.

2 Delays cause you to lose money, but what is to be done?

1 Sickness will cause you to have a setback.

13 T'UNG JEN: COOPERATION
WHEN THE FAMILY HAS HARMONY HEAVEN SMILES ON YOU

6 Wherever you wish to move to you will have good fortune.

5 Partnerships expand as good fortune brings happiness.

4 Marriages are favored—promise of long-lasting happiness.

3 Love relationships will have a happy ending.

2 Any new commitments will be a mistake.

1 Old friends support you while new friends stay indifferent.

14 TA YU: GREAT POSSESSIONS
YOU HAVE POSSESSIONS IN GREAT MEASURE. BE HAPPY

6 People's sentiments are negative. Do not act.

5 Your success will not create problems.

4 What you have lost is sure to be returned to you.

3 You will soon meet someone who can be your partner.

2 Your quest for recognition meets with success.

1 Those applying for a job will be successful.

15 CH'IEN: MODESTY
GOOD FORTUNE FALLS FROM THE SKY

6 Work hard—you could discover gold.

5 There is unexpected success.

4 Your new project finds instant success. Be encouraged.

3 Marriage plans move forward easily and without obstruction.

2 Business moves aggressively forward.

1 Influential help comes from important people.

16 YU: HAPPINESS
THE DRAGON IS RELEASED—HE FLIES HIGH INTO THE SKIES

6 Happiness comes from continuous good fortune.

5 Business meets with huge success.

4 Love relationships can lead to marriage.

3 Gossip and slander evaporate into the air.

2 Mentors and influential benefactors bring new business.

1 Marriage misunderstandings are resolved.

THE 64 HEXAGRAM PREDICTIONS

17 SUI: CHANGE
THE ROAD AHEAD SEEMS PAVED WITH GOLD

6 Plans proceed with few difficulties.

5 Sickness and gossip dissolve, bringing good times.

4 This time favors your ambitions.

3 New commitment brings unexpected happiness.

2 There is the possibility of a new family member.

1 What is lost can be found.

18 KU: IMPROVING
CONSIDER CAREFULLY WHETHER YOU WANT TO IMPROVE YOUR SITUATION

6 Acting honorably and with integrity will help you reap rewards.

5 Misfortune comes when you act dishonestly.

4 Traveling for business is a waste of time.

3 No need for tension—what will be will be.

2 What you have lost cannot be recovered—accept this.

1 Slow and steady progress is better than being in a hurry.

19 LIN: APPROACH
COMPASSION ATTRACTS A SPECIAL KIND OF GOOD FORTUNE

6 Commitments are easy to fulfill—no need to worry.

5 Do not make promises too easily. Think first.

4 Getting married will bring you good fortune.

3 The new job sounds very promising indeed—take it.

2 Problems with the boss were only in your mind.

1 You will gain an unexpected promotion.

20 KUAN: OBSERVING
CRANES AND MAGPIES MAKE UNLIKELY PALS

6 There is no harmony within the household.

5 The living situation is cold and unfriendly. Move out.

4 Ducks and hens together at work—no communication.

3 It is advisable to observe without comment.

2 Plans for new ventures find no takers.

1 In the midst of unhappiness comes one bright spark.

21 SHIN HO: WRATHFUL
A STARVING BEGGAR RECEIVES HIS FIRST MEAL IN DAYS

6 Hard times come to a welcome end.

5 You find pleasure in superficial wining and dining.

4 There is a joyous double happiness celebration.

3 In legal tussles you emerge victorious.

2 Good fortune favors you. Proceed with confidence.

1 Lonely singles find meaningful romance.

22 PI: APPEARANCES
LOVE BLOOMS—THE BLUSHING YOUNG WOMAN FINDS HER YOUNG BEAU

6 Thoughts of marriage bring you a most suitable match.

5 This hexagram symbolizes a truly happy wedding party.

4 Happiness comes after months of misunderstandings.

3 Traveling benefits your luck and your career.

2 Whatever you may have lost is now found again.

1 Your life moves smoothly along a prosperous road.

23 PO: DECAY
FLOWERS BLOOM ONLY WHEN DRY LAND GETS RAINFALL

6 An important introduction brings cause for celebration.

5 Journeys prove interesting and exciting.

4 Your job applications are all successful.

3 Legal entanglements will get resolved.

2 Sicknesses find good cures.

1 Misunderstandings get cleared up.

24 FU: REVIVAL
THIS HEXAGRAM SUGGESTS BAD NEWS

6 Harmony evaporates and people get hostile.

5 Even your friend becomes your enemy.

4 This is a bad time to see the great man.

3 You need patience to endure this time of confusion.

2 When things are uncertain it is best to retreat.

1 There is no useful information coming to you.

25 WU WANG
THE IMAGE OF BIRDS IN CAPTIVITY SUGGESTS A TRAP

6 Do not get embroiled in a difficult situation.

5 It is a mistake to be too trusting; you can be betrayed.

4 There is gossip and complication ahead if you proceed.

3 The future for your project looks difficult. Try to withdraw.

2 You have missed the boat—wait for a more propitious time.

1 Your lover is betraying you. Be careful.

26 TA CHU: TAMING THE GREAT
THE TAMING OF THE GREAT CLARIFIES EVERYTHING

6 Business travel yields good results.

5 Good news comes through the mail.

4 New friendships bring opportunities.

3 Clarity emerges where there was confusion.

2 The man proposes and the woman accepts.

1 Unhappiness transforms into happiness.

27 I: NOURISHMENT
THE IMAGE OF NOURISHMENT IS MOST AUSPICIOUS

6 Even the king stops by your home—great honor.

5 All your plans find favor with the authorities.

4 Sickness and problems find cures and solutions.

3 There is an excellent person helping you, a mentor.

2 This period brings the promise of a rise in rank.

1 Hostilities evaporate and misunderstandings are cleared up.

28 TA KUO: EXCESS
AS LONG AS YOU CAN SEE THE PEAK, KEEP WALKING

6 Living in a dream world is harmful. Be realistic.

5 You encounter difficulties at work and in business.

4 You need patience to develop yourself.

3 This is not the time to be arrogant or ambitious.

2 This is a very frustrating time. Try to be philosophical.

1 In life there are highs and lows. This is the low period.

29 KAN: WATER
THE IMAGE OF THE ABYSMAL IS LIKE SEEING A MIRAGE

6 Reflections of glory have little substance.

5 Hard for you to differentiate between real and fake gold.

4 There is no recognition luck, alas!

3 Hopes for a marriage proposal do not materialize.

2 Business partnerships have no foundation.

1 Your sickness finds no cure.

30 LI: FIRE
THE SUN'S LIGHT BRIGHTENS EVEN THE DULLEST MOODS

6 There is continuous good fortune from heaven.

5 All sadness, problems, and sickness evaporate quickly.

4 Everything succeeds because the time favors you.

3 A good time to be bold.

2 There is every reason to be confident.

1 If you get this, be encouraged—success awaits you.

31 HSIEN: ATTRACT
A BEAUTIFUL WOMAN CANNOT BE WON IN AN INSTANT

6 If you take your time you will succeed.

5 The scenario is unexciting but gold lies hidden within.

4 The superior man bides his time and has good fortune.

3 Taking your medicine faithfully brings recovery.

2 An old love comes back into your life—it is auspicious.

1 Dig deeper and you will discover new opportunities.

32 HENG: PERSEVERANCE
A GOOD HARVEST COMES AT A MOST AUSPICIOUS TIME

6 Business luck is encouraging you to be an entrepreneur.

5 Marriage proposal meets with favorable response.

4 Travel luck is good—the longer the journey, the better.

3 A period of ill health is now over. You will become stronger.

2 Friends surround and support you; it is a happy time.

1 There is total release from legal entanglements.

THE 64 HEXAGRAM PREDICTIONS

33 TUN: RETREAT
THE IMAGE OF THE SUN BEING COVERED BY DARK CLOUDS

6 Better to stay at home. Do not travel.

5 Inviting people to your home brings good fortune.

4 Take a conciliatory approach and compromise.

3 Arrogance and anger lead to misfortune.

2 Publicity attracts bad luck; stay low-key.

1 New endeavors meet with obstacles. Postpone plans.

34 TA CHUANG: GREAT POWER
THE POWER OF THE GREAT BRINGS ABUNDANCE

6 This is a fortunate time when everything is blessed with success.

5 You can proceed with confidence and an optimistic outlook.

4 Travel brings many desirable benefits.

3 Disputes will be favorably settled.

2 Meetings with important people proceed without obstruction.

1 The sickness that worries you finds a cure.

35 CHIN: PROGRESS
THERE IS GOLD IN YOUR GARDEN IF ONLY YOU KNEW IT

6 You do not expect it, but wealth will come to you suddenly.

5 Clouds that hide the bright and glorious sun soon blow over.

4 Wait for a positive sign before acting; it will appear soon.

3 Action should happen only when the time is auspicious.

2 Clean your house and you may find forgotten treasure.

1 Family attics can hold hidden wish-fulfilling gems.

36 MING I: DARKENED LIGHT
A DARKENING OF THE LIGHT CLOSES OUT THE SUN

6 Misfortune strikes with ungraceful haste.

5 You should stay inactive but alert.

4 Friends turn against you and supporters desert you.

3 These are troubled times when you should take care.

2 There is no good news on the horizon. Be cautious.

1 It is hard to build bridges at this time. Try at a better time.

37 CHIA JEN: FAMILY
YOUR REFLECTION LOOKS BEAUTIFUL, BUT IT IS ONLY A REFLECTION

6 You are going through a slow period, but things will pick up.

5 Worrying about your situation cannot help.

4 Business partnerships are headed for a breakdown.

3 Irreconcilable marriage differences lead to heartbreak.

2 What has been taken from you will be returned to you.

1 Fame, recognition, and success are hard to come by.

38 KUEI: OPPOSITION
YOU HAVE INCURRED THE DISPLEASURE OF SOMEONE POWERFUL

6 Only time can lessen the venom being directed at you.

5 This is a time when you are walking on thin ice.

4 You can avoid disaster only if you act and react carefully.

3 Be cautious when you travel; there are hidden dangers.

2 If at school or college you can expect a disappointment.

1 Do not walk in haste—take it one step at a time.

39 CHIEN: DANGER
DANGER AND OBSTRUCTIONS ARE PREDICTED

6 The more you move ahead, the more problems you encounter.

5 This is a time to cut your losses and retreat.

4 You need to have patience. Being tough is vital.

3 Marriage goes through a rough patch.

2 Relationships simply cannot succeed.

1 Traveling brings empty returns and there could be danger.

40 HSIEH: GOOD FORTUNE
THE IMAGE SUGGESTS BIRDS FLY OUT OF THEIR CAGES

6 There is a release from serious entanglements.

5 Money problems become less taxing.

4 Help arrives from new friends.

3 Sickness will see a marked improvement.

2 Your social life takes off—suddenly you are very popular.

1 Your project finds backers. New challenges lie ahead.

41 SUN: LOSS
THE CART HAS LOST ITS WHEEL. HOW CAN IT MOVE?

6 Misfortune comes in the form of strong opposition.

5 Arrogance is what has brought you misfortune.

4 When you know humility, you attract good fortune.

3 Help comes to those who are not too proud to ask.

2 At this stage of your life you can be too ignorant for words.

1 Experience will be your best teacher.

42 I: INCREASE
THE WINTER PLUM BLOSSOM BURSTS INTO BLOOM

6 You experience a sudden spurt of good energy.

5 Misfortunes transform into good fortune.

4 Legal problems get harmoniously sorted out.

3 Travel brings benefits personally and professionally.

2 What has been missing is now found. Plans can be revived.

1 After a period of trying times, good fortune arrives.

43 KUAI: DETERMINATION
DETERMINATION GIVES YOU A COMPETITIVE EDGE

6 A new baby brings happiness to your household.

5 Prosperity luck manifests for you. Be alert.

4 A legal complication will be amicably settled.

3 Sickness is completely cured—medicines will work.

2 Business problems get resolved to your satisfaction.

1 You will have success in your examinations.

44 KOU: ENCOUNTER
LONG-LOST FRIENDS MEET UNEXPECTEDLY AND FIND GOLD TOGETHER

6 Everything moves along smoothly for you—no obstacles.

5 It benefits you to cross the great waters.

4 Travel brings huge and unexpected benefits.

3 The wealth luck coming to you will last for a long time.

2 You have the karma to attain high rank and great honor.

1 Your family enjoys the fruits of your advancement.

45 TS'UI: GATHERING
CROSSING THE DRAGON GATE BRINGS A PROMOTION

6 The fish is transformed into a dragon—upward mobility.

5 Despite setbacks and difficulties you achieve your goal.

4 Many months of hard work bring recognition.

3 Honors and prosperity come easily to you.

2 Your enemies lose their teeth.

1 New opportunities open new ways to wealth.

46 SHENG: GROWING
GOOD FORTUNE COMES LIKE THE FIRST BLOOMS OF SPRING

6 There is excellent expansion and growth luck.

5 Communication from around the globe brings good news.

4 The sun shines brightly and benevolently on all your plans.

3 Projects move ahead with no major obstructions.

2 You can attain the level of recognition you want.

1 Your family benefits from your extreme good fortune.

47 KUN: OBSTRUCTIONS
THE IMAGE SUGGESTS FRIENDS LET YOU DOWN VERY BADLY

6 Plans and projects cannot take off.

5 Beware of fair-weather friends; they cause you distress.

4 Take care who you trust to avoid misfortunes.

3 Seek out the company of true friends.

2 Do not desert old friends for new friends.

1 Your job application cannot succeed.

48 CHING: THE WELL
AN OLD WELL SUDDENLY FILLS WITH SPRING WATER

6 After a period of tough times, you encounter good fortune.

5 You enjoy increasing popularity and praise.

4 Misfortunes have left you. All your plans succeed.

3 Money comes to you from many different sources.

2 Abroad or at home, you enjoy good fortune.

1 Marriage luck is at an all-time high—take advantage of it.

THE 64 HEXAGRAM PREDICTIONS

49 KO: UPHEAVAL
TIME FOR A MAJOR UPHEAVAL IN YOUR LIFE

6 With rain falling, there is water to make your garden grow.

5 All your best laid plans move along with great energy.

4 There will be an excellent harvest this time.

3 "Caution" is a good word to guard against arrogance.

2 Traveling brings new opportunities, especially to relocate.

1 An old friend deserves your serious attention.

50 TING: THE CAULDRON
THE CAULDRON CREATES A FRESH NEW BREW: GOOD FORTUNE

6 You will receive word of money coming to you.

5 There is prosperity for all members of your family.

4 Travel is most beneficial at this time.

3 You will find a marriage partner very soon.

2 Legal threats evaporate and everything is settled favorably.

1 Sickness gets cured—the medicines work efficiently.

51 CHEN: THUNDER
THE IMAGE OF THUNDER BRINGS GOOD NEWS

6 Your good name spreads like the peal of the golden bell.

5 You gain recognition in all ten directions.

4 You enjoy excellent money and wealth luck.

3 You will gain a very good business partner.

2 Influential friends help and protect you.

1 You will receive a high appointment.

52 KEN: STILLNESS
THE IMAGE OF THE MOUNTAIN SUGGESTS TIME TO PREPARE

6 Ignore frivolous gossip and form your own opinion.

5 Inaction is the best course to follow at this time.

4 Business plans have a hard time taking off.

3 You need to go back to the drawing board.

2 Think through your expectations before you act.

1 It is a good idea to be cautious. Not a good time to travel.

53 CHIEN: SLOW INCREASE
THE RED BIRD FLIES TO THE WESTERN HILLS

6 Unexpected opportunity comes from an unlikely source.

5 There is prosperity and recognition coming for you.

4 Traveling to another country is beneficial.

3 The medicine and cures work well. You will soon feel better.

2 Misunderstanding evaporates and in its place is goodwill.

1 You find favor with financiers. Proceed with confidence.

54 KUEI MEI: RESOLVING
THE MARRYING WOMAN BRINGS MISFORTUNES

6 Attempting the impossible can lead only to disaster.

5 Despite great efforts there is little attainment.

4 Your time has not yet come, so there are no benefits.

3 This is not the time to do anything—no blame.

2 Contemplating marriage at this time is a mistake.

1 The suitor is insincere. Better to wait, to be patient.

55 FENG: BRILLIANCE
THE REPOLISHED MIRROR SHINES LIKE THE FULL MOON

6 Love and romance enjoy favorable outcomes.

5 Suddenly you see everything clearly.

4 Bad luck gives way to an auspicious period of abundance.

3 You will benefit from travel and long-distance communication.

2 All business deals will bring extra benefits.

1 Marriage problems are resolved harmoniously.

56 LU: TRAVELER
THE IMAGE OF FALLING TREES AND BURNING FORESTS

6 Nothing benefits if you get this hexagram.

5 No one sees merit in your plan. Drop the project.

4 Travel brings no material rewards.

3 A good time to retreat and meditate.

2 Accept defeat with honor and good grace.

1 The superior man bows low. Take a break!

57 SUN: WIND

THE WIND MOVES THE BOAT ALONG—THERE IS SMOOTH SAILING

6 Wind and water bring you extreme good fortune.

5 Marriage plans proceed without a hitch.

4 Business arrangements with partners go smoothly.

3 All your financial expectations are exceeded.

2 Sales improvements lift you to a higher league.

1 You will gain popularity and a great reputation.

58 TUI: CELEBRATION

LIKE GOING TO THE REALMS OF THE GODS

6 A happy prediction foretells great success.

5 There are many excellent opportunities coming.

4 You can attain your heart's desire with little effort.

3 No gossip or slander can hurt you.

2 Plans and projects find willing takers. Be bold.

1 Whatever is in your mind you will achieve.

59 HUAN: SEPARATION

THE IMAGE OF SEPARATION BRINGS FRUSTRATION

6 Your marriage plans meet with obstacles.

5 There is no marriage proposal possible.

4 There is a great divide between you and success.

3 Joint ventures simply do not succeed.

2 There are many obstacles facing you.

1 This is not a good time to start new ventures.

60 CHIEH: LIMITATION

GETTING THE HELP OF THE GREAT MAN, YOUR PROBLEMS EVAPORATE

6 Troubles disappear when the great man arrives.

5 There will be no more legal entanglements.

4 Great success and fame can be achieved—but be humble.

3 When you have good fortune the sky is the limit.

2 Your career takes off when you catch the eye of the big boss.

1 There is useful information coming to you. Use it carefully.

61 CHUNG FU: SINCERITY

MORE A TIME FOR DEEP CONTEMPLATION THAN ACTION

6 This is a time when inner truths will surface.

5 Money luck is elusive—better wait.

4 Sickness can be cured, but it takes a long time.

3 If your business goes through a tough time, hang in there.

2 Work situations are tense—stay calm.

1 At home inner tension causes feelings of insecurity.

62 HSIAO KUO: SMALL ERROR

IF YOU MOVE OR ACT WITH FIRMNESS THERE IS SUCCESS

6 Indecisiveness will cause you to attract misfortune.

5 You do not need to be perfect to succeed.

4 Putting off a good idea is foolish. Be brave.

3 In life there are times to be bold—this is such a time.

2 Remember: faint heart never won fair lady.

1 Speak up now and your relationships will make good progress.

63 CHI CHI: COMPLETION

YOUR NAME IS PLACED UP HIGH ON THE GOLDEN PLAQUE

6 If you retire now you will go in a blaze of glory.

5 You are blessed with many grateful friends and supporters.

4 Your descendants will benefit from your good name.

3 Whatever you may have lost in the past is now recovered.

2 An old adversary greets you with genuine respect.

1 A prosperous and meaningful period lies ahead.

64 WEI CHI: STRATEGY

THE STORY IS ONE OF SADNESS

6 Misfortunes bring a time of tears and sorrow.

5 Business travels cause distress. It is better to postpone.

4 Avoid disputes for they bring troubles.

3 Do not engage in battle because you will lose.

2 Marriage plans do not succeed. It is better to wait.

1 Be patient: misfortunes transform into good fortune.

THE YELLOW EMPEROR ORACLE

THE TUNG SHU (CHINESE ALMANAC) BOASTS A POEM ABOUT THE FOUR SEASONS THAT IS ATTRIBUTED TO THE LEGENDARY YELLOW EMPEROR, HUANGDI. THE POEM OFFERS EVERYONE A PERSONAL DESTINY READING BASED ON THE IDEA THAT SYMBOLICALLY WE ARE ALL BORN ON A PART OF THE EMPEROR'S BODY. CONSULT THE ORACLE AND DISCOVER YOUR FORTUNE.

The Yellow Emperor is considered to be the founder of Chinese civilization and is traditionally said to have reigned from 2698 BCE to 2599 BCE. Some say he devised the principles of Traditional Chinese Medicine—which helped him to live to the grand age of 111—and that he invented the earliest form of the Chinese calendar. His wife Luo Zu was said to have instructed the people in making silk from silkworms and his historian was believed to have devised Chinese character writing. The Emperor himself was responsible for conquering a wide area along the Yellow River. His tribe honored the virtue of the earth and he was therefore given the title Yellow Emperor after the color of earth, the symbol of farming. The Yellow Emperor was thus greatly revered for his many accomplishments, and his patronage and goodwill widely sought.

The Yellow Emperor's poem, which appears in the Tong Shu, reveals general indications about what life holds in store for each newborn baby. Depending on the season of birth and the part of the Emperor's body on which the baby is born,

the baby's life may be destined to be full of burdens or to be very auspicious. It is possible to consult the Yellow Emperor Oracle to discover your own predicted

BIRTH TIMES: HOUR

TIME OF BIRTH	HOUR PILLAR NAME
11 P.M.—1 A.M.	Zi
1 A.M.—3 A.M.	CHOU
3 A.M.—5 A.M.	YIN
5 A.M.—7 A.M.	MAO
7 A.M.—9 A.M.	CHEN
9 A.M.—11 A.M.	SI
11 A.M.—1 P.M.	WU
1 P.M.—3 P.M.	WEI
3 P.M.—5 P.M.	SHEN
5 P.M.—7 P.M.	YOU
7 P.M.—9 P.M.	XU
9 P.M.—11 P.M.	HAI

destiny and at what stage of your life you might enjoy the Emperor's patronage and goodwill. To discover your destiny, follow the simple steps outlined below:

1. Determine which season you were born in:

· Spring (March, April, May)

· Summer (June, July, August)

· Fall (September, October, November)

· Winter (December, January, February).

2. Consider your time of birth in relation to the chart. The twelve earthly branches (Chinese astrological animals) method divides the 24-hour day into twelve time segments of two hours. Each segment has an hour pillar name in Chinese that is the name of the corresponding Chinese astrological animal. Establish which time segment applies to your time of birth (see table, left) and determine your hour pillar name.

3. Turn to the appropriate seasonal illustration of the Yellow Emperor in the following pages. The Emperor wears differently colored robes for each of the seasons—he wears green in spring, red in summer, white in fall, and blue in winter.

4. Your hour pillar name will show you on which part of the Yellow Emperor's body you were born. First locate the hour name on his body and then read your destiny prediction.

THE YELLOW EMPEROR
Huangdi is by legend a powerful force in the creation of Chinese culture and is attributed with devising handwriting, silk making, and Traditional Chinese Medicine.

PREDICTIONS FOR THOSE BORN IN SPRING

If you were born in the spring, refer to the descriptions below to find your destiny.

YOU AND MAO: BORN ON THE EMPEROR'S SHOULDERS

You will never be short of clothes on your back, which means you will always be able to make a good living. There will be no shortage of the basic necessities of life, including owning a home.

SI AND WEI : BORN ON THE EMPEROR'S HANDS

Your attainments will be average and it is more beneficial for you if you work on projects as the second-in-command and not as the leader. You can rise up high being the right-hand person of someone powerful and wealthy.

CHEN AND XU: BORN ON THE EMPEROR'S KNEE

You will have to travel a great deal in your life—you can view this as good or bad depending on whether you enjoy traveling or not. Professionally, your life will be full of journeys. And, like the wanderer's life, your life will be unsettled and transient.

ZI: BORN ON THE EMPEROR'S HEAD

You will hold a high position in life. You have power and great intellectual capability. You are also blessed with wisdom. You have authority, power, and responsibility. You will be well brought up and blessed with a good education.

WU : BORN ON THE EMPEROR'S STOMACH

Your serious good fortune begins only in middle age when you will enjoy great good fortune in terms of the luxuries of life. There is plenty of food, clothing, and all of life's material pleasures.

CHOU AND HAI: BORN ON THE EMPEROR'S GIRTH

You will go through many changes in your life and, as you get higher up the social ladder, you will change a great deal. This transformation may be for good or bad and it is advisable that if you are in this situation, you should strive to change for the better and become more humble as you become more important in your work and life.

SHEN AND YIN: BORN ON THE EMPEROR'S FEET

This indicates that there will be two marriages in your life. This is especially true for women born into this position. For men, being born on the Emperor's feet suggests a restless nature that is not easy to please.

PREDICTIONS FOR THOSE BORN IN SUMMER

If you were born in the summer, refer to the descriptions below to find your destiny.

MAO AND YOU: BORN ON THE EMPEROR'S SHOULDERS

You are very lucky if you have this birth situation, since it brings you a lifetime of wealth and prosperity, lacking nothing. You will amass a fortune during your lifetime, and in your old age you will own plenty of properties. If you live an honorable life, you will be blessed with plenty of grandchildren and live to an old age.

SI AND CHOU: BORN ON THE EMPEROR'S HANDS

This birth situation suggests that you will have more than your share of money and business luck. Your good fortune improves with the years and you will attain great success during the later stages of your life.

CHEN AND XU: BORN ON THE EMPEROR'S KNEES

It will be hard for you to receive the recognition you deserve for the work you do. Obstacles may stand in your way and, unless you can overcome this lack of recognition luck by middle age, you will be exhausted.

WU: BORN ON THE EMPEROR'S HEAD

This is an auspicious indication, since if you were born on the Emperor's head in the summer you will never have any worries. There are no obstacles or difficulties in your entire life. This also suggests that you will have an excellent intellect and will be good at strategic thinking and planning.

ZI: BORN ON THE EMPEROR'S STOMACH

This birth situation indicates there is plenty to eat and more than enough clothes to wear and enjoy. There is good fortune luck from your late forties onward. You will not have to worry about your old age for you will be well looked after.

WEI AND HAI: BORN ON THE EMPEROR'S GIRTH

This birth situation suggests that you will have loving parents and be surrounded by noblemen and important people. What you make of your good fortune at birth will depend on your own efforts.

SHEN AND YIN: BORN ON THE EMPEROR'S FEET

This birth situation brings an easy life where everything comes easily, especially if you are male. If you are male, it is likely you will have more than one wife. Women will find you irresistible. You will be blessed if you have a good attitude and a pure motivation.

PREDICTIONS FOR THOSE BORN IN FALL

If you were born in the fall, refer to the descriptions below to find your destiny.

HAI: BORN ON THE EMPEROR'S HEAD

This birth situation is especially beneficial if you are female, as it indicates you will have a very comfortable and stable life with plenty of good fortune and prosperity luck. But both genders will benefit from the wonderful good fortune of being born on the Emperor's head in the fall.

ZI AND WU: BORN ON THE EMPEROR'S SHOULDERS

This birth situation suggests that there is prosperity luck and you will become rich in your middle age. You will also have the help of your siblings, especially your brothers. You are blessed with many genuine friends.

SHEN: BORN ON THE EMPEROR'S STOMACH

This birth situation indicates that you will keep company with many clever people. They are people who excel in their career and their studies, and their presence in your life will inspire you to be ambitious. Happiness brings good fortune, so you must develop a happy disposition.

SI AND CHOU: BORN ON THE EMPEROR'S HANDS

This is an extremely auspicious situation of birth, as there is the promise of wealth coming from the four directions. Each time you travel, you will meet with a person of high standing who will help you. You will benefit by going overseas to study or to work.

MAO AND WEI: BORN ON THE EMPEROR'S GIRTH

You will enjoy an abundance of food and clothing during your middle age. Your sons and grandsons will bring you much happiness and contentment, so you have quite outstanding descendants' luck. Those with this birth situation will benefit if they get married at a young age and start a family in their twenties.

YIN AND YOU: BORN ON THE EMPEROR'S KNEES

You will need to work very hard during your early years and there may be some setbacks, but you are blessed with good fortune in later life. Those who have this birth situation should rejoice and should never feel discouraged, as their success when they are older will more than make up for setbacks they may experience in their early years.

XU AND CHEN: BORN ON THE EMPEROR'S FEET

Your whole life will be safe and peaceful and there is nothing to fear in terms of being hurt by others. If you are ambitious and have the determination to succeed, you can reach great heights professionally. Even if you do not reach the top, you will nevertheless be content with what you have. Therein lies the secret of your happiness.

PREDICTIONS FOR THOSE BORN IN WINTER

If you were born in the winter, refer to the descriptions below to find your destiny.

SI: BORN ON THE EMPEROR'S HEAD

If you were born on the emperor's head in winter, you will make a brilliant marriage. Your spouse will be a well respected person who comes from a highly regarded family background. You will have luxury in your life with enough food and clothes.

ZI: BORN ON THE EMPEROR'S STOMACH

You are one person who is sure to enjoy singing, socializing, and glamorous parties. You will be lucky enough to enjoy this lifestyle, as there is both prosperity and longevity in your destiny. However, it is important for you to undertake some charitable work or donate to charity during your middle-aged years. This will bring you even more good fortune.

YOU AND MAO: BORN ON THE EMPEROR'S SHOULDERS

You are blessed with exceptional descendants' luck, so there are many sons and grandsons in your life. You will have some problems and setbacks during your growing-up and early career years, but you will enjoy good luck in later life. A great deal of your luck will be brought to you by your spouse and then by your sons and grandsons.

HAI AND WU: BORN ON THE EMPEROR'S HANDS

You will have a good home environment and there will always be occasions for rejoicing. You will be especially successful in your old age, when you have passed your sixtieth birthday.

YIN AND SHEN: BORN ON THE EMPEROR'S GIRTH

You will be blessed with exceptional good fortune in your old age when there is gold, asset accumulation, and a thriving business in your family. You will be lucky enough to grow old with someone you love.

CHOU AND WEI: BORN ON THE EMPEROR'S KNEES

You will have enough to eat and survive on, but little left over, and during your middle-aged years there will be some truly trying times. It is vital for you to do charity work and to devote some time to caring for others. This will dissolve much of the negative chi that surrounds you.

CHEN AND XU: BORN ON THE EMPEROR'S FEET

You should live away from your parents and grandparents, as it benefits you to have your own home. If you have your own home, you will enjoy good fortune. The further away you are from your ancestral home, the better it will be for you.

THE WEN SHU ORACLE

IN ASIAN TRADITIONS, THERE ARE MANY DIFFERENT METHODS OF SEEKING DIVINATION BUT THE MAHAYANA BUDDHIST ORACLE SYSTEM IS ONE OF THE MOST REVERED AND POPULAR METHODS. THE METHOD WE HAVE INCLUDED HERE IS THE SHORT VERSION OF THE WEN SHU ORACLE SUITABLE TO ASK QUICK QUESTIONS THAT GENERALLY REQUIRE A BRIEF RESPONSE.

Wen Shu Pu Sa is the Chinese name of the Buddha of Wisdom Manjushri, and the Wen Shu Oracle is a spiritual method of seeking divination that is based on the Tibetan MO Oracle that uses the mala beads to help one make decisions when faced with a dilemma.

In Asian traditions there are many different methods of seeking divination, but the Tibetan Oracle system—called the MO—is probably the only one that engages the spiritual wisdom of the Buddhist Mahayana tradition. In Tibet many methods of MO divination are used, some with mala beads, some with sticks, and many with two dice. The most highly respected methods are those used by high lamas and many of these are derived from the spiritual power and wisdom of Manjushri.

The accuracy of the divination is said to come directly from the blessings of Buddha Manjushri and it is his wisdom that manifests itself in the counting of the mala beads. The Chinese have also adopted this method of divination because the Buddhism practiced in China is also

Mahayana Buddhism and the Oracle is known as the Wen Shu Oracle to those familiar with it...

VISUALIZATION

The method starts with a visualization. Visualize the Great Buddha of Wisdom Manjushri, whose body is yellow, with one face and two arms. His right arm holds up high a flaming sword of wisdom, which slices through our ignorance and brings clarity to our minds and firmness in our resolve. His left hand holds close to his heart the stem of the blue lotus flower which blossoms near his ears. On it rests the most precious *Prajnaparamita*, the book of the Perfection of Wisdom.

LOOK FOR A MALA

Next you need to look for a mala with which you feel an affinity. A mala is a Buddhist rosary. Malas are made up of seeds, beads, crystals, and even semi-precious stones such as amber, lapis and so forth. You can obtain a mala from any Buddhist or Dharma store. Select a crystal or stone that you like the best or is

deemed to be excellent for you based on your astrological sign.

• Those born in the years of the Rat and the Pig benefit from moonstones, crystal, amethyst, lapis, and turquoise.

• Those born in the years of the Sheep, the Ox, the Dog, and the Dragon will benefit from coral, crystal, amber, citrine, tourmaline, and any kind of yellow- and red-colored stones.

• Those born under the years of the Monkey and Rooster benefit from crystal, amber, citrine, and any white or yellow stones.

• Those born under the years of Tiger and Rabbit benefit from lapis, turquoise, aquamarine, peridot, or any of the blue and green stones, as well as malas made from the seeds of holy trees (such as Bodhi seeds or Rudraksha seeds) and sandalwood.

• Those born under the years of the Snake and Horse benefit from coral and garnets as well as malas made from the seeds of holy trees (such as Bodhi seeds or Rudraksha seeds) and sandalwood.

MALA BEADS

A mala is a kind of Buddhist rosary. You can use it while chanting mantras and also when asking the Wen Shu Oracle for advice on everyday problems.

There are 108 beads in one mala. Hold your mala with both palms and blow on it after you have chanted the mantras. Recite "OM AH HUM" as you feel the mala beads. Note that chanting the mantras has purified your breath. Now concentrate on your question clearly. Spend a few minutes concentrating on your dilemma or the options that face you. This oracle is especially good to help you make important decisions like whether or not to relocate jobs, to change your place of residence, to react to a proposal or a job offer, and so on. If you need guidance on a problem, using this oracle enables you to receive the wisdom of the Buddhas. Usually the answer given is the one that offers the most beneficial way to move forward with the problem or decision at hand. Remember there are no right or wrong decisions, only good and bad ones from your perspective, and it is this kind of dilemma that this oracle addresses.

CHECKING WITH THE MALA BEADS

If you have been using your mala to chant your mantras, it has great spiritual power. To use your mala as an aid to divination, randomly take any two beads leaving a short strand of beads in between. This

WEN SHU PU SA

Followers of Mahayana Buddhism believe that the accuracy of the MO's divination are derived from the spiritual power and wisdom of Manjushri—the Buddha of wisdom. The Chinese refer to the Buddha of wisdom as Wen Shu Pu Sa.

enables you to hold the mala in front of you. Taking three beads from each side at a time, move slowly toward the center of the mala strand. Recite "OM AH HUM" as you move to the center. Stop when you see remainder beads of five beads or fewer between your fingers.

• With no beads left over between your fingers, the answer is excellent. The MO is telling you that your proposed course of action is beneficial to you and everyone else.

• When there is a single bead left over, the answer indicates that your proposed course of action is good but less beneficial and there could be some hindrances, although these can be overcome.

• When there are two beads left over, your intended course of action may benefit you in the short term, but could turn sour in the longer term.

• When there are three beads left over, your intended course of action is neither good nor bad. The outcome is determined solely by your attitudes and actions.

• When there are four beads left over, the outcome of your question is negative. Nothing beneficial comes from your proposed course of action.

• When there are five beads left over, this is the most negative answer and you are advised not to pursue your course of action. Better to cut your losses.

Invoke blessings from Manjushri before you ask for an answer.

MANTRAS

RECITE AS FOLLOWS:
OM, the magnificent Manjushri who unobstructedly sees all the three times, the past, present, and future with eyes of transcendental wisdom.

Please come here and hear me.

I prostrate to Manjushri and take refuge in the three jewels.

Through the power of truth and dependent arising please make clear the best course of action; on what should be accepted, what discarded, when to move ahead, when to withdraw, and when to stay silent.

OM AH RAPA CHA NA DHI
(Recite this 108 times.)

NEXT RECITE THE LONG MANTRA OF DEPENDENCE ARISING
OM AH HUM OM YEDHARMA HETU PRABHAWA HETUNTE KHEN TATHAGATO HAYA WATETTE KHEN TRAYO NIRODHA EWAM WADI MAHA SHRA MANA SOHA
(Recite three or seven times.)

TEA-LEAF ORACLE

FOR MORE THAN A THOUSAND YEARS, TEA-DRINKING HAS GIVEN GREAT PLEASURE TO THE CHINESE—IT IS THE DRINK MOST LAVISHLY PRAISED, ABOVE WINE. DRINKING TEA IS ASSOCIATED WITH A SPECIAL PREPARATION RITUAL, WHICH ALLOWS THE MIND TO SETTLE. WHEN ONE WISHES TO CONSULT THE TEA-LEAF ORACLE, DRINKING TEA TAKES ON CONNOTATIONS BEYOND ASSUAGING THIRST.

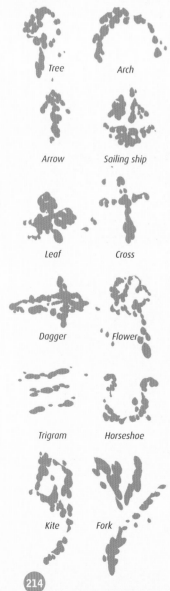

Tree   *Arch*

Arrow   *Sailing ship*

Leaf   *Cross*

Dagger   *Flower*

Trigram   *Horseshoe*

Kite   *Fork*

Different symbols represent different meanings—even among the Chinese the meanings can differ according to variations of dialect interpretations.

INTERPRETING THE SYMBOLS

• Shapes that are sharp or that represent weapons, arrows, and pointed objects denote danger and threats.

• Enclosed shapes, like a full square or circle, signify being hemmed in, a loss of freedom or independence.

• A bow and arrow shape indicates jealousy and spitefulness.

• Three solid lines or three broken lines are auspicious indications, the former for the man in the family and the latter for the woman. Three broken lines can also indicate the possibility of marriage.

• Seeds indicate new beginnings.

• Trees and plants indicate growth, friends, and auspicious developments.

• Mansions and houses indicate security.

• Flowers, bouquets, and bushes suggest celebrations, joyousness, and prosperity.

• Sailing ships mean coming wealth.

• Aeroplanes mean forthcoming travel.

• Birds often indicate new opportunities, although it depends on whether the bird is looking up (good) or down (bad).

• Trigrams and three-pointed symbols are auspicious. A fork indicates an important trade-off confronting you soon.

• Comets indicate betrayals and deceit.

• Crosses indicate troubles, obstacles, and impending loss.

• Fish and bats indicate increasing incomes.

• Flags indicate victory of some sort while umbrellas and turtles indicate protection from some accident.

• Full arches signify a marriage while a half-arch indicates danger.

• Horseshoes and horses indicate good luck and money are coming.

• A leaf, a shell, or a letter indicate significant news coming—often about a rise in station or a promotion.

• Balloons and kites signify a wish fulfilled.

• Numbers that total two or five indicate illness; a total of three indicates court cases; a total of four suggests forthcoming literary or educational success; and a total of six or eight is auspicious.

MAKE THE TEA

Tea symbolizes earthly purity so the preparation calls for the most stringent standards of cleanliness. Two teapots are required, one for preparing the tea and keeping the tea leaves moist but not soaked in water, and the other to contain the freshly brewed tea. The water used must be properly boiled and teacups are warmed before use. Teapots should have texture that allows the tea to "breathe." New teapots must be "seasoned" with tea leaves soaked in water boiled to high temperatures, prior to their first use. This will get rid of any lingering odors that can affect the accuracy of the oracle.

1 Pour boiling water into an empty teapot to warm the pot. Make certain that all the bubbles have settled.

2 Empty the teapot and put in the tea leaves. As you do so, think of the question you wish to ask. The teapot should be filled up to about half-way with tea leaves. Ensure you do not block the spout, which is inauspicious.

3 Pour the boiled water into the teapot until the water overflows. Quickly pour away the water to "cleanse" the tea leaves.

4 Pour boiling water into the teapot along the edge of the pot once again until it overflows. Replace the lid and give the lid and the whole teapot a dash of boiling water as well.

5 All of the tea and some of the leaves can now be transferred into a second, more lavishly decorated teapot.

6 Pour the tea into three cups, allowing the leaves also to fall into the cups. Allow the tea to cool for a while and as you wait, close your eyes lightly and think of the question you wish to ask the oracle.

7 When the tea has cooled a little, drink the first cup in one continuous gulp, until only the leaves are left stuck to the bottom of the teacup. Do the same with the second and third cups.

8 Study the tea leaves left over in the teacup very carefully. Perform the reading in order of the three cups, so that you can get a chronology of the oracle prediction. The first cup describes the medium-term situation and the third cup describes the ultimate situation.

Check against the dictionary of meanings and indications opposite. If you cannot see any equivalents, drink another three cups to see whether some outcomes may be more forthcoming. You do not need to be psychic to use the tea leaf oracle—what is required is focused concentration. You do, however, need to have an "eye" for seeing symbols, patterns, images, and shapes in the tea leaves. The more you practice, the better you will be. Do not doubt the intuitive links and leaps you make between what you see in the leaves and events currently happening in your life. After a while, you will come to know when your intuition is seriously telling you something and when it is not.

APPENDIX: THE CHINESE CALENDAR 1912–2068

THE CHINESE CALENDAR COMPRISES HEAVENLY STEMS AND EARTHLY BRANCHES. IN THE CALENDAR ALL DATES, MONTHS, AND YEARS ARE EXPRESSED IN TERMS OF THESE STEMS AND BRANCHES. THERE ARE TEN STEMS WHICH SIGNIFY THE FIVE ELEMENTS WITH A YIN OR A YANG DIMENSION, AND THERE ARE TWELVE BRANCHES AND THESE ARE THE TWELVE ANIMAL SIGNS.

CHINESE CALENDAR 1912–2068

ANIMAL (ELEMENT)	CHINESE NEW YEAR DATES	EARTHLY BRANCH	HEAVENLY STEM
RAT (WATER)	February 18, 1912–February 5, 1913	Water	Water
OX (EARTH)	February 6, 1913–January 25, 1914	Earth	Water
TIGER (WOOD)	January 26, 1914–February 13, 1915	Wood	Wood
RABBIT (WOOD)	February 14, 1915–February 2, 1916	Wood	Wood
DRAGON (EARTH)	February 3, 1916–January 22, 1917	Earth	Fire
SNAKE (FIRE)	January 23, 1917–February 10, 1918	Fire	Fire
HORSE (FIRE)	February 11, 1918–January 31, 1919	Fire	Earth
SHEEP (EARTH)	February 1, 1919–February 19, 1920	Earth	Earth
MONKEY (METAL)	February 20, 1920–February 7, 1921	Metal	Metal
ROOSTER (METAL)	February 8, 1921–January 27, 1922	Metal	Metal
DOG (EARTH)	January 28, 1922–February 15, 1923	Earth	Water
BOAR (WATER)	February 16, 1923–February 4, 1924	Water	Water
RAT (WATER)	February 5, 1924–January 23, 1925	Water	Wood
OX (EARTH)	January 24, 1925–February 12, 1926	Earth	Wood
TIGER (WOOD)	February 13, 1926–February 1, 1927	Wood	Fire
RABBIT (WOOD)	February 2, 1927–January 22, 1928	Wood	Fire
DRAGON (EARTH)	January 23, 1928–February 9, 1929	Earth	Earth
SNAKE (FIRE)	February 10, 1929–January 29, 1930	Fire	Earth
HORSE (FIRE)	January 30, 1930–February 16, 1931	Fire	Metal
SHEEP (EARTH)	February 17, 1931–February 5, 1932	Earth	Metal
MONKEY (METAL)	February 6, 1932–January 25, 1933	Metal	Water
ROOSTER (METAL)	January 26, 1933–February 13, 1934	Metal	Water
DOG (EARTH)	February 14, 1934–February 3, 1935	Earth	Wood
BOAR (WATER)	February 4, 1935–January 23, 1936	Water	Wood
RAT (WATER)	January 24, 1936–February 10, 1937	Water	Fire
OX (EARTH)	February 11, 1937–January 30, 1938	Earth	Fire
TIGER (WOOD)	January 31, 1938–February 18, 1939	Wood	Earth

CHINESE CALENDAR 1912–2068 CONTINUED

ANIMAL (ELEMENT)	CHINESE NEW YEAR DATES	EARTHLY BRANCH	HEAVENLY STEM
RABBIT (WOOD)	February 19, 1939–February 7, 1940	Wood	Earth
DRAGON (EARTH)	February 8, 1940–January 26, 1941	Earth	Metal
SNAKE (FIRE)	January 27, 1941–February 14, 1942	Fire	Metal
HORSE (FIRE)	February 15, 1942–February 4, 1943	Fire	Water
SHEEP (EARTH)	February 5, 1943–January 24, 1944	Earth	Water
MONKEY (METAL)	January 25, 1944–February 12, 1945	Metal	Wood
ROOSTER (METAL)	February 13, 1945–February 1, 1946	Metal	Wood
DOG (EARTH)	February 2, 1946–January 21, 1947	Earth	Fire
BOAR (WATER)	January 22, 1947–February 9, 1948	Water	Fire
RAT (WATER)	February 10, 1948–January 28, 1949	Water	Earth
OX (EARTH)	January 29, 1949–February 16, 1950	Earth	Earth
TIGER (WOOD)	February 17, 1950–February 5, 1951	Wood	Metal
RABBIT (WOOD)	February 6, 1951–January 26, 1952	Wood	Metal
DRAGON (EARTH)	January 27, 1952–February 13, 1953	Earth	Water
SNAKE (FIRE)	February 14, 1953–February 2, 1954	Fire	Water
HORSE (FIRE)	February 3, 1954–January 23, 1955	Fire	Wood
SHEEP (EARTH)	January 24, 1955–February 11, 1956	Earth	Wood
MONKEY (METAL)	February 12, 1956–January 30, 1957	Metal	Fire
ROOSTER (METAL)	January 31, 1957–February 17, 1958	Metal	Fire
DOG (EARTH)	February 18, 1958–February 7, 1959	Earth	Earth
BOAR (WATER)	February 8, 1959–January 27, 1960	Water	Earth
RAT (WATER)	January 28, 1960–February 14, 1961	Water	Metal
OX (EARTH)	February 15, 1961–February 4, 1962	Earth	Metal
TIGER (WOOD)	February 5, 1962–January 24, 1963	Wood	Water
RABBIT (WOOD)	January 25, 1963–February 12, 1964	Wood	Water
DRAGON (EARTH)	February 13, 1964–February 1, 1965	Earth	Wood
SNAKE (FIRE)	February 2, 1965–January 20, 1966	Fire	Wood
HORSE (FIRE)	January 21, 1966–February 8, 1967	Fire	Fire
SHEEP (EARTH)	February 9, 1967–January 29, 1968	Earth	Fire
MONKEY (METAL)	January 30, 1968–February 16, 1969	Metal	Earth
ROOSTER (METAL)	February 17, 1969–February 5, 1970	Metal	Earth
DOG (EARTH)	February 6, 1970–January 26, 1971	Earth	Metal
BOAR (WATER)	January 27, 1971–February 14, 1972	Water	Metal
RAT (WATER)	February 15, 1972–February 2, 1973	Water	Water
OX (EARTH)	February 3, 1973–January 22, 1974	Earth	Water
TIGER (WOOD)	January 23, 1974–February 10, 1975	Wood	Wood
RABBIT (WOOD)	February 11, 1975–January 30, 1976	Wood	Wood
DRAGON (EARTH)	January 31, 1976–February 17, 1977	Earth	Fire
SNAKE (FIRE)	February 18, 1977–February 6, 1978	Fire	Fire
HORSE (FIRE)	February 7, 1978–January 27, 1979	Fire	Earth
SHEEP (EARTH)	January 28, 1979–February 15, 1980	Earth	Earth
MONKEY (METAL)	February 16, 1980–February 4, 1981	Metal	Metal
ROOSTER (METAL)	February 5, 1981–January 24, 1982	Metal	Metal

CHINESE CALENDAR 1912-2068 CONTINUED

ANIMAL (ELEMENT)	CHINESE NEW YEAR DATES	EARTHLY BRANCH	HEAVENLY STEM
DOG (EARTH)	January 25, 1982–February 12, 1983	Earth	Water
BOAR (WATER)	February 13, 1983–February 1, 1984	Water	Water
RAT (WATER)	February 2, 1984–February 19, 1985	Water	Wood
OX (EARTH)	February 20, 1985–February 8, 1986	Earth	Wood
TIGER (WOOD)	February 9, 1986–January 28, 1987	Wood	Fire
RABBIT (WOOD)	January 29, 1987–February 16, 1988	Wood	Fire
DRAGON (EARTH)	February 17, 1988–February 5, 1989	Earth	Earth
SNAKE (FIRE)	February 6, 1989–January 26, 1990	Fire	Earth
HORSE (FIRE)	January 27, 1990–February 14, 1991	Fire	Metal
SHEEP (EARTH)	February 15, 1991–February 3, 1992	Earth	Metal
MONKEY (METAL)	February 4, 1992–January 22, 1993	Metal	Water
ROOSTER (METAL)	January 23, 1993–February 9, 1994	Metal	Water
DOG (EARTH)	February 10, 1994–January 30, 1995	Earth	Wood
BOAR (WATER)	January 31, 1995–February 18, 1996	Water	Wood
RAT (WATER)	February 19, 1996–February 6, 1997	Water	Fire
OX (EARTH)	February 7, 1997–January 27, 1998	Earth	Fire
TIGER (WOOD)	January 28, 1998–February 15, 1999	Wood	Earth
RABBIT (WOOD)	February 16, 1999–February 4, 2000	Wood	Earth
DRAGON (EARTH)	February 5, 2000–January 23, 2001	Earth	Metal
SNAKE (FIRE)	January 24, 2001–February 11, 2002	Fire	Metal
HORSE (FIRE)	February 12, 2002–January 31, 2003	Fire	Water
SHEEP (EARTH)	February 1, 2003–January 21, 2004	Earth	Water
MONKEY (METAL)	January 22, 2004–February 8, 2005	Metal	Wood
ROOSTER (METAL)	February 9, 2005–January 28, 2006	Metal	Wood
DOG (EARTH)	January 29, 2006–February 17, 2007	Earth	Fire
BOAR (WATER)	February 18, 2007–February 6, 2008	Water	Fire
RAT (WATER)	February 7, 2008–January 25, 2009	Water	Earth
OX (EARTH)	January 26, 2009–February 13, 2010	Earth	Earth
TIGER (WOOD)	February 14, 2010–February 2, 2011	Wood	Metal
RABBIT (WOOD)	February 3, 2011–January 22, 2012	Wood	Metal
DRAGON (EARTH)	January 23, 2012–February 9, 2013	Earth	Water
SNAKE (FIRE)	February 10, 2013–January 30, 2014	Fire	Water
HORSE (FIRE)	January 31, 2014–February 18, 2015	Fire	Wood
SHEEP (EARTH)	February 19, 2015–February 7, 2016	Earth	Wood
MONKEY (METAL)	February 8, 2016–January 27, 2017	Metal	Fire
ROOSTER (METAL)	January 28, 2017–February 15, 2018	Metal	Fire
DOG (EARTH)	February 16, 2018–February 4, 2019	Earth	Earth
BOAR (WATER)	February 5, 2019–January 24, 2020	Water	Earth
RAT (WATER)	January 25, 2020–February 11, 2021	Water	Metal
OX (EARTH)	February 12, 2021–January 31, 2022	Earth	Metal
TIGER (WOOD)	February 1, 2022–January 21, 2023	Wood	Water
RABBIT (WOOD)	January 22, 2023–February 9, 2024	Wood	Water
DRAGON (EARTH)	February 10, 2024–January 28, 2025	Earth	Wood

CHINESE CALENDAR 1912–2068 CONTINUED

ANIMAL (ELEMENT)	CHINESE NEW YEAR DATES	EARTHLY BRANCH	HEAVENLY STEM
SNAKE (FIRE)	January 29, 2025–February 16, 2026	Fire	Wood
HORSE (FIRE)	February 17, 2026–February 5, 2027	Fire	Fire
SHEEP (EARTH)	February 6, 2027–January 25, 2028	Earth	Fire
MONKEY (METAL)	January 26, 2028–February 12, 2029	Metal	Earth
ROOSTER (METAL)	February 13, 2029–February 2, 2030	Metal	Earth
DOG (EARTH)	February 3, 2030–January 22, 2031	Earth	Metal
BOAR (WATER)	January 23, 2031–February 10, 2032	Water	Metal
RAT (WATER)	February 11, 2032–January 30, 2033	Water	Water
OX (EARTH)	January 31, 2033–February 18, 2034	Earth	Water
TIGER (WOOD)	February 19, 2034–February 7, 2035	Wood	Wood
RABBIT (WOOD)	February 8, 2035–January 27, 2036	Wood	Wood
DRAGON (EARTH)	January 28, 2036–February 14, 2037	Earth	Fire
SNAKE (FIRE)	February 15, 2037–February 3, 2038	Fire	Fire
HORSE (FIRE)	February 4, 2038–January 23, 2039	Fire	Earth
SHEEP (EARTH)	January 24, 2039–February 11, 2040	Earth	Earth
MONKEY (METAL)	February 12, 2040–January 31, 2041	Metal	Metal
ROOSTER (METAL)	February 1, 2041–January 21, 2042	Metal	Metal
DOG (EARTH)	January 22, 2042–February 9, 2043	Earth	Water
BOAR (WATER)	February 10, 2043–January 29, 2044	Water	Water
RAT (WATER)	January 30, 2044–February 16, 2045	Water	Wood
OX (EARTH)	February 17, 2045–February 5, 2046	Earth	Wood
TIGER (WOOD)	February 6, 2046–January 25, 2047	Wood	Fire
RABBIT (WOOD)	January 26, 2047–February 13, 2048	Wood	Fire
DRAGON (EARTH)	February 14, 2048–February 1, 2049	Earth	Earth
SNAKE (FIRE)	February 2, 2049–January 22, 2050	Fire	Earth
HORSE (FIRE)	January 23, 2050–February 11, 2051	Fire	Metal
SHEEP (EARTH)	February 12, 2051–January 31, 2052	Earth	Metal
MONKEY (METAL)	February 1, 2052–February 18, 2053	Metal	Water
ROOSTER (METAL)	February 19, 2053–February 7, 2054	Metal	Water
DOG (EARTH)	February 8, 2054–January 27, 2055	Earth	Wood
BOAR (WATER)	January 28, 2055–February 14, 2056	Water	Wood
RAT (WATER)	February 15, 2056–February 3, 2057	Water	Fire
OX (EARTH)	February 4, 2057–January 23, 2058	Earth	Fire
TIGER (WOOD)	January 24, 2058–February 11, 2059	Wood	Earth
RABBIT (WOOD)	February 12, 2059–February 1, 2060	Wood	Earth
DRAGON (EARTH)	February 2, 2060–January 20, 2061	Earth	Metal
SNAKE (FIRE)	January 21, 2061–February 8, 2062	Fire	Metal
HORSE (FIRE)	February 9, 2062–January 28, 2063	Fire	Water
SHEEP (EARTH)	January 29, 2063–February 16, 2064	Earth	Water
MONKEY (METAL)	February 17, 2064–February 4, 2065	Metal	Wood
ROOSTER (METAL)	February 5, 2065–January 25, 2066	Metal	Wood
DOG (EARTH)	January 26, 2066–February 13, 2067	Earth	Fire
BOAR (WATER)	February 14, 2067–February 2, 2068	Water	Fire

GLOSSARY

Basket of elements The combination of four "heavenly stems" and four "earthly branches" that offers clues to your future good and bad luck.

Chi The intrinsic life force (vital energy) of the universe, which may be either auspicious or inauspicious.

Chi luck The five types of chi luck with which everyone is born: fate chi, family chi, mentor chi, prosperity chi, and opportunity chi.

Chinese animal signs The 12 animal signs (Rat, Ox, Tiger, Rabbit, Dragon, Snake, Horse, Sheep, Monkey, Rooster, Dog, and Boar) of Chinese astrology.

Destructive cycle of elements In this chi cycle, water destroys fire, which destroys metal, which destroys wood, which in turn destroys earth, which destroys water.

Earth element The element associated with the middle of the year and the intersection between the seasons.

Earthly branch The lower character in each of the "four pillars;" there are 12 earthly branches, each with a corresponding element and astrological animal (see Chinese animal signs).

Exhaustive cycle of elements In this chi cycle, wood exhausts water, which exhausts metal, which exhausts earth, which in turn exhausts fire, which exhausts wood.

Family luck This signifies a nesting period and a sense of contentment.

Fate luck The most dramatic chi luck, suggesting a major turning point in your life.

Feng shui Literally, this means "wind and water" and refers to the Chinese system of balancing the chi patterns of our natural environment.

Fire element The element associated with summer.

Five elements Water, wood, fire, earth, and metal—the five types of chi that dominate at different times; they are known in Chinese as wu xing.

Four pillars of destiny The hour, day, month, and year of your birth: one of the main divinatory tools of Chinese fortune telling.

Friendship luck element This is represented by the element that is the same as your self element.

Heavenly stem The upper characters in each of the "four pillars;" there are ten heavenly stems, each with a corresponding element and yin or yang aspect.

Hexagram A symbol made up of six broken or unbroken lines, comprising two sets of three lines, or trigrams; there are 64 hexagrams in the *I Ching*.

I Ching A famous Chinese oracle, also known in the West as the *Book of Changes*, which contains practical wisdom on the human condition; its 64 hexagrams may be used as a method of divination.

Intelligence luck element This is represented by the element that is produced by your self element.

Lo shu A magic square of nine numbers in a three-by-three grid, which contain significant information about your future luck; each year a different lo shu chart governs the fortunes of the different directions and animal signs.

Metal element The element that is associated with harvesting time.

Mentor luck This generally signifies the appearance of an important patron in your life and/or promotion.

Opportunity luck This represents the chance of a lifetime, which forces you to make decisions.

Paht chee The "eight characters" method of fortune telling, which uses the "four pillars of destiny" to create a chart that contains the codes of your destiny.

Pa kua An eight-sided symbol containing the directions, numbers, and symbols that are used in feng shui analysis.

Power luck element This is represented by the element that destroys your self element.

Productive cycle of elements In this chi cycle, wood produces fire, which produces earth, which produces metal, which in turn produces water, which produces wood.

Resources luck element This is represented by the element that produces your self element.

Self element This element is represented by the heavenly stem of the day pillar, and helps to reveal the influences that will shape your life destiny; it is either weak or strong.

Sheng chi Beneficial chi that brings good fortune.

Stars There are 12 special stars that appear in the paht chee chart and indicate good or bad luck as well as aspects of your character: the Star of the Nobleman, Star of Scholastic Brilliance, Star of the Aggressive Sword, Star of Prospects, Star of Peach Blossom, Star of the Flower of Romance, Commanding Star, Star of the Traveling Horse, Star of Spirituality, War Star, Warrior Star, and the Star of Powerful Mentors.

Tai Sui The Chinese name for the planet Jupiter, one of the nine planets of the solar system, regarded by the Chinese as a powerful deity, the "God of the Year."

Ten-year luck pillars These pillars indicate the energy influences that prevail in each ten-year period, causing either good or bad luck to occur.

Trigram A set of three lines (broken or unbroken) in a hexagram; there are eight possible trigrams.

Tung Shu A Chinese almanac also known as the "Book of Auspicious and Inauspicious Dates," which contains information on astrology, codes, and symbols, as well as the secret meanings of facial and body moles; see also Yellow Emperor.

Water element The element associated with winter.

Wealth luck element This is represented by the element that is destroyed by your self element.

Wen Shu Oracle A spiritual method of divination based on the Tibetan MO oracle, which uses mala beads to help you make decisions when faced with a dilemma; Wen Shu Pu Sa is the Chinese name of the Buddha of Wisdom, Manjushri.

Wood element The element associated with spring.

Yang One of the fundamental principles of Chinese philosophy, yang is positive, bright, active, dry, hot, and masculine.

Yellow Emperor Huangdi (c.2698–2599 BCE), considered to be the founder of Chinese civilization; his oracle, a poem in the Chinese Almanac known as the Tung Shu, may be consulted for personal destiny readings (based on the idea that we are all born on a part of the Emperor's body).

Yin One of the fundamental principles of Chinese philosophy, yin is negative, dark, passive, cold, wet, and feminine.

INDEX